Applied Linguistics as Social Science

Alison Sealey and Bob Carter

With a foreword by Derek Layder

continuum
LONDON • NEW YORK

Continuum

The Tower Building	15 East 26th Street
11 York Road	New York
London, SE1 7NX	NY 10010

British Library Cataloguing-in-Publication Data
A catalogue record for this book is available from the British Library.

ISBN   0-8264-5519-0 (hardback)
          0-8264-5520-4 (paperback)

Library of Congress Cataloging-in-Publication Data
A catalogue record for this book is available from the Library of Congress.

Typeset by YHT Ltd, London
Printed and bound in Great Britain by MPG Books Ltd, Bodmin, Cornwall

Contents

Acknowledgements   vii

Foreword   ix
Derek Layder

Preface   xiii
Christopher N. Candlin and Srikant Sarangi

Introduction   1

1   Making connections: some key issues in social theory
    and applied linguistics   5

2   Sociology and ideas about language   34

3   Language as a cultural emergent property   60

4   Researching language learning: theories, evidence,
    claims   85

5   Social categories and theoretical descriptions   107

6   Social domain theory: interpreting intercultural
    communication   128

7   Language in the world: properties and powers   156

8   A social realist approach to research in applied
    linguistics   183

References   211

Index   235

Acknowledgements

As a project spanning two disciplines, this book necessarily owes a debt to a large number of contributors to both applied linguistics and social theory. Many of those who have influenced the ideas presented here are cited in the text, and some of them have had a more direct influence through discussions and debates. Amongst these we would particularly like to thank participants in the ESRC-funded seminar series *Realizing the Potential: Realism and Empirical Research*, as well as delegates to recent conferences of the British Association for Applied Linguistics and Sociolinguistics Symposia. Support from the University of Warwick is acknowledged in providing one of us with a period of study leave to work on the manuscript.

We have also benefited from discussions and correspondence with Margaret Archer, Allan Bell, Grace Boas, Dave Byrne, Lynne Cameron, Guy Cook, Geoff Hall, Martyn Hammersley, Alan How, Susan Hunston, Paul Kerswill, Caroline New, Ray Pawson, Andrew Sayer, Michael Stubbs, Paul Thompson, Eddie Williams and Malcolm Williams, many of whom have offered constructive criticism on earlier drafts of parts of the text. We are also grateful to the series editors, Chris Candlin and Srikant Sarangi, for their support of the project and their detailed and helpful comments on a draft of the complete book, and Jenny Lovell at Continuum for her editorial assistance. Finally, we are especially indebted to Derek Layder, both for his important contribution to social theory, on which we have drawn extensively, and also for his careful reading of, and constructive response to, our text. Its shortcomings, of course, are entirely our own responsibility.

Chapter 5 uses material from Sealey, A. and Carter, B. (2001) 'Social categories and sociolinguistics: applying a realist approach' which appeared in the *International Journal of the Sociology of Language* 152, 1–19, published by Mouton de Gruyter.

Foreword

In this innovative and incisively argued book Alison Sealey and Bob Carter attempt something all too rare in present-day academic debate. They straddle disciplinary boundaries in an effort to constructively bring together elements that cry out for some kind of rapprochement or integration. They start out with a simple but far from obvious question 'how may applied linguistics benefit sociology and how can social theory benefit applied linguistics?' Of course, although such questions may appear deceptively simple on the surface, they actually pose some very complex problems that require rather extended and sophisticated consideration.

Perhaps one reason why attempts at establishing creative connections are not common is that they inevitably attract negative critical responses. This is often because interdisciplinary explorations are regarded with suspicion by those concerned to 'protect' their home discipline from uninvited incursions from 'outside' – presumably for fear of dilution or destabilization. I have no doubt that this present work will be met with some hostility by self-appointed disciplinary 'minders', but any truly innovative work must inevitably bump up against the forces of conservatism that are typically organized against radical advances in knowledge. On the other hand, a book that makes some giant leaps, as this one does, will also be embraced and recognized by those who are more receptive to challenging and progressive ideas.

Of course, any attempt at productive dialogue and interchange will involve some critical confrontation and painful self-examination and Sealey and Carter do not shrink from these important and challenging issues. But they do so in an even-handed and charitable manner that makes their arguments and style of presentation seem amenable and fair to the sternest of critics. Moreover, by endeavouring to extract the positive 'cores' from applied linguistics and realist social theory while subjecting each to far-reaching critique, they salvage something of inestimable value.

Chapter 1 outlines the broad lineaments of their argument by indicating both the overlaps and the differences between the study of society and the study of language. They go on to specify what they mean by realist social theory and applied linguistics – the two disciplinary strands with which they are most concerned. A central reason why they prefer 'realist' social theory is because it claims that 'agency' and 'structure' have distinct properties and powers and sees language as a property emergent from their interplay.

The authors develop this theme by examining the way that sociology has dealt with the relationship between language and society (Chapter 2) and the continuing debate between 'autonomous' linguists and 'applied' linguists about the importance of language practice to the analysis of language (Chapter 3). But these considerations are not simply of theoretical pertinence. From the vantage of their realist framework Sealey and Carter consistently bring together questions of social theory and research methods, with substantive questions.

Thus practical research problems are employed as illustrative examples throughout the book, such as, what works in foreign language teaching (Chapter 4), how groups and the language they use are identified in sociolinguistic research (Chapter 5), intercultural communication (Chapter 6), literacy, language and literacy education policy in England and global and threatened languages (Chapter 7). The dovetailing of theoretical and empirical concerns is a great strength of the book and further contributes to the coherence and continuity of their overall argument.

During the course of their explorations and discussions Sealey and Carter raise some important questions and cover a wide range of ground – all of which are succinctly tied together in the concluding chapter. I cannot hope to do justice to this full range here but there are some issues I find irresistible. In particular I find their argument about the nature of the relationship between agency and structure and its implications for wider theoretical accounts of social phenomena, as well as for the practice of social research, very compelling.

Now this may be, in part, because they draw on and develop some of my own (and others') ideas in this respect and so I am already in tune with the general drift of some of their arguments. But insofar as they develop independent ideas about the agency–structure connection in relation to examples from sociolinguistic research, they add an interesting new emphasis and angle to this topic. Sealey and Carter's overall assessment is that the structuration account does not do justice to the detailed interplay between agency and structure. Instead, agency and structure must be understood as possessing distinct properties and powers and structuration theory does not allow for this. It simply compacts and conflates the two into a unity that dissolves their very properties and hence cannot account for their mutual impact or causal interrelationship.

Again, for Sealey and Carter the social research implications are never very far away from the surface of such seemingly abstract issues. In this respect the concluding chapter rounds off the discussion by returning to the contribution that realist social theory can make to the design and evaluation of social research in general and more specifically to that concerned with applied linguistics. A great advantage of the realist position in this respect is that it appreciates the way in which measurement and theory are closely related. It thus provides for the possibility of steering a course between the two extremes of rejecting all (quantifiable) measurement or elevating its importance out of all proportion.

This also allows Sealey and Carter to adopt a stance that 'stresses the links between theory and the empirical world, seeking to steer between an approach in which the world tells us, as it were, what theories to have, and an alternative approach which suggests that the connection between the empirical world and theory formation is arbitrary or contingent: that is that theories can be of little help with developing knowledge of the empirical world'. This also is a position that I feel happy with mainly because it seems to offer a constructive alternative to some of the more restrictive and 'closed' research positions to be found in the social and human sciences.

For those who expect this book to be a comfortable or easy read, the quotation above is a stark reminder that these are inherently difficult and complex issues. They are so, I think, for two reasons. First, basic issues of theory and practice like this are at an important juncture in which established and entrenched positions are being questioned and new alternatives being offered. Articulating new conceptual space is a difficult process which, for the reader, is often quite demanding. But the difficulty is also to do with the profundity of the issues that are being posed, involving as they do protean questions of epistemology and ontology. It is to Sealey and Carter's immense credit that they have produced such a lucid and coherent argument that shines through the book as a whole.

More generally for sociology and applied linguistics this book opens up new areas of debate that could only have arisen from the cross-fertilization of ideas that follows from interdisciplinary investigation. Sociology has always had something of an ambivalent relationship with the topic of language – both its study and by way of acknowledgement of its importance more generally for social analysis, interpretation and theory. As Sealey and Carter note, while there have been strands of sociology that have recognized the pivotal importance of language, it remains at the periphery, as it were, of mainstream preoccupations. It is crucial that in the future it should occupy a more central position.

On the other hand, applied sociolinguistics is in need of a social theory that can do justice to the variegated nature of social reality and is not content with easy answers to the agency–structure problem – especially ones that simply obviate the problem by erasing or dissolving the dualism itself. Moreover, the social theory in question must have an analytic apparatus and set of research strategies that are able to productively engage with a variegated social reality without doing violence to its properties and characteristics. In this book Sealey and Carter have gone some way in providing for the needs of both sociology and applied linguistics in this respect by focusing on their common problems and suggesting the kinds of solutions that potentially may be acceptable to both.

Derek Layder

Preface

Applied Linguistics as Social Science is a welcome addition to the
Advances in Applied Linguistics Series, partly because, unlike its
predecessors, it makes applied linguistics the subject of its enquiry and
achieves this by bringing together two voices – that of an applied
linguist and a social scientist. Not that we wish to emphasize polar-
ities, but it is clear that although the book as written is a monologic
text, it is not difficult to see how much dialogue has gone into the
process of writing, and how much effort has gone into orienting the
book to an interdisciplinary audience, evident from the authors'
explicit signposting of what can be skim-read by whom, and without
appearing in any way to be 'writing-down'.

As we see it, the title underscores an ecological relationship
between the two disciplines, which is far from casting them in hierarchical terms, as if one discipline is in the process of colonizing the
other. It represents the first book-length study to engage with this
relation, pursuing as its key theme how the ways in which applied
linguistics has viewed the social world have in turn defined how the
social is constructed in applied linguistics. The presence in the book of
an authoritative Foreword from the sociologist Derek Layder, identifying for the reader the significant themes from his perspective, makes
it necessary for us to highlight only briefly the significance of the book
from our applied linguistic persuasion.

The book as a whole is an exercise in (inter)disciplinary reflection, but not at a level of generality. It goes beyond a sheer reminder
about the language-society interrelationship, but makes a definitive
stride towards delineating the different levels of this interrelationship,
illuminated through adequate exemplification. A distinct hallmark of
the book is Sealey and Carter's engagement with the core tensions in
social science between agency – the self-conscious reflexive actions of
human beings – and structure – the enduring, affording and constraining influences of the social order – and the ways in which they
make this engagement relevant to issues of explanation in applied
linguistics. In turn, their identification of, and detailed analytic attention to, a set of core themes in mainstream applied linguistics such as
language teaching and learning, language planning and policy, lit-

eracy, standardization, language corpora, intercultural communication, enables them to situate their particular social realist perspective, and from that position to challenge the utility and relevance of socio-theoretical constructs, including those of structure and agency.

This book can be seen as an extension of the interdisciplinary debate initiated in Coupland, Sarangi and Candlin (2001), where the focus was placed on the nature of the relationship between socio-linguistics and social theory. As do many of the contributors to the Coupland *et al.* volume, Sealey and Carter vigorously argue here how neither language nor the societal context can be taken for granted by social scientists and applied linguists respectively. The study of language, especially language use in real life situations, and its role in social representation or categorization cannot be seen as the pre-rogative of any particular discipline. This is cautionary for applied linguistics, especially at a moment where some practitioners are making claims to provide explanations for problematic issues and critical moments in social interaction. By a similar token, language cannot be taken for granted as some surface level operational device – a slippage many social scientists can be held accountable to. A key message from this book is for both disciplines to treat concepts such as *language* and *society* not as unitary givens, nor as simple combinations, but as instances of interdisciplinarity *par excellence*. In short, the authors argue in favour of a re-specification, including a shift from periphery to centre, but not, as they put it, 'linguistifying social theory' or 'sociologising applied linguistics' – neither of which can foster a relationship on an ecological footing. Language, or more particularly, discourse is central to this ecological relationship as it becomes a resource for 'creative agency'.

One pathway to realizing this interdisciplinarity is to focus on common issues and concerns in methodology and research practice. Here the book is again reflexive, but in another sense, offering critical insights about research practice both in applied linguistics and in social science more generally, as the authors explore the links to be made between theory building and the empirical world. Not that this project is in any way unproblematic, as we point out in a recent Editorial (Sarangi & Candlin 2003). In the same vein as Funtowicz and Ravetz (1992) posit their claim in favour of 'a post-normal science' which marks the end of 'applied science', we are here faced with the limitations of linguistics or sociology as source disciplines in their own right for straightforward application to solve real-world problems. Claims by experts (as here applied linguists or social scientists) to explain the conditions of the empirical world by reference to linguistic or social theory in discrete ways are likely to be frustrated by the stakeholder values attached to such theories, by the loss of any pre-rogative of the expert over the increasingly knowledgeable subjects of research, and by the ability of such 'subjects' to access and appropriate for themselves applied linguistic and social science expertise.

References

Coupland, N., Sarangi, S. and Candlin, C. N. eds. (2001) *Sociolinguistics and Social Theory*. London: Pearson.

Funtowicz, S. O. and Ravetz, J. R. (1992) 'Three types of risk assessment and the emergence of post-normal science', in S. Krimsky and D. Golding eds., *Social Theories of Risk*. Westport, Connecticut: Praeger, 251–273.

Sarangi, S. and Candlin, C. N. (2003) Trading between reflexivity and relevance: new challenges for applied linguistics. *Applied Linguistics* 24(3) 271–285.

Introduction

The aim of this book is to make a case for regarding the discipline of applied linguistics as a social science. This requires a theory of language and a view of social analysis as social science, both of which the book attempts to provide. 'Applied linguistics' is construed here very inclusively, to refer to those areas of language description and analysis which locate language itself within the social world, and which understand language use as a form of social practice. The social theory on which we draw allows us to describe issues in applied linguistics with reference to the properties and powers of language and of language users. The concept of properties and powers is associated with some developments in contemporary social theory which are broadly identified as 'social realism'. A central feature of this approach is to argue that the social world consists of different kinds of things: namely human beings and the products of their interactions, which are social relations and cultural creations. The idea that each of these has distinctive properties and powers will be explored in detail throughout the book. Our argument includes the proposition that a social scientific account of applied linguistics helps to explain the interaction between these different kinds of things: social structures, human agents and language. We suggest that some aspects of linguistic behaviour are more accurately described with the aid of insights from social science disciplines other than those which are primarily concerned with language. What we have tried to do is to illuminate questions and topics which are of concern to applied linguists with reference to such insights, without losing sight of what is distinctive about language itself and not reducible to any other dimension of the social world.

Social theory and applied linguistics, then, share some common areas of interest, although the concepts used by each to discuss these have their own emphases and history. Throughout the book, we shall be considering what each discipline can contribute to our understanding of a number of key questions in the social sciences. Both disciplines are, in effect, concerned with ways of knowing the social world. In pursuit of this, each deals with a range of objects of knowledge. That is, each makes claims about: what exists in the social world (ontological claims); to what extent and in what ways these objects can be known about (epistemological claims); and the appropriate methods for achieving that knowledge (methodological claims). Any proposition about the world will entail engagement with all three sorts of claim – although these are not always made explicit. Moreover, most kinds of knowledge are linguistically mediated. This accounts for the unique status of language, as both an object of knowledge and the means by which that knowledge is comprehended, expressed and discussed. Thus, none of the social sciences can avoid a concern with language. Conversely, as we have suggested already, applied linguistics cannot escape involvement with social theory.

In recent years, most of the social sciences have turned their attention to the study of language in social life, and various approaches to the analysis of discourse have been developed beyond linguistics itself. While we obviously believe that both disciplines can benefit from this exchange, we also want to delineate their respective boundaries, and maintain a commitment to the distinction between different forms of knowledge and appropriate ways of accessing these. In other words, we are wary of 'linguistifying' social theory, as well as of 'sociologizing' applied linguistics.

In Chapter 1 we identify some ways in which the study of language and the study of society overlap. Readers who are conversant with sociological ideas and debates will find much that is familiar in the first part of this chapter, although the distinctively realist angle we are taking to these ideas and debates may be novel even to those from a sociological background. Likewise, those readers with a background in applied linguistics will recognize the issues discussed in the second part, although, again, it does serve to outline our particular position, rather than attempt to cover the area in its entirety. It is also difficult to avoid falling on the wrong side of a metaphorical line between taking too much for granted and stating the obvious, particularly when addressing a readership with a range of different backgrounds and prior knowledge. We hope we have not strayed too far in either direction.

In Chapter 2 we consider in more detail the relationship between language and society, as it has been explored in sociology. In order to evaluate the usefulness to applied linguistics of social theory, it is obviously important to establish the nature of the insights it provides into the relationship between language and social action. Conversely, any shortcomings in accounts of language will indicate the nature of the potential contribution applied linguistics may make to social theory. The chapter considers three distinct kinds of position within social science: those which consider language as the basis of social interaction; those which emphasize the central role of language in the discursive construction of social life; and those which seek to develop a view of language as having systemic features as well as being a source of creative agency.

We consider in Chapter 3 the continuing debate between autonomous linguists and applied linguists about the extent to which the practice of using language is relevant to the analysis of language itself. Applied linguists, we argue, are obliged to confront evidence of 'real' language – in the sense of what speakers actually say – by virtue of their involvement with social issues in which language is a feature. These include most obviously the practice of teaching and learning additional languages, but other 'real-world' problems are also relevant, such as decisions about which language is to be the official variety in a nation-state, or where writers can turn for adjudication about the 'real' meaning of a disputed term. The chapter explores some different senses in which language and languages may be thought of as 'real', going on to examine the implications of conceptualizing them as 'cultural emergent properties'. This approach seeks to identify what distinguishes human languages from other phenomena in the natural and social worlds, and we also look briefly at the claim that the notion of emergence may help to explain how languages develop over time.

In the next chapter, the emphasis shifts from questions of ontology (what is language like? what is society like?) to issues of epistemology and method. The area we explore is the most extensive in applied linguistic research, and in some interpretations is almost synonymous with it, namely the practice of teaching and learning languages other than the variety learned in infancy. We survey the most influential approach to researching 'what works' in second and foreign language teaching, which is that based on the identification and correlation of salient variables, as well as considering alternative approaches which seek to give greater weight to social context and holistic descriptions. We also examine the theories of causality on which both kinds of approach tend to rest, and explain how the social realist theory we are using offers alternative explanations, based on the properties and powers of the different denizens of the social world.

The next four chapters extend and develop the ideas introduced in the first four. Chapter 5 furthers the critique, broached in Chapter 4, of the use of variables in social research. It is routine in sociolinguistic and similar areas of research to group speakers with reference to their membership of a range of social categories, such as age-group, ethnicity and class. In line with the theory we are proposing, we suggest that the basis on which these categories are conceptualized warrants more detailed scrutiny, and that they each depend on somewhat different properties of aspects of the social world.

Whereas social categories are a key concept for sociolinguistic research, there is another branch of applied linguistics in which the salient divisions are those between speakers of different languages and, relatedly, members of different cultures. Chapter 6 explores the topic of intercultural communication from the perspective developed in the book, introducing the idea of 'social domains' as a refinement of the analytical dualism separating structure and agency.

Chapter 7 takes four further areas of applied linguistic interest to illustrate the significance of a 'properties and powers' approach to understanding language in the social world: language itself; literacy; language and literacy education policy in England; and global and threatened languages.

The final chapter reviews the concepts explored and developed in previous chapters to outline how a realist social theoretical approach might inform an applied linguistic research programme. It provides the conclusion to the book in summarizing the key principles of social realism, going on to apply these to an exploration of some actual studies carried out in various areas of social science. In this chapter, we indicate how many of the questions which are of concern to applied linguists could benefit from the social realist perspective developed throughout the book.

1 Making connections: some key issues in social theory and applied linguistics

Introduction

In this chapter, we introduce some of the key terms and concepts we shall be employing in subsequent chapters to examine the relationship between language and society. Part 1 (which, as we have indicated, contains material likely to be more familiar to sociologists) considers the structure–agency debate, outlining the different ways in which the relationship between structure and agency has been explained; the key concept of emergence is also introduced. The question of the possibility of objectivity in knowing the social world is then discussed, before we sketch out the implications of a realist account of structure and agency for the study of language, to be developed in subsequent chapters. Part 2 (containing material which will be more familiar to applied linguists) provides an outline of the issues with which the discipline of linguistics is currently concerned, as a context for an interpretation of applied linguistics.

Undertaking these summaries is an invidious task, since each of the topics sketched so briefly here is a large area of study in its own right, which means that the discussion will necessarily be simplified and very introductory. However, many of the issues raised are revisited at greater length in subsequent chapters.

Part 1: Some key issues in social theory

Structure and agency

One of the major themes of sociological debate since the discipline was established in the late nineteenth century has been the relationship between human beings and the social context within which they seek to realize their intentions, aspirations, needs and desires. This social context, made up of political and legal relations, institutions, distributions of wealth and income and so on, may frustrate or enable people's efforts to achieve what they want. The desire to go to university, for example, is much more likely to be realized by an individual who comes from a middle-class, rather than a working-class, background.

Broadly speaking, the sociological interest in this relationship stems from the fundamental question to which it gives rise: do people make society or does society make people? Put in this crude way, of course, there can be no straightforward answer. Nevertheless, if we convert the question to a continuum in which the two elements of the question represent opposite ends, it is possible to see that sociologists have inclined towards one or the other. That is, some sociologists (such as Durkheim, Parsons or Lévi-Strauss – see Chapter 2) have favoured an emphasis on the role of society or social structures in shaping people's values, cultures and choices. Other sociologists (such as Goffman or Becker) have regarded the role played by individuals in sustaining social interactions and interpreting meanings as more central to accounts of social life.

Wherever a theorist lies on this continuum, however, the nub of the issue remains constant, namely the extent to which it may be claimed that individuals construct or create society and, conversely, the degree to which social structures may be said to impress or socialize individuals. This issue was not one invented by sociology, although sociologists have explored it in distinctive ways (Nisbet 1966). The much older philosophical debate about free will and determinism is also concerned with exploring the extent to which human beings are free to shape the world according to their own desires, wishes and intentions.

In this book, concerned as it is with social theory and language, we shall adopt the characteristic sociological formulation of the issue as one of the relationship between structure (society) and agency (human beings). The 'structure–agency debate' is, as one recent commentator has put it, 'widely acknowledged to lie at the heart of sociological theorising' (Archer 2000: 1). It occupies this salient position precisely because of the fundamental nature of the relationship it seeks to examine: that between human beings (the source of agency in the social world) and the social relations (structures) that are generated on the basis of their interaction. As we have seen, there are a number of possible ways in which the relations between structure and agency may be interpreted. We shall start at the structure end of the continuum, but before doing so we should enter an important caveat about the notion of structure which is raised by Lopez and Scott (2000). They argue that the meaning of the term 'structure' is itself ambiguous. Generally speaking, sociologists have employed the term in two senses: to refer to normative institutions (the legal system, ideological system and so on) and to relational groupings (capitalist and proletariat, for example). Relational structure and institutional structure are connected but distinct aspects of structure and irreducible each to the other. This cautionary note should be borne in mind in the following discussion of different approaches to the agency–structure debate. That is, structures are always 'macro' features of society, which persist over time; however, for some of the writers discussed in what follows, the term refers primarily to social institutions – such as the economy, schooling and so forth – while for others the emphasis is on social relations such as employer–employee, teacher–pupil and so on.

Structuralist accounts of structure-and-agency

In structuralist accounts of the structure and agency relation, human beings are viewed as determined by the social world, such that if we wish to account for the social world we should concentrate on the role played by social structures. This role can take a variety of forms. For example we may want to argue that the values and attitudes that people hold, or the ambitions that they have, are a consequence of the ways in which they have been socialized. Radical versions of this thesis replace socialization with ideological hegemony; postmodernist versions replace socialization with discourses which 'subject-ify'. The core feature of such 'structuralist' accounts is that, in explaining the social world, social structures are afforded causal primacy in shaping and fashioning agency.

Thus, the work of Lévi-Strauss (1958, 1966) focuses on the underlying structures of cultural codes that are responsible for the surface variety of human mythologies. In a similar vein, Barthes' (1973) semiological studies of such apparently disparate phenomena as the VW Beetle car, wrestling and striptease sought to demonstrate their conceptual unity in an underlying schema of myths and dramatic codes. From a different tradition, that of structural functionalism, Parsons (1937, 1951) has sought to identify the functional prerequisites that underlie all social action.

One of the major problems with approaches which concentrate on the structural end of our continuum is how to explain social change. This is unsurprising perhaps, since an emphasis on the role of structures is necessarily accompanied by a diminished view of agency, one in which human beings scarcely figure as movers and shakers of the social world. The need to account for change, for the dynamic features of social life, has attracted many theorists towards the other end of our continuum where the focus is much more on agency, on people as active participants in the making of the social world.

Interactionist accounts of structure-and-agency

We have termed agency-centred approaches interactionist, and although this is a rather rough and ready description it will serve our central purpose of identifying those theories which reverse the direction of the structuralist's explanatory flow. Causal primacy in explaining the social world in the interactionist approach goes to human beings. Social structures are sometimes reduced to the status of convenient sociological descriptions (as in certain forms of ethnomethodology – see Chapter 2); or viewed as simply the accumulation of habit and routine; or as the discursive product of social conversation (as in some forms of social constructionism – again, see Chapter 2).

Movement towards the agency end of the continuum introduces the obverse problem to that raised by moving towards the structure end, namely the problem of social persistence. Here the emphasis on the role of agency is often accompanied by an impoverished view of structures, one in which social relations become more plastic, offering only a flimsy resistance to human reworking. It thus becomes difficult to explain why situations of injustice or inequality continue when they clearly work to the disadvantage of many.

So it would seem that an overemphasis on structure brings the problem of explaining social change, whilst an overemphasis on agency brings the problem of explaining social persistence or stability. Understandably enough, many social theorists have hovered more or less in the centre of our continuum, convinced by neither structure nor agency as adequate bases for explanation of the social world. However, political and social changes such as the collapse of the Communist bloc and the increasing dominance of a global capitalism have renewed the demand for a social theory able to account for both social stability and social change. Additionally, the emergence of the so-called 'linguistic turn' in social theory has raised doubts about the value of earlier formulations of the structure and agency relation. Together these developments have prompted some fresh approaches to the structure–agency issue.

Structurationist accounts of structure-and-agency

One possible resolution of the debate is to suggest that the two terms cannot be considered separately, since they are effectively only referring to two sides of the same coin. This line of argument has been persuasively developed in the structuration theory of Giddens (1976, 1979, 1984). Giddens rejects the idea of structural forces which constrain and determine human behaviour 'from the outside' as it were, and objects to the notion that 'social systems' have properties of their own that can be analysed independently of human needs and purposes. On the other hand, for Giddens the problem with the agency end of the continuum is that the subjective experiences of individuals, and the meanings that they attach to them, become the central point of analysis. There is a tendency to regard social reality as the outcome of the actions of free agents; the influence of the persistent, institutional features of the social world on these agents is difficult to incorporate analytically.

Giddens suggests, therefore, that rather than think in terms of a *dualism* of agency and structure, in which the two terms are taken to refer to separate and opposed phenomena, we should think in terms of a *duality* of structure, in which structure is seen as having twin aspects. According to this perspective, structure and agency are intrinsically united through social practices. When people interact with each other, they draw upon a vast range of skills and resources: cognitive, linguistic, perceptual, physical. Many of these will have been acquired through experience, through their routine practical application in the living of a life (how to ride a bike, how to make yourself understood in a common language). Other skills and resources will, however, be part of a stock of socially shared knowledge and skills (how to chair a department meeting, how to get an article published). Nevertheless, how we as unique individuals deploy these skills and resources will depend on how we interpret the rules governing the contexts in which they are relevant: there are many ways of riding a bike or chairing a meeting.

Thus for structuration theory, social practices reflect the ability of human beings to modify the circumstances in which they find themselves (by creatively interpreting rules and deploying resources), whilst simultaneously recreating the social conditions (rules, knowledges, resources) which they inherit from the past. Thus, each doctor–patient consultation – or employer–employee job interview, or classroom lesson – both draws on existing routines for carrying out these interactions and interprets them afresh through the specific medium of the individuals 'instantiating' these routines on this occasion. Structure and agency are thus two sides of the same coin: in order to develop purposes and do things we draw upon rules and resources, and in doing so we endorse and enact them, thereby contributing to their continuance.

The persuasiveness of the structuration approach, as both Archer and Layder have pointed out, depends heavily on Giddens' novel definition of structure (Archer 1995; Layder 1994). By recasting structure as 'rules and resources', he separates it from the idea of system, of an 'objective' social reality independent of the activities of people. So, for Giddens, social structures possess only a *virtual* existence until they are instantiated by people, that is insofar as people knowingly take them into account in social action and thereby either reproduce or modify them. Social relations are thus dependent on the activities of extant human beings and cannot be separated from them. Since structure and agency are held to be mutually constitutive, their properties are not real except in conjunction with each other, and it is impossible to examine the interplay between them.

In our view this constitutes a major limitation to the structurationist model. While we would accept that, at the level of the consultation, interview or lesson, people's understandings of these interactions do influence how they are conducted, we would also argue that social relations shape such interactions in ways that the people involved in them may not be fully aware of. For example, asylum-seekers who cannot access health-care in the country they find themselves in, or unemployed workers in a period of economic recession, find themselves in situations that are significantly structured by social relations of political power and economic influence. These structures are not confined to those aspects of the role of patient or interviewee which are instantiated in the interaction itself – most obviously if participation in that interaction is precluded by one's social location.

Realist accounts of structure-and-agency

A fourth view of the agency–structure relation is also possible and it is the one that we shall be advocating here. It is derived from the recent work of authors who subscribe to a version of the philosophical tradition known as 'realism', and it claims that structure and agency possess distinct properties and powers. As we argue elsewhere (Sealey and Carter forthcoming), there are important distinctions to be drawn between different versions of realism, particularly as this philosophical tradition is better established in the natural and physical sciences than in the social disciplines. (See also the discussion in Sarangi and Candlin 2001.) For the social realist, in direct contrast to the structuration model of Giddens, the terms 'structure' and 'agency' denote different types of things in the social world.

The claim, then, is that social structures are one particular kind of entity, whose properties are of a different kind from those of other entities. The distinctive properties of social structures include their anteriority: the fact that, for example, legal systems and property relations precede us, are always already features of the world into which we are born. This points to another distinguishing property of social structures: they are relatively enduring. Amongst the powers possessed by social structures are those of enablement and constraint: structures of discrimination will constrain the discriminated-against and enable the discriminators; inegalitarian distributions of wealth and income will constrain the poor and enable the rich.

Amongst the distinguishing properties and powers of agency are self-consciousness, reflexivity, intentionality, cognition, emotionality and so on. As reflexive beings capable of highly sophisticated symbolic communication, people are able to formulate projects, develop plans, have ambitions, pursue interests. This ontological endowment means that it is people who make history, not least because they are the only denizens of the social world able to reflect upon, and so seek to alter or reinforce, the fitness of the social arrangements they encounter for the realization of their own interests. This cardinal power of agency – the power to maintain or modify the world – is not only dependent on the property of self-consciousness. People collectively can exert an influence simply by virtue of their numbers, a property we might call demographic agency. Thus the unemployed or the homeless, if their numbers reach a threshold of political or social visibility, can prompt changes in economic or housing policy (or, of course, changes in policing policy). The point is that such effects do not rely on the homeless or the unemployed knowing about or reflecting upon their condition and formally organizing as *the* homeless or *the* unemployed. (Although, of course, they may arrive sooner at the threshold of political visibility if they do so.)

The distinct properties and powers of structure and agency thus entail their irreducibility to each other. This undermines the mutually constitutive, structurationist view of the relationship between structure and agency we summarized above. It also entails a rejection of the 'structuralist' view, since without an active notion of agency, that is, without being able to enquire about who is doing what to whom and why, we cannot arrive at a convincing explanation for structures at all. Once we recognize the powers and properties of agency, it becomes difficult to see people as passive puppets, cultural dopes or discursive effects.

However, a corresponding recognition of the enduring and anterior properties of social structures, and the consequent patterns of constraint and enablement that they generate, undermines the second view of structure and agency summarized above. If social structures are ineffectual in their own right because they are at any given moment nothing more than the product of the conversations or interpretive strategies of currently existing people, then the social theorist is hard pressed to explain how human agency is shaped by social contexts. The realist view that we are advocating, on the other hand, is committed to an explanatory model in which the interplay between pre-existent structures, having causal powers and properties, and people, possessing distinctive causal powers and properties of their own, results in contingent yet explicable outcomes.

Emergence

In the previous section we observed that structural features of the contemporary social world are emergent from earlier social interaction. The term 'emergence' is gaining currency in many areas of research, in both the natural and social sciences, and we shall be drawing on some of these developments in later chapters. For the moment, it is important to clarify its relevance for the structure–agency debate which is our current concern. An 'emergent property' is generated from its constituent elements, but is not reducible to them. For example, although people are comprised of cells, and they possess the power to think, '[w]e would not try to explain the power of people to think by reference to the cells that constitute them, as if cells possessed this power too' (Sayer 1992: 119).

To take an example from the social world, let us consider the institution of marriage as an emergent property of social interaction. It is difficult to establish the primary (or 'first order' (Archer 1995)) constituents of marriage, since it is an institution which has changed over a long historical frame. It is the emergent product of previous emergent products, as contemporary social practices nearly always are. Among the constituents of marriage are the social resources which make institutions possible, such as systems of law, property and inheritance. Another constituent is the interpretive understanding of human beings: for marriage to operate as an 'institutional fact' (Searle 1995), people must understand what it signifies, whether they wish to get married, or to struggle against the institution of marriage because it is oppressive or iniquitous. These two constituents – interpretive meanings and a legally binding contract – are different kinds of things, and the institution of marriage is not reducible to either one.

The relationship between these constituents is a necessary one: without either we could not talk of marriage as a *social* institution. This fact illustrates a second feature of emergent properties: the relations between the constituent elements are necessary rather than contingent. That is to say, it might seem plausible to propose that another constituent feature of marriage is that, in the words of the English marriage service, it involves 'the union of one man with one woman', since at the present time marriages in the United Kingdom are invariably 'occupied' by just one incumbent of each sex. However, on closer analysis it turns out that this correlation, between 'married people' and 'one man and one woman', is a contingent feature rather than a necessary one, since at other times and in other places the institution of marriage has involved a partner of one sex and several partners of the other (as in polygamy and polyandry), or two same-sex partners. So the involvement of two partners of opposite sex is a contingent feature of one manifestation of marriage, albeit a very widely occurring one, whereas the constituents of human under-standing and a legal system stand in a necessary relation to each other for marriage to be an emergent product.

A third feature of emergent properties is their power to condition the contexts in which subsequent social interaction takes place. As an institution – legal, political, economic, cultural and conventional – marriage has proved relatively enduring and stable. (This is not to deny the enormous cultural and temporal variability in marriage practices and customs, of course.) The pressure to get married, to get married in particular sorts of ceremonies, to see marriage as an aspiration and to regard it as the most appropriate form of cohabitation, all provide conditioning influences on the power of human beings to effect choices about their lives. It should also be noted that the influ-ence of structures on agency, their power to constrain and enable, is not an abstract property, but attains relevance only in the context of particular projects by particular people in particular situations. Thus those with no interest in getting married do not experience the insti-tution of marriage in this way – although they may well be affected by it, nonetheless, perhaps by feeling stigmatized, on the one hand, or privileged, on the other, as a 'single person'.

Emergence is what makes the identification of structures poss-ible, for the irreducibility, endurance and autonomous influence of emergent properties entails that they pre-date any particular set of incumbents. Marriage has the capacity to modify the powers of its constituents. People's understanding of what it is to be married often changes when they become married. They may find themselves embroiled in relations (and with relations) which frequently can come to seem oppressive, disappointing, or not at all what either (or both) of the partners had in mind. Even couples who, conversely, regard themselves as 'happily married' may still need to make considerable adjustments to their perceptions of self in relation to others. The legal system which makes marriage possible is itself altered by the institu-tion of marriage: the legal entitlement to certain sorts of privileges becomes restricted to those who have participated in the socially recognized form of marriage. Marriage depends on people getting married, but it doesn't depend on particular individuals getting married. This means that the interplay between marriage, as an institutionally embedded and expressed form of cohabitation, and people, as socially situated actors, can be analysed and researched.

In summary, then, the defining features of emergent properties are three-fold: relative endurance; necessary, not contingent, relations between the constituent elements; and the possession of causal powers (Archer 1995: 167).

Throughout this book we shall be illustrating how these social theoretical ideas relate to the concerns of applied linguistics, but let us give one further example here. When language learners seek accreditation in their capacity to write in the language they have been studying, they are involved in processes resulting from a number of emergent features of the social world. There are the linguistic resources which make up the variety in which the learners wish to be qualified; these have already been codified by groups of people who can lay convincing claim to expertise in doing so; this claim is dependent on the institutionalization of assessment practices, which generates the possibility of careers for those qualified as language testers, and the procedures for assessment are developed over time. The well-known 'washback' effect of examinations (e.g. Bachman 1990) influences teaching practices as teachers try to ensure that learners are as likely as possible to succeed in the test. At the same time, the grammar and vocabulary deemed acceptable in the language variety in question acquire prestige, while other variants become stigmatized, so that the linguistic resources themselves are to some extent modified by language testing institutions.

We now turn to consider some of the epistemological implications of these ideas.

Objectivity

Perhaps the most obvious of these implications (obvious not only from our account above of the anteriority of social structures, but also from realism as a more general philosophical position) is that realists are able to defend a commitment to objective knowledge. We understand objective knowledge in a dual sense, although these senses are intimately connected. Firstly, following Popper, we would distinguish between subjective knowledge – what any particular individual knows – and objective knowledge – knowledge expressed in theories, propositions, conjectures. The important feature of objective knowledge is that it is 'totally independent of anybody's claim to know; it is also independent of anybody's belief, or disposition to assent, or to assert or to act. Knowledge in the objective sense is *knowledge without a knower*; it is *knowledge without a knowing subject*' (Popper 1972: 109). The second sense in which we understand objective knowledge is that, precisely because it is 'knowledge without a knower', it is capable of refinement and methodological development. The social practice of knowledge production has this as an aim, albeit one which is often imperfectly and only partially realized. Without objective knowledge it is hard to make any case for improving theoretical understanding or for the epistemic authority of research.

We should perhaps say a word or two about the term objectivity, since it has come to carry some pejorative meanings. Let us dispose of some of these to begin with. Firstly, objectivity must be distinguished from objectivism. This latter term denotes the popular idea that there is one (true) point of view from which reality can be apprehended. Sometimes this view is referred to as a 'God's eye' view or, in Nagel's apt phrase, the 'view from nowhere' (Nagel 1986). It goes without saying that such a view cannot be found; knowledge is always knowledge from a particular place and time and cannot provide us with a 'complete' view of the world.

However, and secondly, this should not lead us to underestimate or dismiss the importance of objectivity (as opposed to objectivism). As Sayer (1992: 83) puts it, '[t]he world can only be understood in terms of available conceptual resources, but the latter do not determine the structure of the world itself'. Knowledge may always be historically specific and socially located, must always be knowledge *from* some-where, but it is also knowledge *of* something. The interesting issue is not that knowledge is always knowledge from somewhere, but rather how, given this commonplace, we come to have knowledge of anything at all. In fact, as Nagel has argued, those who dismiss objectivity as well as those who overrate it share a common error, which stems from their insufficiently robust sense of reality and of its independence of any particular form of human understanding. They both significantly underestimate the difficulties and the possibilities of human know-ledge: the one by denying that there is a reality to be known, the other by assuming that it can be known simply by occupying the objective viewpoint. (For a discussion of these issues as applied to socio-linguistics, see Sarangi and Candlin 2001.)

It is, of course, central to realist accounts that the world is in an important sense mind-independent. But this, as we have just seen, both limits and justifies objectivity, since 'as small creatures in a big world of which we have only very partial understanding, ... how things seem to us depends both on the world and on our constitution'

(Nagel 1986: 5). The structure–agency debate is important precisely because it attempts to capture analytically this distinction between the social world and ourselves. Here also lie the roots of our opposition to the non-realist accounts of the relationship between structure and agency outlined above. In making agents the puppets of structures, or structures the creation of agents or, in the case of structuration theory, making them mutually constitutive of each other, these accounts make it difficult to examine the interplay between the world and ourselves. This has implications for our notion of objectivity.

As particular individuals we confront a world that is not directly produced or constructed by us, but is rather the complex, emergent outcome of the interactions between structural contexts (structure) and ourselves (agency). For the realist, therefore, there may be a divergence between how things are and how people take them to be. This follows logically from the temporal priority given to structures. (For example, we learn to speak in a particular language from infancy; the anteriority of the language to us as particular individuals ensures that we have little choice about which language this will be.) Furthermore our grasp of these structures will necessarily be partial (and for many of us in the case of language remains so), partly because their systemic features may become accessible only to theoretical excavation and partly because of their temporal precedence. A crucial feature of structures in our realist account then is 'that they exist and act independently of the knowledge of which they are objects' (Bhaskar 1979).

Realism and language

A core argument of this book is that language is itself an emergent property of the interplay between structure and agency. Language, to use Marx's expression, is practical consciousness. The key term here is practice. For the moment we will take this to refer to the practical, embodied engagement we have with the world from the moment of birth. As an emergent property of this engagement, language develops its own powers of constraint and facilitation, as we shall see in later chapters, and itself makes possible the general discursive domain of culture. Nevertheless, the ontological primacy placed here on practice is likely to raise a few hackles amongst those who take a more imperialistic view of the place of language in the social world. We shall return to this later.

Part 2: Some key issues in applied linguistics

This section is intended particularly for those readers who are less familiar with the discipline of applied linguistics, and its aim is to introduce some of the key concepts, terms and controversies that will be referred to elsewhere in the book. However, since the discipline is itself fairly heterogeneous, readers from within it may also find the section of interest as an indication of our position within this broad field. The general reader may be baffled by the distinction between 'applied' linguistics and simple 'linguistics', so we shall explain some of the background in what follows. The term 'applied' linguistics reflects in part the nature of the work which its practitioners do, but the fact that 'linguistics' and 'applied linguistics' each have their academic 'territory' also indicates a degree of debate about more conceptual matters, such as the nature of language, and how to identify means of describing it, classifying it, and explaining the way people use it.

It is traditional in introductions to applied linguistics to begin with linguistics and then explain what is applied about it. For example, Carter (1993) indicates that '... applied linguistics is the application of linguistic theories, descriptions and methods to the solution of language problems which have arisen in a range of human, cultural and social contexts' (p.3). If '... linguistics reifies "language"', asks Brumfit (1997: 90), 'what does applied linguistics reify? More than just language – "language practices".' What applied linguists do could be considered a definition of what the discipline is (Davies 1999), so, since (on strict quantitative measures) by far the majority of its work is concerned with foreign language teaching, this is what it is perceived to be by many. But this overlooks a great deal. Cook (2003: 8), for example, lists a significant number of areas that '... fall within our definition of applied linguistics and are claimed as areas of enquiry by organizations and journals concerned with the discipline'. This list includes the following three main areas and their subcategories: Language and education: first-language education, additional-language education (subdivided into second- and foreign-language education), clinical linguistics, language testing; Language, work and law: workplace communication, language planning, forensic linguistics; Language, information and effect: literary stylistics, critical discourse analysis, translation and interpretation, information design, lexicography. From this broader perspective, applied linguistics may be redefined as 'problem-based researching into communication-mediated issues in social life' (Candlin pers. comm.). In such explorations, applied linguistics draws on a range of communication-interested disciplines and tools. Linguistics features among these, but certainly not to the exclusion of the others; indeed our claim that applied linguistics needs to be understood as a social science exemplifies the fact that descriptions of language and languages alone are inadequate to account for language-related practices and the problems associated with these. Thus 'applied linguistics' is a somewhat problematic label, but one that is convenient and has become established despite its problems.

What then are the core issues with which applied linguistics is concerned? Obviously, language itself is one key area of enquiry; the motivated practice of human agents as they use language is another; and the nature of the structured social contexts within which people seek to pursue their interests – where language is usually a medium for doing so, and is sometimes also an objective of those interests – is a third. In this part of the chapter, we sketch out some of the ways in which applied linguists have contributed to our understanding of these overlapping dimensions of language in social life, influenced as they are by a range of disciplinary perspectives. The division of topics into these three sections is necessarily somewhat arbitrary, since, as we explain in subsequent chapters, the social theoretical position we advance takes account of the *interplay* between the different domains, or strata, of the social world. However, in order to structure the material in a way which is consistent with the preceding part, we start with those topics which are most closely linked to language itself, move on to those concerned with situated practices, and conclude with an outline of some of the wider social issues to which applied linguistics makes a contribution.

Applied linguistics and descriptions of language

What does it mean to describe 'language'? What does such a description need to include? 'Language' may be conceptualized variously as a form of human behaviour, sounds in the air and marks on the page, a system of symbolic communication, an innate cognitive competence; and the answers to these questions may depend on who is asking them and why: the researcher recording the characteristics of a nearly-extinct language is likely to need different kinds of information from that required by the minister devising the language policy of a newly independent territory, or a language teacher, or a translator and so on. For some of these purposes applied linguistics draws on linguistics, especially when what the applied linguist needs to do is to give some account of the properties of a language, for example in the context of courses for the teachers of language learners or of children learning literacy. It might be assumed that the descriptions of the properties of languages which linguistics has made available would be ideal for such purposes, but this does not always turn out to be so, partly because the aims of the two enterprises are far from identical.

Linguistics is sometimes referred to as 'autonomous' linguistics, a phrase which signals its concern with the formal system of language as independent from other disciplines (Crystal 1991). The goal of linguistic enquiry, in this tradition (which is associated particularly with Chomsky), is the abstraction from the ubiquitous and polymorphous phenomenon which is language, towards greater understanding of the universals of the human mind. Describing a language is synonymous with 'describing part of the minds' of its speakers (Salkie 2001: 107, 110). The data of speakers' actual behaviour (their 'performance'), in this context, '... are disregarded ... because they are of little theoretical interest: they do not provide reliable evidence for the essential nature of human language' (Widdowson 1996: 70). A summary statement of this essential nature, of what is common to human languages, is provided by Pinker (1999: 92): '... the ingredients of language are a list of memorized words, each an arbitrary pairing between a sound and a meaning, and a set of productive rules that assemble words into combinations'. Units such as individual sounds, which are normally meaningless on their own, are elements in a combinatorial system. The finite number of elements – such as the distinct sounds which contrast with each other in any one language – can combine to generate exponentially larger numbers of units of meaning. According to the Chomskyan tradition, human beings, endowed as they are with linguistic 'competence', are genetically programmed to be able to process language – any language – and what is of interest is the interface between language and mind.

The area of second language acquisition provides one overlap between the concerns of autonomous linguists and those of applied linguists. Some would claim, with Gregg (1993), that the basic focus of this research is '... L2 competence, in the Chomskyan sense of the term: How do L2 learners acquire competence in a second language? or, Why do learners not acquire the same competence as native speakers of the L2?' (p.278). However, the more 'applied' this interest is, and the more pressing the need not just to investigate these questions but to actually teach particular learners, the greater the priority given to speakers' linguistic *performance*. Applied linguistics thus necessarily concerns itself with language *behaviour*, with speaking, listening, reading and writing. As conceived within theoretical – or autonomous – linguistics, such behaviour involves those features of language which are 'secondary ..., incidental, and peripheral' in

19

contrast to those which are 'essential and primary' (Widdowson 1996: 24–5).

The question of how far the study of language should involve attention to empirical evidence will be revisited in this and subsequent chapters, but at this point it may be useful, particularly for those readers who are less familiar with the linguistic disciplines, to provide a very basic, and necessarily greatly simplified, outline of what is thought to be involved in human linguistic competence.

Language 'rules'

One academic who has made some efforts to popularize the study of language, Jean Aitchison, maintains that 'almost all linguists, not just psycholinguists, are trying to find out about a speaker's mental "grammar" – the internalized set of rules which enables someone to speak and understand their language' (1989: 164). It is so common for rules of this kind to be conflated with the social, extralinguistic rules which are invoked to pronounce an utterance in a non-standard dialect, for example, as 'ungrammatical', that we feel it is worth pointing out the distinction, as introductory textbooks about linguistics always do. Yet in our own experience, academics from a range of disciplines lack confidence in their students' – and often their own – knowledge of linguistic (particularly grammatical) 'rules'. In this they share with the public at large some of the attitudes about local accents and class dialects which within linguistics are classified as norms of a quite different kind from the descriptions which indicate which combinations are possible and which not within a given language variety. At the risk of labouring the point, here it is made by the author of one of the textbooks of the kind referred to above:

> Sometimes you will hear people object that certain expressions or constructions are 'not English' or 'ungrammatical'. Some teachers still like to say this about *ain't* or the use of the double negative, as in *I ain't got no money*. But this is not so. Something is only ungrammatical if it fails to follow a rule in the way it is formed. *I ain't got no money* doesn't follow the same rule in its construction as *I haven't any money* but it's not without one. People who use this construction wouldn't dream of saying *got I have money n't no*, which would be uninterpretable.
>
> (Finch 1998: 3)

This injunction to draw a distinction between extralinguistic and intralinguistic 'rules', the latter being 'internalised in us as native speakers of the language' (*ibid.*: 9), is by no means the end of this discussion. It will resurface in our consideration of lay discourse and epistemic authority, as well as in our exploration of natural and social realism, but for now it is sufficient to allow that languages do at least *appear* to be subject to rules which fall somewhere between the evaluative norms of the social world and the 'universal' laws of the natural world.

Traditional description of how the units of language are combined assumes a basic pattern that can be visualized as a vertical axis and a horizontal axis which intersect. Within a sentence, the vertical axis is the 'syntagm', which represents the sequential order of words in a language, created by its syntax. The horizontal axis is the 'paradigm', which represents 'the set of alternative words which could be used equally legitimately in a particular position in the syntagm' (Graddol *et al.* 1994: 72). This pattern can be illustrated by presenting some of the variations on a simple sentence which are possible in English.

She	read	a	long	poem
The student	wrote	some	interesting	essays
Bob	likes	these	difficult	problems
Alison	asked	one	simple	question

The pattern going across the horizontal axis illustrates some features of English syntax, linking in a familiar order words which can be classified as having particular properties. So we are able to process 'one simple question', but would be puzzled by 'question simple one'. The pattern going down each of the vertical axes illustrates alternatives among words which have something in common with each other. Thus 'long', 'interesting', 'difficult' and 'simple' are all examples of words said to belong to the same 'word class' (also known, more traditionally, as 'part of speech').

A similar pattern can account for the relations between sounds. In English, for example, it is very common for words of one syllable to consist of the sequence consonant-vowel-consonant, and several examples illustrated together (transcribed here – and thus idealized – as letters) can contribute to a grid which can vary horizontally and vertically.

p a t
b i d
t o p

Variations both across and down the elements of this three by three square can generate multiple combinations.

Traditionally, linguistics is concerned to describe this system of patterns (or rules) among the elements of language, working from sounds, through words to syntax. (Another level of analysis is 'mor-phology', concerned with the internal structure of words, but it is not important to discuss this here.) Single sentences are often held to be the largest unit of analysis for the 'core' of linguistics, as the patterns involved in longer stretches of language are nowhere near as suscep-tible to description of this kind.

Methodologically, the appeal to internalized, mental representa-tions of 'rules' such as these is via 'native speaker intuition'. In other words, if you as a reader grew up with English in your linguistic repertoire, you would be expected to know that *got I have money n't no* violates the rules of English grammar, even if you are not able to parse the construction and explain in technical terminology why this is. The emphasis, as we have remarked, is on competence rather than perfor-mance. However, this view competes with alternative approaches to language description which put much greater weight on performance data.

Integrationist and functionalist accounts of language

The most thoroughgoing rejection of the separation of linguistic form from social function is perhaps that articulated by Harris and his associates. Harris (2001) draws a distinction between 'autonomists' – those who believe language is a set of verbal tools, and communication just the use to which those tools happen to be put – and 'non-autonomists', those who believe language *is* communication. He defines himself as an 'integrationist', and thus among those who take 'the most radical position' (p.131) on this issue. Integrationists see the extrapolation from individual cases to general rules as illegitimate, because language is a negotiated protocol between individuals which varies with each negotiation. (Other interpretations of integrationism also challenge mentalist versions of linguistics, though from slightly different positions. See, for example, Lieb 2002.)

Another approach which denies a distinction between language 'competence' (the abstract mental capacity, or potential, to deploy language) and 'performance' (the realization of this capacity in actual utterances) is defined as 'functional', associated particularly with Halliday, who proposes that 'language is as it is because of what it has to do' (Halliday 1978: 19), and that the way to understand language is to start from the principle that 'the linguistic system is a sociolinguistic system' (*ibid.*: 72). There is considerable integration, in Halliday's system, of the uses to which language is put and the patterns of its grammar and vocabulary. The functions of language include not only the communication of ideas (the 'ideational' function), and the organization of texts themselves (the 'textual' function) but also the participation in communicative acts, enabling human beings 'to take on roles and to express and understand feelings, attitude and judgements' (Bloor and Bloor 1995: 9). The descriptive system which has developed from this perspective on language as practice includes categories and labels such as 'Actor', 'Goal' and 'Process' which signal a concern with meaning, including interpersonal meaning. Rather than seeing the sentence as the largest unit of analysis, and sentences as composed of aggregations of smaller units, this perspective posits the text as 'the basic unit of the semantic process' (*ibid.*: 107). For Hallidayan functionalists, it is more useful to see text as *encoded in* sentences rather than *composed of* them, and the emphasis on understanding what language is is much more inter- than intra-individual. As Chouliaraki and Fairclough (1999: 140) express it, 'the social is built into the grammatical tissue of language'.

In this approach there is a shift of emphasis from the invisible workings of the individual mind towards the empirically observable behaviour of the language user. Many applied linguists would argue that this is more useful to them than the formalist approach to language description associated with Chomsky. As Carter (1993) puts it:

> There is a primary focus on language in use rather than on language as an abstract system and the models of analysis developed within functional linguistics are therefore of particular use for the analyses of naturally occurring spoken and written texts, often those produced within educational contexts.
>
> (p.31)

A concern with empirical evidence of language-users' behaviour underpins another development in language description, whereby researchers have developed large, electronically stored 'corpora': 'collection[s] of pieces of language, selected and ordered according to explicit linguistic criteria in order to be used as a sample of the language' (Sinclair 1996 in Aston and Burnard 1998). A key objection made by corpus linguists to traditional descriptions is the weight placed by the latter on the intuition of the native speaker of a language, a procedure which Sinclair (1991) likens to 'that of the physical sciences some 250 years ago' (p.1). Corpus linguistics uses the computer to store and to search very large quantities of language data which have been produced for actual communicative purposes by (usually) large numbers of speakers and/or writers. The corpus known as the Bank of English, for example, includes over 400 million words of running text drawn from newspapers, magazines, fiction and non-fiction books, brochures, leaflets, reports and letters, as well as transcripts of every-day conversations, meetings, discussions and radio programmes.

The software used to investigate a corpus allows the identification of recurring patterns; in particular, *concordancing* programs identify the contexts within which particular linguistic items, such as a specific word or group of words, occur. *Collocations* are patterns of co-occurrence of words – 'You shall know a word by the company it keeps', wrote Firth (1957: 11, cited in Stubbs 1996) – and corpus investigations have identified some facts about such patterns which had not been identified by earlier methods of analysis. Corpus linguists have found reason from their research to challenge the adequacy of traditional grammatical categories. They argue that corpus evidence points to a different kind of classification, of 'patterns' functioning differently from the paradigm/syntagm matrix described above. Again, communicative function is foregrounded:

> As communicators we do not proceed by selecting syntactic structures and independently choosing lexical items to slot into them. Instead we have concepts to convey and communicative choices to make which require central lexical items, and these choices find themselves syntactic structures in which they can be said comfortably and grammatically.
>
> (Francis 1995 in Hunston and Francis 2000: 31)

In Chapter 3, we explore in much greater detail the implications of corpus linguistics for a realist theory of language, as well as considering how social realist theory might illuminate the enterprise of empirically based descriptions of language, including corpus linguistics.

Applied linguistics and human practice

As we have argued, within applied linguistics, concerns about what people do with language make it difficult to be satisfied with accounts which confine language, and descriptions of language, to internalized mental rules. In this section, we consider some ways in which language is researched less as a set of rules and more as a human practice, and highlight some applied linguistic activities which are conducted from this perspective.

Language corpora and applied linguistics

Although it has generated much useful information for the enterprise of language description, the original impetus for the development of a corpus like the Bank of English was pedagogic, so that reference books for language learners, such as grammars and dictionaries, could be based on evidence rather than intuition. Those involved in syllabus design can, if they wish, make decisions about when to introduce certain items based on their relative frequency, or can teach words as they appear in their most typical contexts (Nattinger and DeCarrico 1992). The ambition of many learners to sound 'authentic' may be aided by this kind of approach. Other areas of applied linguistic activity which are supported by corpora of various kinds (including parallel corpora in different languages) include for example translation, stylistics and forensic linguistics (Hunston 2002).

Discourse analysis and applied linguistics

Another area of research in which applied linguists are active is the analysis of discourse, where the aim is not so much the identification of the patterns and systems that constitute a language as the use of that language for specific communicative purposes. The term 'discourse analysis' carries a number of different meanings, and those who practise it operate within a range of disciplines, from the more sociological to the more linguistic. Work more strongly associated with the former tends to explore how 'discursive practices [may be] constitutive of knowledge', while that linked with the latter has been termed 'textually oriented discourse analysis' (Fairclough 1993: 38).

Insights from both orientations, though more usually the latter, are 'applied' in language teaching, where learners need to be familiar not only with sentence level constructions but also with the larger patterns which characterize a wide range of text types and social interactions. For discussions of different methods and models of discourse analysis in respect of their usefulness to teachers and students of (English as a) foreign language, see, for example, Cook 1989, McCarthy 1991, McCarthy and Carter 1994. The different genres into which discourse can be subdivided have also been explored in applied linguistics, and research continues into how different text types may be classified, and how the discourse of particular kinds of practice, particularly academic practice, is constituted and learned. Some relevant literature here includes, for example, Dudley-Evans 1994 and Swales 1990. Research into the discourse of various written genres has also been used in suggestions for the teaching of mother-tongue literacy to schoolchildren (Lewis and Wray 1997; Martin 1989; Rothery 1989).

Sociologists may well be more familiar with the approaches to discourse analysis which have developed out of ethnomethodology, with its interest in how people produce and interpret conversation. The seminal theorists associated with this kind of conversation analysis (CA) include Garfinkel, Sacks, Schegloff and Jefferson, some of whose ideas we explore in Chapter 2. These conversation analysts have sought to identify, for example, the ways in which speakers open and close conversations, and how turns and transitions between speakers are managed within fractions of a second. Some applied linguists have sought to explore how the findings of CA may be utilized in pedagogic contexts (e.g. Seedhouse forthcoming; Wong 2002), while Firth (1996) uses a CA approach to look at intercultural encounters, analysing interactions in English between non-native speakers.

Sociocultural and ecological theories in applied linguistics

Many applied linguists whose work involves them in the field of additional language learning have developed ways of thinking about the process which draw on ideas, from disciplines such as psychology and education, where learning is conceived of as significantly inter- as well as intra-individual. '... [S]pecifically human forms of mental activity are not processes that occur invisibly inside someone's head but are instead the activity of socio-historically constituted people engaged in the historically situated activity of living' (Dunn and Lantolf 1998: 427). Particularly influential here is the work of Vygotsky and his sociocultural theory of mind, which has been taken up by a number of applied linguists – see, for example, Lantolf 2000a, Lantolf and Pavlenko 1995, Smagorinsky 2001.

A further development in culturally situated accounts of language use and language learning, to which some of the same researchers have contributed, makes use of the metaphor of ecology. Rejecting the implications of likening language learning either to the input–output process associated with machines and computers, or to the linear acculturation process associated with a period of apprenticeship, ecological approaches invoke a concept of language learning as 'a nonlinear, relational human activity, co-constructed between humans and their environment, contingent upon their position in space and history, and a site of struggle for the control of power and cultural memory' (Kramsch 2002a: 5).

This much more global view of what applied linguists are interested in takes us beyond applicable descriptions of language itself, and accounts of language learning and use as intersubjective practices, into the third section of this part. Here we consider a selection of the ways in which the discipline intersects with the study of social institutions and issues of power.

Applied linguistics and social contexts

It has been claimed that 'social processes, sociology, anthropology, and media studies recently seem to have replaced pedagogy, linguistics, and psychology as the major preoccupations in British applied linguistics' (Rampton 1995a: 233). This may be something of an overstatement, given in particular the size of the continuing enterprise of language teaching in which applied linguists are involved. However, there are many areas where the discipline overlaps with those social sciences whose focus is on more macro phenomena, and we touch on some of them here.

Critical discourse analysis

While applied linguistics contributes to the description of communicative practices partly through its work in discourse analysis, some of its theorists and researchers are committed to analyses which not only describe 'what is', but also enquire into 'how it has come to be, and what it might become, on the basis of which people may be able to make and remake their lives' (Chouliaraki and Fairclough 1999: 4). For example, a virtual research group concerned with 'language in the new capitalism' is interested in 'the language and meaning of contemporary capitalism, and the links between economic, social and linguistic change in the contemporary world', in the belief that 'a better understanding of how language figures in the new capitalism ... increases our capacity to question and critique it, and to change it' (LNC 2003). The 'critical linguists' and, later, 'critical discourse analysts' who have used the analysis of language practices to illuminate issues of power and inequality include, for example, Chouliaraki and Fairclough (1999), Fairclough (1989, 1995, 2001), Fowler *et al.* (1979) and Kress (1985). Amongst their data are texts produced by institutions, such as universities, government departments or commercial corporations, the output of news media (both print and broadcast) as well as the discourse of political speeches, and there is, again, a particular affinity between the systemic functional description of language associated with Halliday (see above) and the enterprise of exploring large-scale political issues through the analysis of language (see particularly Chouliaraki and Fairclough 1999).

The methods available to corpus linguists are also drawn on in studies of social and cultural values. According to Teubert (1999), corpus linguistics 'is based on the concept that language is a funda-mentally social phenomenon, which can be observed and described first and foremost in the empirical data readily available, that is, in communication acts'. Corpus linguists have explored cultural pre-occupations in their data, such as various examples of specific lexical items being repeatedly found with other words that have one kind of connotation rather than another, leading Stubbs (1996) to propose that the analytic methods made possible by these methods could enhance new versions of the kind of social commentary carried out by Raymond Williams in his *Keywords* (1976), and he provides examples here and in Stubbs 2001a.

In the previous section we highlighted the link between discourse analysis with an applied linguistic provenance and the conversation analysis conducted by sociologists. The critical discourse analyst Billig (1999a, 1999b) has attacked traditional conversation analysis on the grounds that it 'conveys an essentially non-critical view of the social world', but there are many analysts who use the CA approach to explore the role of talk in the constitution and maintenance of asym-metrical social relationships, particularly in institutional discourse. For example, the collection edited by Drew and Heritage (1993) reports on the interactions between professionals and 'clients' in a wide variety of settings, including doctor–patient consultations, legal hear-ings, news interviews, visits by health visitors, psychiatric interviews, and calls to the emergency services. Contributors include sociologists and applied linguists, some of whom are well-known for developing the branch of the discipline which has drawn particularly on anthro-pological and ethnographic methodologies.

Ethnography and applied linguistics

If mentalist accounts of language are criticized by applied linguists for their inadequacy in describing language practices, and conversation analysis attracts criticism for its failure to deal with social conflict, corpus linguists have been criticized for taking language data out of the context of its production (Widdowson 2000), and some applied lin-guists who are committed to the detailed study of language practices eschew the analysis of decontextualized corpus data in favour of research methods developed by anthropologists and ethnographers. In the 1970s, Hymes described an approach to language description (partly as a reaction against Chomsky) which he termed 'an ethno-graphy of speaking', by which he meant 'a description that is a theory – a theory of speech as a system of cultural behaviour' (Hymes 1974: 89), and since then a number of scholars have conducted detailed studies in diverse social settings of various 'speech communities', looking at the range of language choices open to speakers and the ways in which variation is patterned. Examples of such studies are found in Gumperz (1982), whose introduction claims that 'communication cannot be studied in isolation; it must be analyzed in terms of its effect on people's lives. We must focus on what communication does: how it constrains evaluation and decision making, not merely how it is structured' (p.1). Gumperz and his associates have long been involved in the close observation of the ways in which different social identities and different language practices can lead to miscommunication among individuals and groups (see, for example, Roberts *et al.* 1992; Roberts and Sarangi 1999), and one practical effect of such work has been the involvement of applied linguists as consultants to companies and organizations seeking to ameliorate problems in communication, such as those of doctors in training or between managers and their work-forces. The British Association of Applied Linguistics recently established a special interest group to foster developments in con-temporary theories and practices in linguistic ethnography, and their research involves areas such as literacy practices, institutional dis-course, urban heteroglossia, multilingualism and children's home and school learning. The study of 'intercultural communication', which is the topic of Chapter 6, has also benefited from some ethnographic studies, as advocated by Blommaert (1998, 2001a), with an increasing interest in using ethnographic approaches also in the *teaching* of languages and 'intercultural competence' (see Byram and Fleming 1998; LARA 2003).

Sociolinguistics

The contributions of researchers such as Hymes and Gumperz span approaches which appeal to both applied linguistics and socio-linguistics. The latter sub-discipline is quite broad in scope, but it is basically concerned with exploring how people use language differ-ently in different social contexts. Practitioners whose interest is predominantly in language description, particularly language change, often use a quantitative approach in the measurement of linguistic variables, and 'correlating linguistic variation as the dependent vari-able with the independent variables such as linguistic environment, style or social categories is the primary empirical task of socio-linguistics' (Chambers 1995: 17). For others, the legitimate concerns of sociolinguistics are deemed to extend to issues which are elsewhere delineated as 'the sociology of language', while there is also a great deal of potential common ground between this broader interpretation of 'sociolinguistics' and the broader interpretations of 'applied linguistics'. The most inclusive definitions of either discipline may make the distinction between the two effectively redundant, and indeed in the chapters which follow, some of the issues we discuss might equally well be considered 'sociolinguistic' as 'applied linguistic'. To give just one example here, a widely publicized controversy was sparked in the late 1990s by the decision of the Oakland School Board in California to recognize 'Ebonics' as 'the primary language of African American children'. Sociolinguists who have studied the detail of phonological, lexical and grammatical variations between varieties of English spoken by black and white Americans suddenly found themselves in the media spotlight (Rickford 1999a). The extremely heated debate concerned *both* the status and characteristics of a language variety *and* the political and pedagogic issues of what language and literacy teaching practice should be.

Responding to social problems with applied linguistics

The foregoing discussion has provided an indication of some of the areas of social life in which applied linguists are active. As we have noted, the realm of education sees a significant proportion of this activity, and this extends from research into how the individual learner – including learners who may have some clinical condition affecting language interpretation or production – processes spoken language or written text, through analyses of what goes on in language and literacy classrooms, and on to questions about the global influence of specific languages, notably English, as education systems all over the world are involved in decision-making about which languages are to be taught in their schools. We have also illustrated how the language of social interactions and institutions from a much wider range of contexts than education is not only analysed but also subject to suggested alterations as a result of some of the projects in which applied linguists are involved. Commercial institutions, workplaces, media texts, family conversations, intercultural encounters, hospitals and emergency services: all of these sites have been investigated in the course of applied linguistic research. As a final illustration of the scope of the discipline, we outline how some of the work applied linguists do is incorporated into another powerful social institution – the legal system.

Forensic linguistics

It is an indication of just what a crucial role language plays in social life that being – or indeed failing to be – the author of a particular text or utterance can result in severe punishment. Forensic linguistic enquiry scrutinizes language such as statements allegedly made by an accused person or witness, the assessed work of students suspected of plagiarism, suicide notes apparently written shortly before death, threatening letters or telephone calls and disputed police interview records. Methods of analysis include linguistic and statistical measures to establish authorship and whether texts have been altered, and phonetic procedures used to aid 'earwitness' testimony in voice line-ups. A number of applied linguists have acted as expert witnesses in court cases, demonstrating once again the range of activity covered by this discipline.

As people's language behaviour comes under ever-increasing scrutiny, the informed accounts provided by applied linguistics of linguistic *performance* as well as *competence* is likely to continue to be in demand.

Conclusion to Part 2

In this discussion of applied linguistics, we have, while fully aware of the danger of adopting the 'science of everything position' (Davies 1999: 11), taken an inclusive view of the subject. The relationship between linguistics and applied linguistics is largely a matter of historical contingency, and readers are referred to more extensive descriptions of the events which have led to the areas of activity currently occupied by the respective disciplines (for example Cook 2003; Davies 1999; Brumfit 2001; Pennycook 1994a). The questions we address in subsequent chapters will, we hope, make it clear that our view of language locates it within the social world, and that many of the issues with which we are concerned are also the concerns of applied linguistics, defined, as here, very broadly.

Summary and conclusion

Our main task in this chapter has been to provide an introductory outline of relevant key concepts in realist social theory and applied linguistics, suggesting that the theme which unites them is that they are both concerned with ways of knowing the social world. Applied linguistics is concerned partly, but unavoidably, with the study of social relations; social theory is partly, and equally unavoidably, concerned with the study of language. Further, we have noted that language itself is the medium of theoretical exploration in both disciplines. For these reasons we have argued strongly that applied linguistics and social theory have a great deal to gain from an explicit collaboration.

We have tried to identify those concepts which can facilitate this collaboration, and in this concluding section we aim to exemplify it further. In presenting our introduction, we posed some dichotomies, most notably that between structure and agency. We suggested that structure and agency constitute distinct entities in the social world, each with their own *sui generis* properties and powers. One characteristic power of agency is human beings' capacity to use language as a means of self-expression. Social structures have the power to facilitate or frustrate human projects and purposes, within which language features as a resource. Brumfit (2001: 55–6) has captured this dual aspect of language well:

> Language has simultaneously a public and a private face. On the one hand, it is the most subtle means for our classification of the world, our clarification of our own ideas, our establishment of self-identity. On the other, it is the major means of communication with other people that we possess, and thus has to fit in with the conventions that other people have collectively accepted. It pulls in one direction to the private and individual, and in the other to the public and ritualized.

Whilst we remain in broad agreement with this description, subsequent chapters will seek to refine the distinction between private and public. Importantly, we will argue for a view of language as a cultural (not a material) emergent property, not detachable from human beings but emergent from their biological attributes and their practical engagement with the world. Access to linguistic resources is conditioned by material relations but language, as emergent, has a degree of autonomy both from individual speakers and from material relations. Thus the working-class child can learn to speak with an upper-class accent; girls can talk 'macho'. Conversely, an upper-class accent may not protect you from bankruptcy; native-like fluency in a language is not an absolute prerequisite for business success in your adopted country.

A benefit of the realist perspective on language – which sees it as a property emergent from the interplay between structure and agency – is that it allows us to pose questions that are of concern to both applied linguistics and social theory. These are questions about, for example, the role of language in national and cultural identity; the performative functions of language in social relations; the role that language plays in the constitution and reproduction of social life; the relationship between languages and forms of political oppression and indoctrination; and the central place of symbolic communication in social interaction. The next chapter explores the kinds of answers to such questions which have been provided by various sociological traditions, thus developing some of the ideas raised in this chapter about the connections between language and the social world.

2 Sociology and ideas about language

Introduction

The previous chapter argued for the cardinal importance of ideas about structure and agency within social theory, and also signalled that similar ideas are at the heart of debates about language. That is to say that as soon as we observe the ways in which speakers use language we are engaged with the analysis of the social world. For this reason, we have claimed that it is in applied linguistics that theories about language are put to the test. This chapter will suggest that insofar as social theorists neglect the insights of those who study language in use, their accounts of language will be under-developed. Conversely, insofar as the issue of structure and agency is inherent in the concerns of applied linguists, neglect of the work carried out by social theorists will lead to under-developed accounts of the social world. Accounts of *both* the social world *and* language require contributions from both disciplines. (The relevance of this point for research in applied linguistics is demonstrated particularly in Chapters 4 and 8.) This is not to deny the particular expertise to be found in each field, nor to claim that every concern of each is shared by the other.

This chapter will explore some sociological accounts of the relationship between language and society. We are not, of course, aiming to provide a comprehensive survey, but will focus on a particular set of concerns within the structure–agency problematic which we outlined in the previous chapter. These include the kinds of claim made in each tradition about what language is like, what it can do and what people can do with it. We also explore the extent to which these claims are based on empirical evidence.

The chapter unfolds as follows. Sociology has a longer history than linguistics, and a concern with language is evident in the writings of its founding figures – Durkheim, Marx and Weber, whose work we briefly discuss to begin with, as it sets the context for later sociological work about language. We examine next those approaches which view social relations as symbolic enactments and performances carried off by social actors, and which have regarded language as a key element in social interaction and as central to the elaboration of the meaningful nature of social life. We then consider those perspectives which have directed their attention to various aspects of what has come to be called 'the linguistic turn' in social theory. The emphasis here is on the discursive nature of social life, the importance of the linguistic mediation of social relations and the role of language in human knowledge and the understanding of social action. Finally, we discuss those writers who develop a dualistic view of language, seeing it as having systemic features as well as being the medium of social interaction.

Early accounts of language and society

In the work of the classical social theorists, and particularly that of its pre-eminent trio Durkheim, Marx and Weber, there is little in the way of a *systematic* treatment of language. This is unsurprising perhaps, given amongst other things the rudimentary development of a discipline of linguistics. Yet it is clear that the social theories advanced by the social scientists of the late nineteenth and early twentieth centuries often made claims about language (or rested on implicit assumptions about it) that, without an adequate theory of language, were merely hopeful or naïve. Durkheim, for example, recognized the centrality of the symbolic to his notion of the *conscience collective*, that is, the normative order external to, and constraining of, individuals (Durkheim 1965, 1982). Ritual and ceremonial practices were important *symbolic* practices whereby the individual experienced both the transcendental nature of the social (it is a bigger force than the individual) and its immanence (by becoming part of something bigger than oneself, one commits oneself to the social). However, there is little account in Durkheim of how, and in which ways, symbolic meanings are linguistically mediated.

This tendency – to emphasize the symbolic without elaborating on language – is more marked in the work of Weber, partly because of his emphasis on the role of meanings in the explanation of social action (Gerth and Mills 1948; Weber 1964, 1974, 1978). In particular, his insistence that people act on the basis of reasons whose content can be identified in terms of their beliefs and motives introduced an interpretive dimension to social analysis. Weber sought to reconcile this focus on meanings and their fundamental role in the interpretation of social action with a commitment to the discovery of causal connections and to a notion of a social *science*. There is some question still about how far Weber succeeded in this enterprise, but for our present purposes two points should be noted. First, Weber's stress on the meaningful nature of social action provided a powerful input into those sociologies that viewed the recovery, articulation and understanding of social meanings as *the* primary objective of social explanation. We shall consider these shortly. Second, Weber, like Durkheim, did not concern himself systematically with the linguistic mediation of meanings. (For a discussion of the relevance of Weber and Durkheim to sociolinguistic enquiry, see Sarangi and Candlin 2001.)

By contrast, Marx regarded language as a distinctive capacity of human beings, one that crucially allowed for conscious reflection on their activity (Marx 1959). Unlike other animals, human beings were thus freed from a fixed sequence of behaviour and so could modify and improve upon earlier forms of production. As Callinicos notes, 'Marx's conception of human labour as necessarily a social activity is closely related to his view of language as "the immediate actuality of thought: [as] practical, real consciousness that exists for other men as well, and only therefore does it exist for me" ' (Callinicos 1989: 27–8). However, linking language in this way to human practice, suggestive though it is (and we will return to this later), does not amount to a fully developed theory of language (Kitching 1988).

In short, it is difficult to discover in the founding figures of the sociological tradition more than the raw material for treating language sociologically. (This is not, of course, a matter of personal culpability or dereliction of sociological duty, but rather a case of theorists working within their own historically limited social and intellectual horizons.) Despite this, and in their different ways, Durkheim, Marx and Weber have imparted to social theory particular sets of interests in language and its relation to social life. In the next section, we outline the work of the symbolic interactionists and ethnomethodologists, for whom language is a key constituent of social interaction.

'Getting things done': language and social interaction

Symbolic interactionism

The approach within social science that seeks most explicitly to develop Weber's insights about the meaningfulness of social action is symbolic interactionism, whose central figure is Mead. Weber was not the only influence on Mead; he was also strongly influenced by the work of Darwin, using the latter's evolutionary account of the natural world to ground a notion of human beings as dynamic and changing rather than as merely playing out a fixed repertoire of personality traits (Charon 1998). For Mead, the distinguishing feature of human beings was their capacity for symbolic communication, particularly linguistic communication. This capacity freed them from the passive, instinctual relation to nature of other animals, allowing them to think and reflect upon nature and, crucially, to act upon it. Indeed, as Charon notes, citing Becker, '. . . humans are emergent in nature precisely because of the symbol' (Charon 1998: 56). Meaning itself becomes an emergent product of social interaction, rather than being simply contained within the object being studied: for instance, the meaning of criminality is not given in the behaviour of people identified by some as 'criminals', but rather is defined by the interaction between those doing the identifying and those being identified. This is an attractively radical notion and it can be applied to querying the meaning of many terms and concepts such as gender, race and ethnicity, deviance, identity and so on (although such application is not without its own methodological difficulties, as we see in Chapter 5).

The signs and symbols that constitute language enable the development of a fund of common meanings, ideas and under-standings, or what we refer to, following Popper (1972), as the 'World 3' of the products of human consciousness. In this schema, 'World 1' is the physical world, 'World 2' is the subjective experiences emerging from the engagement of human consciousness with World 1, and World 3 is the realm of the externalized products of the engagement of human consciousness with the world beyond itself. World 3 is pre-eminently symbolic. Although Mead, and symbolic interactionists generally, do not dwell on the ontological status of such a concept as 'World 3', they do insist on the emergent nature of shared meanings, which, though the product of human social interaction, are irreducible to it. Furthermore, this allows for more and more complex forms of social interaction as people's access to, and manipulation of, common meanings and symbols becomes more extensive and sophisticated.

This active social conversation based upon these common meanings and symbols, and through which individuals come to negotiate their place in the world, is not only directed towards other people. Mead argues that we 'talk to ourselves', are constantly engaged in an inner conversation as we manage our social world: 'Give the human the self and the words to communicate with the self, and the active person emerges, manipulating words, thinking and creating' (Charon 1998: 100).

It should be clear, as Layder (1994) notes, that this emphasis on the importance of meaning is the key distinguishing feature of symbolic interactionism. Furthermore, meanings are mediated through an interpretive process that is, to a very considerable degree, linguistic. However, those who developed Mead's work (such as Blumer, Becker and Goffman) undertook little in the way of practical linguistic research. Their work focuses overwhelmingly on negotiated interaction, on the strategies – 'saving face', 'maintaining role distance', 'turn taking' and so on – that individuals deploy in the course of everyday life. That is to say, the concern of symbolic interactionism is less with the *linguistic* mediation of social interaction, and more with its dramaturgical (socially enacted) forms. This may be because, beyond the recognition that human beings are symbol-users, symbolic interactionism (like many other traditions in social science) does not pay much attention to how people's social relations are related to the ways in which they use language. There is, in other words, an assumption that social relations and the languages people use to interpret and negotiate them are separate entities.

Ethnomethodology

One approach that seeks to overcome this assumption, by insisting that social relations are practical accomplishments, is ethnomethodology. A central source of inspiration for ethnomethodology was the work of Schutz (1943, 1953, 1967). Schutz developed his ideas through a critique of the Weberian conception of interpretive sociology discussed above. While agreeing with Weber that people experience the social world as a socially meaningful reality, he took issue with Weber's insistence that meanings were subjective (that is, Weber's claim that meanings were attached by the individual to their actions, were provided by the individual, as it were, to make sense of, or to orient, their actions towards definite, intentional purposes). The core of Schutz's reservations lay in his affirmation of the intersubjective nature of meanings. By this, Schutz refers both to the emergent nature of meanings, a theme we have already identified as characteristic of symbolic interactionism, and to the ways in which this emergent nature leads us to experience the everyday world as a common, 'shared' world. In our practical doings in the world we come to take for granted these common meanings: we expect to be understood, to be served when we queue for the checkout, to be recognized as a lecturer by students and so on. In short, individuals *experience* the world as external, orderly and pre-existing.

However, it is also the case that each of us has to negotiate and make sense of this world whose 'reality' at a practical level has simply to be taken for granted. The basis of our ability to interpret the social world routinely, and by and large successfully, is what Schutz calls our 'common-sense knowledge'. This is the knowledge we gain by virtue of living in and being part of the everyday world, and it enables us to categorize and order the world through the stock of typifications it provides us with. Importantly for the argument we wish to advance later, this stock of typifications is not our own invention, argues Schutz, but is embodied in the language we share with others. Such typifications, the shorthand of commonsense knowledge, are enabled by language.

Ethnomethodology was also partly a reaction to the structural functionalism of Parsons, although it continued to share some of its assumptions, particularly those to do with the consensual basis of social action (Williams 1992). Structural functionalism presents a model of society in which the persistence of social stability and the orderliness of social life are accounted for in terms of externally defined norms and values which people learn and incorporate into their behaviour. The common, shared nature of social life is attributed to the 'shared' normative commitments that social actors are given by the processes of socialization. Ethnomethodologists reject the deterministic emphasis on an external value system pressure-moulding a stream of social actors predisposed to conformity. Instead, following Schutz, they want to insist that social order is not something guaranteed from *without*, but is rather generated from *within* social settings by the practical activity of those involved. It is people's commonsense knowledgeability, their adroitness at interpreting symbolic cues, at assessing paralinguistic signs, at communicating intentions, that makes social life run in a relatively orderly fashion. It is therefore to the means of 'local production', that is, the ways in which social life is sustained and accomplished by people in everyday settings and on an everyday basis, that social research must turn. This emphasis on how people produce their social worlds through negotiation and interaction inevitably brings language to the fore.

The situated, local nature of social meanings, their rootedness in specific social contexts (what ethnomethodologists refer to as the indexical nature of meanings), leads these theorists to reject approaches to language use which focus on the formal aspects of language structure. When, for example, theorists concern themselves with formal sentences there is an implication, directly analogous to that found in sociological accounts which focus on formal norms and rules, that a lexicon exists with obvious meanings for all competent speakers. Such approaches, precisely because they ignore the indexical nature of meanings, obscure the implicit ways in which the standardized character of the culture or society is presumed as obvious to its members. Garfinkel, regarded as the founder of ethnomethodology, would illustrate this for his students by getting them to enact 'breaching experiments', such as pretending when they went home that they were lodgers rather than family members; this often provoked hostility and anger, demonstrating that there are many aspects of the everyday 'moral order' which are usually taken for granted (Garfinkel 1967).

Ethnomethodology is thus drawn to a methodological focus on how individuals make norms and meanings relevant to themselves, and claims that this is accomplished through social conversations. As we shall see, this leaves the approach with the problem of how to account for constraints on what people are able to accomplish through their social conversations. The issue of constraint, of course, entails a consideration of power and conflict, features of the social world which interactionist sociologies have found notoriously difficult to explain. This problem of accounting for power is compounded in the case of ethnomethodology by the construal of social interaction *as* language (a position which we described in Chapter 1 as conflationary). Methodologically, interaction is accessed by observing conversation. One attempt to attend to these limitations is made by Goffman, who, although he belongs to the broadly interactionist tradition, introduces the notion of the 'interaction order' (Goffman 1983), as a means of linking these micro-processes to wider issues of social order and social structure (Layder 1997: 211). However, like many of the writers discussed here, he pays little detailed attention to language as such.

A writer who is regarded by some ethnomethodologists as departing from the mainstream because he insists on distinguishing between interaction and language, and who has also concerned himself with the linguistic aspects of social action, is Cicourel. Cicourel's concern with the significance of language starts from where symbolic interactionism stops. Whilst concurring with symbolic interactionism on the crucial role of meanings in the negotiation of everyday social life, Cicourel regards this as only the beginning of analysis, since the more fundamental question is 'How does the actor in everyday life order and assign meanings to objects and events in his environment?' (Cicourel 1973: 12). This is also a direct challenge to the structural functionalist tradition which, in viewing the orderliness of social life as a product of normative patterns inducted by socialization processes, fails to get to grips with the issue of how individuals decide what norms are operative or relevant in any situation.

There are two aspects to this claim that are relevant to our present argument. The first is a methodological one and concerns the assumption often made by certain variants of sociological theory that the (sociologist's) identification of patterns of norms and values is also an account of people's attachment to such norms and values. Consensual behaviour is seen to be an outcome of shared norms and values. Cicourel regards this a 'gloss', by means of which the sociologist smuggles into the analysis an implicit model of how individuals assign meaning and relevance to symbols, rules and values, interpret them in the context of everyday situations and engage them through appropriate behavioural displays. There are some similarities between Cicourel's arguments here and those of Archer concerning the 'myth of cultural integration', which we consider in Chapter 6. Both sets of arguments suggest that identifying 'cultural' or 'ethnic' groups on the basis of a supposed commitment to certain values and norms is far from straightforward; not only is there the general problem of how persons establish roles and statuses in everyday action (how does one know when one is conforming to role expectations? which role?), but also the specific problem of how the researcher establishes goals and norms for the individual, let alone for some group or wider community. As Cicourel notes, this 'is not obvious theoretically, nor procedurally clear methodologically' (*ibid.*: 15).

The second aspect of the ethnomethodological insistence that sociological research must make the role of interpretive procedures in social life explicit concerns the central role of language in such procedures. Again, this goes beyond the symbolic interactionist position that meanings are the basis of social interaction, and stresses social *performance*, that is, the question of how, and by what means, people come to assign relevance to meanings. It is individuals themselves who decide what is relevant, what is influential, what they are to take into account in their social behaviour. They do this through what Cicourel terms 'interpretive procedures':

> Interpretive procedures provide the actor with a developmentally changing sense of social structure that enables him to assign meaning or relevance to an environment of objects. Normative or surface rules enable the actor to link his view of the world to that of others in concerted social action, and to presume that consensus or shared agreement governs interaction.
>
> (*ibid.*: 30)

We are continually modifying our interpretive procedures as we acquire new context-bound lexical items; the study of language use is important for understanding how we do this and thereby 'place' our environments, rendering them comfortable and familiar, or threatening and strange, or something in between. Interpretive procedures are thus the practical methods by which social order is constructed and sustained through everyday interaction. The notion of interpretive procedures clearly indicates the importance for Cicourel of the sociolinguistic element in sociological research.

However, Cicourel is not abandoning the effort of sociological analysis, nor necessarily confining it to the (linguistic) analysis of actor conversation. The purpose of his work, rather, is to suggest 'a more explicit foundation for integrating social process with the structural or institutionalized features of everyday life' (*ibid.*: 11). The crucial issue here is 'how much we feel we can genuinely know about social structure through the analysis of local practice' (Coupland 2001a: 17).

Cicourel does provide some grounds for developing a model of social life which is not composed solely of social conversations. From his work, there would appear to be two elements in the social world that are irreducible to, although clearly the product of, linguistically mediated social interaction: interpretive procedures and syntactical rules. We have considered the former's objective status above; according to Cicourel they are 'invariant properties of everyday practical reasoning necessary for assigning sense to the substantive rules sociologists usually call norms' (Cicourel 1973: 52). Syntax, too, shares the same property of irreducibility and so has an independence from social actors which allows them to shape the actors' interpretive repertoire:

> ... formal syntactic rules can be generated in cultural settings or can remain oral traditions: once they are available and used in socially prescribed and sanctioned ways, however, they constrain (although not completely) interpretations assigned by members.
>
> (*ibid.*: 48)

So, although it would seem that the social world comprises more than human beings and their conversations, the nature of the formal properties of language, and of the invariant properties of interpretive procedures, is unclear. Furthermore, the links between them and local practices are not made explicit, making it difficult to grasp the interplay between, say, the systemic features of a language such as its grammar, and the ways in which these might enable or constrain particular sorts of utterances. As we shall argue, a social realist applied linguistics offers the potential for making these links more explicit.

Conversation analysis

The ethnomethodological approach developed to accommodate the research known as conversation analysis, whose aim is to explore how language is used in social action. This work is probably the area in sociology which has paid the closest attention to linguistic detail – 'actual occurrences of conduct in interaction' – and how these provide indications of social structures, in the sense of 'what sort of social scene is being constructed' (Schegloff 1991: 48, 46). Core principles in conversation analysis are close attention to authentic empirical data and a reluctance to admit concepts such as social categories or social structures as relevant to the interaction unless this is demonstrably warranted in the utterances of the participants themselves. Conversations themselves display 'patterns ... with robust and consistent properties' (Wooffitt 2001: 58), and it is these 'indigenous features of talk-in-interaction' (Schegloff 1991: 67) which should be appealed to first, while social structures should be considered extrinsic, unless there is empirical evidence that they are relevant enough to participants to affect their talk-in-interaction.

Conversation analysis attracts similar criticisms to those levelled against ethnomethodology. Those most relevant to our concerns here are, firstly, that conversational participants are deemed to have knowledge sufficient to generate the analysis, and, secondly, the denial of the influence of social structures on social life. What is needed, argue the critics, is an approach which considers the relations between irreducible structures and social interaction in a 'balanced manner' (Mouzelis 1995). This would emphasize a conception of structure as providing the deterministic conditions of action, whilst recognizing that 'interaction can be understood to be the product of determinate structures which are irreducible, but which none the less do not vitiate the importance of the interpretive capacities and intentions of social actors' (Layder 1981: 87).

There is a further important consequence to the 'unbalanced' view of structures in ethnomethodology and conversation analysis, namely their empiricism. Several writers (Bauman 1978; Mouzelis 1995) have made this point, but Layder (1990: 61) puts it most forcefully:

> I would argue that the idea that social structures do not exist independently of the activities they govern and the agents' conception of what they are doing is only true within the terms of an exclusively empiricist epistemology, and thus an individualist/voluntarist conception of social structure.

Moreover, the essentially empirical task of understanding human interaction, as Bauman (1978: 189) puts it, 'by throwing light on the procedures through which meanings are produced in practice' engenders a radical moral neutrality. By forcing attention on to the *practices* of meaning production, rather than the meanings themselves (providing formal knowledge of interpretive procedures and their application as opposed to substantive knowledge of whether people's interpretations are 'true' or 'false'), these approaches avoid the problem of truth. The impoverished view of structures coupled with the empirical concern with *how* actors accomplish or 'do' social life leaves ethnomethodology and conversation analysis with little to say about any possible correspondence between the meaning actors assign to topics and the intrinsic, extra-discursive features of the topic itself (Bauman 1978). This is a feature they have in common with the approaches that we consider in the next section.

'Having things done': language and discourse

The previous section examined what interactionist sociologies, and especially symbolic interactionism and ethnomethodology, had to say about the relationship between language and social action. In this section we shall concern ourselves with more contemporary developments, directing attention to various aspects of what has come to be called 'the linguistic turn' in social theory. The emphasis here is on the discursive nature of social life, the importance of the linguistic mediation of social relations and the role of language in human knowledge and the understanding of social action. Clearly, a full account of 'the linguistic turn' in social theory (which may also be regarded as a social/discursive turn in linguistics – see Coupland *et al.* 2001) would be out of place in the present book; rather the concern is with the views on the links between language and social action proffered by various perspectives.

The 'linguistic turn' in social theory is often associated with two other currents within social science: postmodernism and post-structuralism. Much has been written about these overlapping, but distinct, 'movements', but their significance for our argument rests on the criticisms they advance of the interactionist, phenomenological approaches we considered in the previous section. These centred on the privileging in such approaches of the human subject as both the origin of meaning and as the end point of analysis. These criticisms owed much to the work of writers such as Lévi-Strauss, Barthes and Althusser in the 1950s, 60s and 70s who were, in different ways, responsible for establishing structuralism as an intellectual current in Western social theory. (See, for example, Anderson 1976 and Thompson 1978.)

Broadly speaking, structuralism took issue with those traditions of thought which emphasized the freedom of the individual and which regarded meanings as the creation of human consciousness. Against this view, structuralists pointed, on the one hand, to the powerful social and material forces (such as the distribution of wealth and political power) arrayed against the individual and severely curtailing their freedom, and on the other, to the equally powerful forces which shaped and structured social meanings. In the latter case, rather than seeing meanings as an emanation of individual consciousness – in which human beings creatively devise various ways of interpreting the world – structuralists saw them as the product of social discourses. Through the social organization of symbolic representations, social discourses confront people with historically limited and specific repertoires of meanings. Of course, the practices that people engage in influence social discourses in their turn, but practices and discourses are social, rather than individual, phenomena. In this way, structuralism 'decentres the human subject', and entails a radical break with the sociological perspectives considered earlier, with their emphasis on the importance of some notion of subjective understanding.

Post-structuralists make this break yet more decisive by insisting that the very idea of a subject is itself a social construction produced through social discourses. These discourses position people within particular sets of practices, already constructed through other social discourses, and it is these practices which provide the basis for the construction of human subjectivity. So the notion of the rational and autonomous human being that has been at the heart of much Western philosophy since the seventeenth century is extinguished; the autonomy has been much exaggerated and the rationality is the product of social discourses about rationality. These discourses structure the human psyche in complex and contradictory ways, often imperfectly understood (both by the individuals concerned as well as those seeking to analyse or interpret their behaviour) and poorly managed. This fragmentary self spells not only the end of any unitary or mechanical relation between human subjects and the class or power positions they occupy – this is the 'post' element of post-structuralism – but also brings to the fore the role of language (and discourse more generally) in the constitution of the self and in the social relations of everyday life.

The pivotal role assigned to *discourse* by those writers influenced by post-structuralism requires a closer exploration of the term. We shall do this first by looking at the notion of discourse as it is developed and employed in the work of Foucault, possibly the most influential wielder of a discourse approach, and second by taking one or two examples of the use of a concept of discourse in contemporary social research. Our central argument will be that the notion of discourse employed in the Foucauldian tradition conflates practices and knowledge (or culture and agency, to use the vocabulary deployed in this book). That is to say, while it may be true that power effects are inscribed in practices, the two are not identical (Layder 1994).

Foucault's work has had a major influence within the social and human sciences, and this makes hazardous the enterprise of summary and interpretation. Furthermore, the status of the conception of discourse shifts in Foucault's work. In his earlier work (Foucault 1974) the focus is on 'discursive formations', on discourse as rules for constituting areas of knowledge; in the 'genealogical studies', such as *Discipline and Punish* (Foucault 1977), the emphasis is on the relation between knowledge and power; and towards the end of his life, Foucault became more concerned with the issue of 'ethics', with how the subject actively constitutes herself (Foucault 1978). Talk of a Foucauldian 'perspective' might be regarded in this light as premature. Bearing this in mind, the account that follows is narrowly concerned with the implications of Foucault's uses of a notion of discourse for an understanding of the relation between language and social action. There are, of course, many others who have considered his ideas within a much broader context. (See, for example, Barratt 1991, Carter 1996, Coupland *et. al.* 2001, Dean 1994, Dreyfus and Rabinow 1982, Fairclough 1993, Gordon 1980, Hoy 1986, Miller 1993, Owen 1994, Rabinow 1984, Simons 1995.)

Despite the various modifications in Foucault's use of the notion of discourse, we want to suggest that his definition in *The Archaeology of Knowledge* is compatible with the position we adopt insofar as it recognizes the irreducibility of discourse to either individual speakers or to linguistic structure in the Saussurean *langue* sense (Foucault 1974). This notion of discourse posits a stratified social ontology comprised of linguistic structure, discourse and individual speech activity, each with their distinctive properties and each irreducible to either of the others. Foucault expresses it thus:

> Discourse lies at the level of pure atemporal linguistic 'structure' (*langue*) and the level of surface speaking (*parole*): it expresses the historical specificity of what is said and what remains unsaid.
>
> Discourses are composed of signs, but what they do is more than use these signs to designate things. It is this move that renders them irreducible to the language and to speech. It is this 'move' that we must reveal and describe.
>
> (*ibid.*: 49)

As writers such as Pennycook (1994a) and Sarangi (2001) have noted, this view of discourse has considerable potential relevance to applied linguistics. Nevertheless, there is a certain 'openness' about this definition that allows for less moderate interpretations. A discursive formation consists of 'rules of formation' for the particular set of statements that belong to it and in this way discourses both enable and constrain actors and agents through the rules that govern their operation. These rules, to follow Fairclough's (1993: 41–9) useful typology, concern the formation of objects, the formation of enunciative modalities or 'subject positions', the formation of concepts and the formation of strategies. The last two of these refer to the ways in which intra- and inter-discursive relations of complementarity, competition, analogy and so on operate to shape the meanings and possibilities available within a discursive formation. (Note that such relations are possible precisely because of the ontological status of discourse and its irreducibility, although there is little in Foucault's work to justify a strong claim that discursive relations may be realized independently of social agency.) However, it is the first two sets of rules of formation that have been subject to readings which have pushed Foucauldian discourse in a decisively postmodern direction.

Common to the discursive formation of both objects and of subject positions is Foucault's view of discourse as constitutive, '... as contributing to the production, transformation, and reproduction of the objects ... of social life' (Fairclough 1993: 41). So discourse is not only constitutive, in significant or important ways, of our ideas about reality, it is also productive of the ideas we have about all sorts of social relations and thus about the social practices – of measurement, accounting, examining and imprisoning – that we found upon these ideas.

Besides this constitutive role in the formation of objects, discourses, on this account, also constitute subjects and their subjectivities. They accomplish this via the subject positions that are associated with discursive activity: for example, 'immigrant' and 'British' are two subject positions constituted by discourses about race and immigration in postwar Britain. Subject positions are historically specific, and therefore liable to change, and are able to exert a conditioning influence on those subjects positioned in particular ways.

Both of these constitutive functions can be interpreted in what we shall call, following Rosenau (1992), 'weak' and 'strong' ways. In their 'weak' sense they have a great deal to offer. In particular, they can draw attention to what Taylor (1985: 234) has termed the expressive aspects of language and the ways in which they serve to '... express/constitute different relations in which we may stand to each other: intimate, formal, official, casual, joking, serious, and so on'. Our reservations about using discourse to analyse the social world arise from the 'strong' interpretations. With these the 'de-centring' of agency becomes the elimination of active social agency in any meaningful sense. The social world is seen as constructed by authorless discourses which themselves become agents; rather than tension between actors, agents and discourses, concretely negotiated in particular historical settings, there are merely discourses constructing objects and human subjects. Consequently, efforts to develop accounts using such a notion of discourse often get into difficulties when it comes to identifying agency in a specific, empirical sense.

One approach to researching social behaviour using a notion of discourse is that of 'discursive psychology', and we have taken a study by Wetherell and Potter (1992), concerned with the 'language of racism', as an illustration of the problem outlined above. In this study of the attitudes of New Zealand 'whites' towards the Maori population, Wetherell and Potter make several claims about the nature and role of discourse. Most importantly, they argue that discourse is actively constitutive of both social and psychological processes. 'The psychological and social field – subjectivity, individuality, social groups and social categories – is constructed, defined and articulated through discourse' (*ibid.*: 59). Consequently, they place an 'over-riding stress on the study of discourse in action rather than language as an abstract system' (*ibid.*: 71).

The emphasis on 'discourse in action' conflates social practices with the ways in which such practices are thought about and enunciated through speech. The texts employed in their study – extracts from their interviews with 22 New Zealanders – are interpreted by the authors as instances of 'discourse in action'; others might interpret these texts differently. As we have argued elsewhere, viewing discourse as a practice raises other problems. Two in particular are pertinent here. Firstly, the actual content of discourses becomes secondary to its effects in defining and identifying them. Thus:

> Racist discourse ... should be seen as discourse (of whatever content) which has the effect of establishing, sustaining and reinforcing oppressive power relations. ... Racist discourse is discourse which has the effect of categorizing, allocating and discriminating between certain groups ... it is discourse which justifies, sustains and legitimates ... practices.
>
> (*ibid.*: 70)

On this model, the identification of racist discourse becomes a task of Herculean proportions. How do we establish empirically what the effects of a discourse are? How do we distinguish these from the effects of other discourses? Such questions bring us to the second problem, namely the tension between reducing discourses to practices, which makes difficult analysis of their specific properties and the ways in which these may influence practices, and at the same time needing to render them distinct in order to account for people's decisions to construct certain forms of identity or to utilize certain types of narratives. The status of discourse is indeterminate: it is both a constitutive practice and yet it circulates as a resource:

> ... identity and forms of subjectivity which become instantiated in
> discourse at any given moment should be seen as a sedimentation
> of past discursive practices. A sense of identity and subjectivity is
> constructed from the interpretative resources – the stories and
> narratives of identity – which are available, in circulation, in our
> culture.
>
> (*ibid.*: 78)

In some ways, this formulation comes close to the emergentist model
we are advocating of regarding social and personal identities as products of the engagement of people's consciousness with a World 3 of
cultural forms (including 'stories and narratives of identity'). However,
the emergentist view entails a consistent analytical distinction
between culture, in the form of World 3, and agency, that is what
human beings do with culture, precisely so that their mutually influential effects of constraint and enablement may be assessed. It is to
those social theorists who have suggested that such a distinction is key
to sociological accounts of language that we turn in the next section.

A dualistic approach to language

Besides the approach which sees social interaction as generating the
social world and the one which sees discourses as constructing it,
there is a third approach, which resists the conflation of either structure to conversation or of agency to discourse. It is, perhaps, stretching
the point to refer to the writers considered below as constituting an
approach. Nevertheless, they share at least a common commitment to
exploring the notion that language and agency are distinct and that
social analysis is, to an important degree, about examining their
interplay. They also share a view of language as social action. In doing
so writers such as Habermas, Bourdieu and Bernstein have engaged
explicitly with the linguistics of Saussure, Chomsky, Austin and
others.

Habermas and communicative interaction

The work of Habermas has consistently placed language at the centre
of social analysis. Moreover, Habermas has a strongly emergentist view
of language, one in which '... sensory contact with the world is
reworked into something meaningful through the use of symbols'
(Habermas 2001a: 7). The development of symbolic communication is
the defining feature of human existence; also, the 'objectifying force of
symbolic mediation' creates the distance from the world which makes
reflexivity possible. From our perspective, this 'objectifying force' is

49

also the principal means by which a World 3 of the products of human consciousness is sustained.

This view of the central role of symbolic mediation fuels Habermas's critique of scientism, the notion that empirical knowledge is derived from the direct apprehension of reality and is therefore the only reliable form of knowledge. Symbolic mediation rules out a direct understanding of the world in the sense of an understanding 'uncontaminated' by theory. There are two important senses in which this has to be the case for Habermas.

Firstly, sensory apprehension of the world, if it is to be generalized beyond the experiencing individual, has to be expressed through language, that is symbolically; the communication of sensory experience requires a communicative practice. Secondly, the reality encountered by human beings is a symbolically prestructured reality, which is why, for Habermas, when people engage in interaction they encounter the world and one another as meaningfully structured (Habermas 1984, 1987). Therefore, access to this reality cannot be gained through observation alone (Outhwaite 1994). The core of Habermas's position was worked out in his extended debate with Gadamer (1975). Gadamer argued that people understand each other, insofar as they do, from within their own framework or tradition – what he termed their 'horizon'. This perspective is very much that of the tradition known as 'hermeneutics', with which he is closely associated. The necessarily partial perspectives (or 'prejudices'), which are a condition of these 'horizons', are not just obstacles to understanding (what we would describe as 'constraints') but also a possible means towards understanding others (what we would describe as 'enablements'). There is a significant realist element in Gadamer's account of the influence of tradition on the resources for symbolic communication that people encounter (see Davey 1993, How 1995). It is this element that Habermas reworks into a distinctive view of language.

Acknowledging Gadamer's insistence that the hermeneutic process is not the replacement of one horizon by another, 'better' one, but a dialogical process in which horizons are mutually extended, Habermas nevertheless wants to identify two important limits to the hermeneutic approach to language. Language, argues Habermas, is not just a means of communication which mediates our experience of the world, but is also a medium of domination and social power. A social science cannot therefore be reduced to interpretation, as is implied by hermeneutics. The second limit to the hermeneutic approach, argues Habermas, is that it is inattentive to the dependence of language on wider social processes (Habermas 1990). This is important because it is

50

this dependence that generates what Habermas terms 'systematically distorted communication'. 'What raises us out of nature', claims Habermas, 'is the only thing whose nature we can know: language' (Habermas 1986: 314). Language thus performs a double function in Habermas's model of social analysis: as the means through which our apprehension of the world is expressed and as the basis for our claims to truth and knowledge. The roots of rationality are to be found in the structures of everyday communication for Habermas, since such communication expresses our desire to be understood, to achieve an unconstrained consensus with our interlocutors. This claim is the core of Habermas's theory of communicative action.

Communicative action is distinguishable from communication, since it designates a form of social interaction that is managed through speech acts but is not reducible to them. This is because, for Habermas, reaching mutual understanding requires a speaker and hearer to operate at two levels: the level of intersubjectivity on which they speak with one another and the level of objects or states of affairs about which they communicate. These two levels are interdependent – all speech acts have a cognitive and a communicative dimension, that is to say they are both to do with the accomplishment of social interaction (getting somebody to do something) and with the expression of knowledge (claiming that something is the case) (Habermas 2001b: xiii).

Communicative action is therefore irreducibly intersubjective and emergent. Moreover, and this is the legacy of Gadamer, social actors are 'always already' situated within a 'lifeworld' of taken-for-granted assumptions on which actors can draw in trying to understand others. The lifeworld is the world of intersubjectively shared meanings that provides, in Habermas's words, 'a constantly operative context of relevance' (*ibid.*: xvi). Habermas contrasts the intersubjectively shared nature of the lifeworld, where people strive for consensual under-standing as the means of managing social interaction, with the nonconsensual nature of the system, driven by the impersonal forms of instrumental rationality. This distinction has been criticized on vari-ous grounds (see, for example, Giddens 1984, Layder 1997, Mouzelis 1991, 1995, 1997, Outhwaite 1994), and we do not wish to comment on these here. Rather we want to note the significance for our account of Habermas's emergent view of language and the 'depth ontology' that he proposes with the distinction between lifeworld and system.

Bourdieu and linguistic capital

Another figure who has placed a stress on language as a central feature in the analysis of social life is Bourdieu. Like Habermas, Bourdieu focuses attention on language as social action, arguing strongly that social science must reject 'the core intention of linguistics, namely the intellectualist philosophy which treats language as an object of contemplation rather than as an instrument of action and power' (Bourdieu 1991: 37). For Bourdieu, social relations are symbolic interactions and linguistic exchanges are also relations of symbolic power in which the power relations between speakers or their respective groups are actualized.

This claim sets Bourdieu at odds with both Saussure and Chomsky, since it entails a rejection of dichotomies between *langue* and *parole* (in the case of Saussure) and *competence* and *performance* (in the case of Chomsky). The Saussurean emphasis on language as an autonomous system of codes realized through actual utterances is seen as unacceptable on a number of counts. In its concentration on meaning as deriving from the internal relations between the semiotic elements of a text, it tends to disregard the empirical manifestations of languages through actual speech. This inattention to the empirical frequently leads to a reification of language and to a neglect of the social and historical conditions surrounding the production and reception of texts. It may also result in an unreflexive account of the researcher's own position, since it implies a clear distinction between the object of enquiry (language as *langue*, as semiotic system) and the researcher, such that the latter's social location and its implications for the account of language that he or she develops are taken for granted. In other words, the structuralist model conceals in a methodological distinction (between language as a system and languages as actually uttered, either as spoken or written texts) a series of substantive assumptions about what is to count as language in terms of social research. So, for example, for Bourdieu the idea of homogeneous, identifiable languages or speech communities is chimerical, simply an idealization of a particular set of historically determinate linguistic practices. It is the linguist who produces the illusion of a common language through the theoretical strategy of treating a particular set of linguistic practices as a normative model defining who belongs to this or that speech community.

Bourdieu's rejection of the structuralist model, whether in the form of Saussure's semiotic system or Chomsky's transformational grammar, has a further aspect pertinent to our own arguments, namely that it is insufficient to account for the kind of competence and creativity that actual speakers possess. Bourdieu's argument does not compel him to deny that human beings possess the capacity to generate grammatical sentences, that they have a biological or organismic capacity for language use, but it does lead him to point out that such a capacity cannot satisfactorily explain the practical competence of actual speakers. Practical competence, for Bourdieu, requires not only that speakers produce grammatical sentences, but also that they produce utterances appropriate to the context of their utterance. To speak (or to write) is not only to produce sentences that make sense in the obvious linguistic sense; it is also to recognize who has the right to speak and in what sorts of terms one is likely to be listened to. Practical competence therefore deals with the profoundly sociological question of the forms of power and authority implicit in all communicative situations. It is, as Bourdieu quoting Proust points out, about 'the infinitely varied art of marking distances' (Bourdieu 1986: 66).

The concern with language as practical social action prompts Bourdieu to take a much more sympathetic view of Austin than he does of Saussure and Chomsky. The significance of Austin's work for Bourdieu is its concern with performative utterances and the accompanying recognition that such utterances presume an institutional setting which defines the conditions that must be fulfilled in order for an utterance to be effective. For example, the utterances of a judge in passing sentence obtain their force from the judicial setting in which they are uttered, which places the judge in a position of authority in relation to the defendant and so on. Although in Bourdieu's view Austin left undeveloped the nature of the 'conventional procedures' that underpinned performative utterances (what Austin (1962) termed 'illocutionary acts'), he sees the insight as fundamental to a social scientific account of language.

This critical scrutiny of the work of Saussure, Chomsky and Austin provides the foundation for Bourdieu's own distinctive approach, including the two concepts that are core to his perspective on language and social life: habitus and practice.

Broadly speaking, 'habitus' for Bourdieu refers to the 'durable motivations, perceptions and forms of knowledge that people carry around in their heads as a result of living in particular social environments and that predispose them to act in certain ways' (Layder 1997: 236). The concept of habitus is Bourdieu's resolution of the structure–agency problem that we have identified elsewhere. The concept explains why everyday, routine activities are to some degree regular and predictable, since our social backgrounds delineate ways of seeing, patterns of thought, even physical posture. However, habitus only provides a general, loose series of predispositions, and these are not determining of what people do in specific social contexts. This is in part due to the emergent quality of social action, the fact that for Bourdieu what people actually do in a particular setting is an outcome of the relation between the habitus, on the one hand, and the specific social contexts (or 'fields' in Bourdieu's terms) within which the individual acts. A 'field' may be seen as 'a structured space of positions in which the positions and their interrelations are determined by the distribution of different kinds of resources or "capital" ' (Bourdieu 1991: 15).

In this way, Bourdieu seeks to escape the trap of objectivism (the Saussurean, Chomskyan flaw in which actual language use is merely an epiphenomenal instance of a structural code or a language acquisition device) through an emphasis on practice, the concrete negotiation of social settings by people predisposed by their habitus to certain ways of doing things but capable of adapting such ways appropriately to particular contexts. At the same time, Bourdieu's perspective seeks to avoid subjectivism, the intellectual orientation to the social world that epistemologically privileges immediate experience. This is close to what we refer to as 'experiential empiricism', which rests upon the presupposition that it is possible to apprehend in an immediate sense the lived experience of others (as in some forms of sociology, such as ethnomethodology).

It is a source of some contention how far Bourdieu has managed to accomplish this twin ambition. For example, Bourdieu's notion of practice has been criticized for being defined *against* theoretical discourse (Archer 2000: 151). That is, Bourdieu's practical knowledge is exactly that: knowledge of how to practically effect social competence. It is not obvious why this should count as 'knowledge' (Pleasants 1999), but more significantly, it rules out an adequate account of 'World 3' theoretical discourse as itself the emergent product of our practical relations with the world (Archer 2000: 151). The position we are advancing here would therefore want to argue for a more foundational role for human practice than Bourdieu's. Indeed, the emergentist model of language development and acquisition that we are advocating is one based squarely on a realist, materialist view of human practice.

Nevertheless, Bourdieu's notion of social fields has much to offer. Layder, for example, has made a convincing case for regarding social fields as similar to his social domains of 'contextual resources' and 'social settings' which we explain in Chapter 6 (Layder 1997: 116–17). Furthermore, Bourdieu's view of various forms of capital as emergent (habitus + field = value) is one which we find appealing. In particular, there are strong similarities between what Bourdieu terms the realization of capital and what we have described as the realization of constraints and enablements:

> The dispositions constituting the cultivated habitus are only formed, only function and are only valid, in the relationship with a field which ... is itself a 'field of possible forces', a 'dynamic situation', in which forces are only manifested in their relationship with certain dispositions. This is why the same practices may receive opposite meanings and values in different fields, in different configurations or in opposing sectors of the same field.
>
> (Bourdieu 1986: 94)

We thus have a powerful means of viewing the distributions of linguistic attributes – accent, dialect, patterns of speech and so forth – and their realization as constraints and enablements in particular linguistic markets, where they may become either the source of profit or the cause of bankruptcy. This is a matter we shall return to in our discussion of 'language death'.

Whilst we hope to have demonstrated that both Habermas and Bourdieu attach a good deal of importance to language in the interpretation and constitution of the social world, it remains the case that neither of them systematically analyses language in the ways that applied linguists do. Whilst they reject the structuralist view of language as an autonomous, regulatory system of codes in favour of an approach which regards language and social life as profoundly interlinked, they do not see the task of developing this claim in a rigorous way as one that requires a specifically linguistic knowledge.

Bernstein and social codes

This might also be said to be the case with the third figure we consider in this discussion of language and social action, Bernstein. Indeed, the defence of Bernstein against the charge that his core distinction between an elaborated code (characteristically used by the middle classes) and a restricted code (characteristically used by the working classes) was a normative one, has been to argue that such codes do not refer to dialects or sociolects, but to codes in the more formal structuralist sense discussed above. (See, for example, Atkinson 1985, Grillo 1989.) It is not germane to our purposes to review the extensive debate provoked by Bernstein's formulation and the accusation that it was unavoidably pejorative of working-class modes of language. Rather we shall sketch out an interpretation of Bernstein's work which draws attention to the relation between language and social action that has been the focus of this chapter.

In fact, our view of Bernstein's work is similar to that of Chouliaraki and Fairclough (1999: 107–19) in that we too see Bernstein's primary concern as being with social class relations and symbolic control. Bernstein himself sought to make the notion of the restricted code distinct from that of actual language use:

> It [the restricted code] simply means that there is a restriction on the *contexts* and on the *conditions* which will orient the child to universalistic orders of meaning and to making those linguistic choices through which such meanings are realized and so made public. It does not mean that the children cannot produce at any time elaborated speech in particular contexts. It is critically important to distinguish between speech variants and a restricted code.
>
> (Bernstein 1970: 118)

Bernstein's codes, then, are structural codes which guide and regulate the way language is organized. The public or restricted code uses unfinished sentences, chained clauses, formulaic expressions, whilst the formal or elaborated code is characterized by more complex syntax, greater explicitness and so on. Through associated kinds of language use, codes are linked to particular forms of social solidarity: the working class achieves solidarity through a limited stock of idiomatic expressions, or as Atkinson (1985: 43) expresses it, the 'affirmation and confirmation of pre-existing, shared meanings and orientations', whilst the middle class socializes children more as individuals through the explicit negotiation of meanings.

In view of this it is unsurprising, perhaps, that Bernstein's work was interpreted in ways which suggested that the languages and cultures of the working class were in some sense deficient in, or lacking the capacity for, extended thought. As Grillo (1989: 202) has pointed out, such charges tend to miss the main thrust of Bernstein's work: 'It is undoubtedly the social system whose values the educational system reflects which makes of difference a deficit.' However, our reservations about his approach take a different form.

Principally, Bernstein, in common with theorists of a structuralist provenance, operates with a restricted view of agency (Bernstein 1970, 1996). Like Bourdieu's notion of habitus with which it has much in common, Bernstein's code is the *éminence grise* of social life, relativizing perspectives, individuating human subjects and constraining behaviour. This is, in other words, a 'top down' account of social life and, in common with many such accounts, pays little attention to the emergent nature of social interaction or to the possibility, arising from such interactions, that people might contribute to altering the code.

The theorists we have considered in this section have sought to develop dualistic accounts of the relation between social action and language. That is, Habermas, Bourdieu and Bernstein have placed language at the forefront of their analysis of the social world and have recognized its partial autonomy from individuals and its power to influence directly the nature of their social interactions. However, as we have indicated, their work does not fully incorporate the analysis of language itself into a social theory of language and languages.

Conclusion

This account of some currents in sociological theory has been necessarily brief and selective. The selection was guided by the light shed in each approach on the nature of the relationship between language, social order and social action, as befits this book's themes of language, structure and agency. It is often remarked that sociology has contributed more to the socially situated study of language than linguistics has to the study of society. Attempts have been made to constitute a 'sociology of language', notably by Fishman (e.g. Fishman 1978), but as he himself observed, writing in 1992, 'the two fields are as remote from each other now as they were in the 1960s' (Fishman in Williams 1992: viii). Topics considered within the 'sociology of language', as well as in some interpretations of applied linguistics, would include bilingualism and multilingualism, bilingual and minority education, language planning, language and nationalism, language and ethnicity, and language rights. While we have not explicitly discussed these here – most are explored in subsequent chapters – the reader will no doubt recognize how the sociological preoccupations discussed in this chapter are drawn on in research which does look closely at linguistic issues in their social contexts.

We started with a discussion of the interactionist sociologies, including symbolic interactionism, ethnomethodology and conversation analysis. In applied linguistics, the range of approaches which fall under the heading of 'discourse analysis' includes some which develop and extend interactionist sociologies into detailed studies of language. Conversation analysis is an obvious example, but studies in the 'ethnography of speaking', associated with researchers such as Hymes and Gumperz could also be cited here. Space does not permit us to explore the differences between the various contributors to work in this area, who by no means constitute a homogeneous group. However, approaches such as these share an emphasis on the inter-subjective meanings of members of the 'speech community' to which they are said to belong, and it is, we suggested, a merit of the inter-actionist model that it recognizes an important role for human agency.

We turned our attention next to those approaches which place discourse at the heart of their explanations, and here there is obviously considerable overlap with versions of discourse analysis to which applied linguistics has contributed. If interactionism runs the risk of reducing interaction to nothing more than language, the more extreme discourse sociologies are in danger of reducing social reality to language.

In both cases (that of reducing interaction to language on the one hand and that of reducing social reality to discourse on the other), an abiding problem is how to deal with the notion of constraint, that is, with the ways in which people's conversational strategies and resources are structured. To do so adequately entails considering not only the structuring of language itself, but also issues of power and conflict. Conversation analysis has been criticized for claiming that it attends only to its linguistic data, thereby assuming a voluntaristic, consensual version of the social order:

> Above all, it conveys an essentially non-critical view of the social world. The bedrock situation – or the default option – is implicitly depicted as a world of equality and participation, in which 'members' share systems of social order. Inequality is to be found in the exceptions – in institutional talk, interviews etc. Thus, traditional CA, far from being free of social presuppositions, carries them in the regular deployment of its foundational rhetoric. The warnings against being theoretical, and against using conventional sociological analyses, together with the prescription to keep to the data, can serve to protect these assumptions from analysis.
>
> (Billig 1999a: 552)

Conversation analysts have taken issue with this depiction (Schegloff 1999), and it must be noted that 'ideological' or 'critical' discourse analysis, which does seek to locate discourse within a social world of conflict and inequality, attracts criticisms of its own. For example, in relation to Critical Discourse Analysis, Stubbs expresses uncertainty about 'the extent to which cause and effect relations are being claimed, about the nature of evidence which textual traces are said to provide of social change, and so on' (Stubbs 1997: 105). As we noted, a problem with accounts which draw on a strong notion of discourse is that these often seem to leave agency behind altogether.

The theorists whose work we considered in the third section of this chapter have sought to hold to a distinction between language and social action, and this, we have argued, makes their work a fruitful source for exploring the relations between language and society. In different ways Habermas, Bourdieu and Bernstein have – importantly – recognized the partial autonomy of language from individuals, and its power to influence directly the nature of their social interactions.

However, as we have also indicated, their work does not fully incorporate the analysis of language itself into a social theory of language and languages. Nevertheless, it is our contention that this task needs to be predicated on the distinction between language and agency. The following chapter builds on this distinction to elaborate a view of languages as cultural emergent properties.

3 Language as a cultural emergent property

Introduction

This chapter explores the significance of the core concepts of social realism outlined in Chapter 1 for applied linguistics in order to explore the possibility of a particular view of the relationship between language and social life. We begin by examining how applied linguistics deploys various concepts of 'the real', and how these overlap with and deviate from the concepts of the real in theoretical linguistics. We discuss one particular pedagogical issue, namely the use of authentic language data, in relation to this, before turning to the more philosophical questions involved in distinguishing between domains of reality. The chapter then goes on to discuss what large language corpora and actually existing human languages can tell us about the intersubjective nature of language, concluding by proposing that there is much to be gained by conceptualizing languages as cultural emergent properties.

The philosophy identified as 'realism' has a longer history in the natural than in the social sciences. Within linguistics, its applications have been largely in those areas which come closest to the natural sciences, so that Chomsky's claims about the generative mechanisms which underlie the production of specific utterances are sometimes taken to be typical examples of the kinds of phenomena in which realist philosophers of science would be interested. Our position is rather different, however. Our own orientations, as a social theorist (Carter) and an applied linguist (Sealey), are towards the questions and problems faced by actual speakers as they use language, and towards those who try to understand these issues, whom we might designate 'social linguists'. This chapter is therefore concerned with the ways in which we think the core concepts of social realism illuminate the experiences and ideas about those experiences which interest social linguists.

What's real about real language?

We start with this question for two reasons. Firstly, applied linguists are explicitly concerned with 'the real', although we shall argue that the concept of the real which concerns them warrants further elucidation. Secondly, the non-applied, non-social dimensions of language are often seen to be what constitute its 'reality' in the Chomskyan tradition, so we need to address that line of argument here as well. Indeed, we might suggest that a key contrast between linguistics and applied linguistics concerns their respective concerns with different kinds of 'reality'.

For Chomsky, the concept of language which locates it beyond the brain, and thus 'externalizes' it as 'a "construct" that is understood independently of the properties of the mind/brain' is 'too far removed from reality' (Chomsky 1986: 19, 20). This 'externalized' version of language, or 'E-language', is criticized for being epiphenomenal to 'the data and mechanisms' (Botha 1992: 84) of the internalized, 'I-language', the proper concern of linguistic science. The I-language is 'some element of the mind of the person who knows the language, acquired by the learner, and used by the speaker-hearer'; 'the system of knowledge of language attained and internally represented in the mind/brain' (Chomsky 1986: 22, 24). This internal, unobservable, generic version of language is what is 'real' in this version of linguistics.

As an applied linguist, Brumfit (2001) demonstrates a different interpretation of what is meant by 'real', when he re-presents his definition of applied linguistics as 'the theoretical and empirical investigation of real-world problems in which language is a central issue' (p.169). Cook (2003) makes a similar link: applied linguistics is defined as 'the academic discipline concerned with the relation of knowledge about language to decision making in the real world' (p.5). Cook prioritizes 'the *facts* of language *use*' (*ibid.*: emphasis added), while Brumfit claims that '"real-world problems" are investigated partly as a counterweight to the disconnection of autonomous and idealized disciplines' (p.186), thus contrasting 'real' with 'idealized'.

When the word 'real' is used, as it is in several publications, to denote a characteristic of the language with which applied linguistics is concerned, it is clearly intended to invite approval (cf. Carter 1998). COBUILD, which uses the Bank of English as a source of data for its dictionaries and grammars, includes on its publications the strap-line 'Helping learners with real English'. The Longman book series entitled 'Real Language' describes itself as a 'sociolinguistic series about language in the real world' (e.g. Milroy and Milroy 1993: back cover), whose titles (one of which is *Real English*) 'draw on natural language data from a wide range of social contexts'.

So can we begin to answer the question 'what is real language?'? Two contrasting positions can perhaps be summarized thus:

1. *Real* language is an unobservable property of the human mind. Understanding it requires analytical skill and an ability to deduce generic and generalizable patterns, rather than observations of people communicating in any specific language variety in particular circumstances.

2. *Real* language is what people actually say. Understanding it involves collecting examples of this observable language behaviour. Describing it means describing this behaviour, rather than accounting for some hidden generic mechanism.

Of course, there are many shades of commitment to and modified versions of these contrasting positions, which to some extent echo those held in different traditions of linguistics through the twentieth century. It is possible that misunderstandings based on the connotations of each are responsible for some of the divisions between 'autonomous' and 'applied' linguists today, and for the failure of each to recognize potential common ground between them. Our own position distinguishes us both from the 'ontologically driven' rationalist version of realism which we believe characterizes adherence to hidden generative mechanisms and a derogation of empirical data, and also from the naïve empiricism which privileges observable behaviour over theory. We accept that some aspects of the conceptualization of language may depend on the purposes of the person who is adopting it. It is thus quite conceivable that a literary critic, a translator, a curriculum designer, a teacher, a speech therapist and a neuroscientist (not to mention all of them – and us – in our roles as routine language users) might hold very different concepts of 'language' without any one of these being 'wrong'.

Lest we be accused of side-stepping theory and taking refuge in pragmatism, however (cf. Carr 1990: 71ff), we should make it clear that our position here is not that 'anything goes'. Theory plays a part in conceptions of language, and language itself has properties which limit the ways in which it can legitimately be described. Those who analyse language, whether for 'pure'-ly descriptive or for 'applied' (e.g. pedagogic) purposes, will necessarily have a different understanding of it from those who use it as a medium to get things done. This means that we can rule out the exclusively hermeneutic position, summarized by Pateman (1987) as the requirement for a theory – in this case, a theory about language – that it 'could in principle be recognized as true by those to whom it applies' (p.12). But it also means that we need to add a third conceptualization of 'real language' to the two already identified:

3. *Real* language is what ordinary speakers produce and encounter as they go about their business. In the normal course of existence, language users only intermittently have the need or motivation to analyse the properties and patterns of language, and are likely when they do to turn to 'authorities' such as dictionaries (to establish what words 'really' mean).

This means that there is a potentially greater contrast between what the lay person perceives as significant and what the analyst chooses to highlight, than between the accounts provided by different kinds of analyst. There is a potential paradox here. The 'real' concerns of the 'non-scientist, non-specialist' may turn out to be incompatible with the characteristics of 'real' language as identified by those who analyse it (as Cameron (1995), among others, has pointed out). Or, as Brumfit (2001: 153) puts it, 'Teachers work in a world of real people, real motives, and conflicting interests' so will often see things differently from researchers, whose job is to be reflective about language in particular and explicit ways. Applied linguists thus have to ask themselves whether their version of 'real language' can accommodate position 3 above, including, for example, commonsense definitions of who in the world speaks 'real English', or prescriptivist attitudes to 'correct' language use.

This is one way in which the applied linguistic enterprise of engaging with 'real language' in 'the real world' invites further attention, and it leads us to another one. Even the most practical of applied linguists, whose principal concerns are with helping language learners to make more successful progress in their studies, for example, have to make use of *some* theoretical constructs in conceptualizing language. As Brumfit (2001: 178) points out, 'any theoretical and empirical study involves principled idealization'. In other words, we are arguing that no applied linguist (when being an applied linguist, that is, and thus, by our definition, a social scientist) can take 'real language' as given and unproblematic. Some theorizing and analysis inevitably goes with the territory. This is not to denigrate either the practical abilities or reflective capacities of 'lay' speakers; it is simply to acknowledge that using language and researching language use are not identical activities.

'Real language' in applied linguistics = 'real sentences' in the classroom?

Let us take one topic of debate as an example of how competing theories about what constitutes 'language' are implicated in an applied linguistics problem. This topic is chosen because it relates closely to the issue of 'real' language. It is the question of whether language teachers should make use of invented sentences or should restrict themselves to authentic examples only. Although at one level this is an argument about pedagogy, at another it rests on (possibly competing) beliefs about the 'real' properties of language.

Several applied linguists are explicit proponents of the use in the classroom of attested examples of the language-to-be-learned. One core element of their argument is that what learners are engaged in is the processing (both productively and receptively) of language behaviour. In other words, what they usually want is engagement with those very aspects of language that Chomsky would classify as epiphenomena of 'real language'. As Cook (2001) points out, advocacy of authentic sentences in teaching has a long history, but the arguments have been given new momentum with the advent of linguistic corpora. Thanks to this particular technological development, those responsible for providing learners with examples of the target language (that is, mainly, teachers and textbook writers) now have access to large databanks of examples of language behaviour, for example in the Bank of English (the result of a collaboration between a university, Birmingham, which has primarily scientific purposes, and a publisher, HarperCollins, with its commercial, and thus, indirectly, pedagogic priorities). One of the principal uses to which the Bank of English has been put is to contribute to textbooks for learners of English as a foreign language, and Sinclair has this to say about the approach (emphasis added to key words):

> It is now generally accepted that it is extremely difficult to invent examples which sound *realistic*, and which have all the features of *natural* examples. I am convinced that it is essential for a learner of English to learn from *actual* examples, examples that can be trusted because they have been used in *real* communication.
>
> (COBUILD 1990: vii)

Another corpus with a partly pedogogic motivation is CANCODE (the result of a collaboration between Nottingham University and Cambridge University Press). This corpus comprises transcripts of spontaneous spoken English, and is thus a repository for examples of the kind of spoken language behaviour that non-corpus-based textbooks often omit. The best course of action to remedy this deficit, claim

Carter and McCarthy (1995: 154), 'would seem to be to expose learners to *natural* spoken data wherever possible' (emphasis added).

Now the theories made most explicit in the debate about this topic (e.g. Carter 1998; Cook 1998) are primarily pedagogic, secondarily linguistic and only tangentially ontological: that is, the writers are not explicitly debating the nature of what language 'really is'. Our argument, though, is that ontological claims are entailed by the claims that are made in this debate, and it is these that are most relevant to the issues discussed in this chapter. So, while not intending to impute to the protagonists positions they would not adopt themselves, let us try to elucidate some of the claims about the nature of 'real language' which are implicit in this debate.

Claim 1: The use of the terms 'natural', 'actual', 'attested' and 'authentic' as near synonyms for 'real' points to one ontological proposition: what's real about language is what can be empirically observed. If one wants 'real' language data, one consults a repository of examples collected by observers of language behaviour (in the form of transcribed recordings or of communicative writing).

Claim 2: Language has some properties which are rarely observed empirically, and evidence of these (in this case for teaching purposes) has to be artificially brought into being. One of these properties is a distinction between form and meaning. Thus an example sentence which illustrates the formal, grammatical properties of a language may fail to illustrate its communicative, semantic properties. (Perhaps the most well-known invented sentence used to illustrate this is Chomsky's 'Colourless green ideas sleep furiously', which is grammatically acceptable but semantically obscure at best.) This 'real' property of language (i.e. the potential to be grammatical but communicatively inauthentic) is not revealed in language users' routinely observed behaviour.

Claim 3: Language has some properties which are not reducible to individual instantiations of it, such as utterances. One illustration of this, from a proponent of the use of invented examples, is the observation that, thanks to the human capacity for creativity, language users can, and often do, put even the most bizarre sentences into some kind of imagined context which will render them as discourse (Cook 2001). An illustration of this claim from the opposing position, that is from proponents of corpus-based teaching, is that it is only by looking at lots of examples of individual sentences (or, more accurately, of concordance lines) that some of the properties of language become evident.

In the next section, we discuss an ontological position which we hope will help to accommodate, or at least adjudicate between, those aspects of these claims that seem to be in conflict. But first let us examine where we have reached in respect to determining what might be 'real' about language for these various applied linguists.

If what is real about language could be exhausted by what can be empirically observed, then neither the attested sentence nor the invented one could be an 'example' of any of the properties which might underlie that sentence. The concept, for instance, of 'relative clause' is a theoretical description, and is not given, unmediated, to the observer of any sentence which contains one, invented or attested. Many, perhaps most, speakers of a language manage perfectly well as communicators with no concept of 'relative clause', though this concept may be useful to learners of an additional language, which is why applied linguists concern themselves with how best to teach it: it becomes, pedagogically, 'a target structure'. The idea of a target structure presupposes that language is 'structured'. This claim is largely uncontroversial, although, as we noted in Chapter 1, there are those who are sceptical that 'the resources of the descriptive apparatus available' can capture any supposed 'underlying "system" ' of linguistic universals (Harris 2001: 126). However, if there are such structures within language, then it is often a teacher's goal to illustrate one such aspect of it, to make it more apparent, more central and uncluttered by features which are irrelevant and potentially misleading.

Both putative example sentences share the property of being instantiations of some more generic characteristic of the linguistic system – perhaps of the fact that the system includes structures such as relative clauses. (Indeed, as Cook (2001) points out, the terms 'invented' and 'attested' need not be mutually exclusive: all attested sentences had to be 'invented' by their original speakers; and sentences invented by teachers or textbook writers become attested, even if only in the pedagogic context for which they were produced.) In pedagogic terms, the 'ludicrous' example is said by Cook to have the advantage of being memorable. For Carter and McCarthy, and others, the authentic example scores on another dimension, by illustrating what is typical, and, when contextualized among large numbers of similar examples, by revealing to learners the structure (again) clothed in so many variants of incidental features that it is the *common* property which becomes apparent. Two routes to the same end: to make apparent to the learner what the analyst/teacher knows is there, despite the fact that it is not empirically observable. So protagonists on both sides, it would seem, share (at least implicitly) the realist's belief in two levels of reality: the empirical (i.e. that which can be perceived by the senses), and something distinct from the empirical (i.e. phenomena, such as those labelled by linguists 'relative clauses', which cannot be seen directly but which nevertheless exist as features of language).

The empirical, the actual and the real

So far, then, we have claimed: that language users engage in language behaviours; both language users and applied linguists experience, as sensory impressions, language behaviour, and this is the level of the empirical, that which speakers say and write; this behaviour can be witnessed, and, for the (social) scientist, it becomes data when recorded and subjected to analysis. However, as we have seen, those facts about language which can be empirically observed do not exhaust all that language comprises. In this section, we try to identify some different senses in which we think it is helpful to conceptualize what is 'real'. The discussion necessarily takes a rather philosophical turn at this point, but we believe that the level of abstraction involved is both necessary and productive. Therefore, although at first sight 'empirical', 'actual' and 'real' may seem to be synonyms (see several quotations in the foregoing sections), whose respective meanings are not worth teasing apart, we hope to demonstrate otherwise as this section unfolds.

The distinction between these three 'domains' of reality is drawn by Bhaskar (1978: 56). (Note that the notion of 'domains' employed here is not the same as that used by Layder about the social world as explored in Chapter 6.) The initial context for Bhaskar's argument is the natural world, and, as we have said, there are different issues to consider in the social world of human beings. However, his core claim is that:

> ... the causal structures and generative mechanisms of nature must exist and act independently of the conditions that allow men [*sic*] access to them, so that they must be assumed to be structured and intransitive, i.e. relatively independent of the patterns of events and the actions of men alike. Similarly I have argued that events must occur independently of the experiences in which they are apprehended. Structures and mechanisms then are real and distinct from the patterns of events that they generate; just as events are real and distinct from the experiences in which they are apprehended. Mechanisms, events and experiences thus constitute three overlapping domains of reality, viz. the domains of the real, the actual and the empirical.

In due course we will seek to demonstrate how useful this tripartite distinction may be in understanding applied linguistic problems such as the status of competing varieties in language planning decisions, or of attested versus invented sentences in the language classroom. We should note that we are concerned here with different kinds of phenomena than those in the natural world which are Bhaskar's concern at this point, and our interpretation of the distinction as it applies to language and (applied) linguistics is very much our own.

The real

In this kind of ontology, 'real' phenomena are generative mechanisms underlying empirically observable phenomena. Thus Chomsky is often identified as a linguistic realist because of his concern with the hidden operational code which makes instances of language behaviour possible. There are, of course, a number of challenges to this approach, some of them presented by other realists. Carr (1990), for example, holds to a fairly traditional notion of what it is that linguistics is about. Its evidential base '... is something other than a collection of observed events' (p.30), and what linguists do is attempt '... to describe the mechanisms in the underlying linguistic reality which allow us to characterise these expressions [sets of sentences] as well-formed' (*ibid.*: 33). Carr, however, takes issue with the insistence in the Chomskyan tradition that 'linguistic objects and states of affairs are speaker-internal and ... theoretical linguistics is in some sense a branch of cognitive psychology' (*ibid.*: 3). This is because of his commitment to the intersubjective nature of linguistic reality. Drawing heavily on Popper's conception of intersubjectivity, Carr maintains that '[u]nder this ontological interpretation of the generative enterprise, we may say that a language, constituted by its rules, is a public object' (*ibid.*: 42).

The ontological status of linguistic 'rules' is a matter of continuing debate, and some linguistic realists part company with the Chomskyan tradition over a perceived conflation between two different kinds of 'rule', leading to different positions about the ontological status of unobserved 'realities'. Devitt and Sterelny (1999), for example, are sceptical of the claim that speakers must be possessed of propositional knowledge, represented in the mind and therefore pyschologically real, as grammatical rules which are isomorphic with the rules formulated by linguists. Devitt and Sterelny are concerned not to dismiss the empirically observable reality of language, and to accommodate linguistic symbols as observable outputs into their description of language, as 'datable, placeable parts of the physical world: sounds in the air, marks on the page, and so on. They are not mental entities at all' (p.169). The detail of their argument about the

'... two sorts of rules, the "structure-rules" governing the products of a competence, and the "processing-rules" governing the production of those products, rules governing the *exercise* of the competence' (*ibid.*: 171) is not our main concern. However, their position does illustrate that contemporary interpretations of realist philosophy in linguistics allow a greater role for 'objects or events in the physical world "outside the head"' (*ibid.*: 169) than is associated with the Chomskyan position. Thus, although Devitt and Sterelny take a somewhat different line from Carr (to whose work they do not refer), they too conceptualize linguistic realities as having an existence which is external to, and separate from, individual psychological realities.

One of the differences between Carr's position and that of Devitt and Sterelny is that, despite the commitment of both to the inter-subjective properties of linguistic reality, the former is much less ready to concede the relevance of spatio-temporal events to the study of language. A realism which is so theory-driven that it effectively precludes the description of data is not one we would want to endorse. A critic of generative linguistics who makes the case well is Beaugrande:

> A paradoxical scenario arose: reality being claimed for a technical construction while rejecting the reality of human discourse – inclusive theory with exclusive practice ... . And instead of becoming a genuine *normal science*, generativist linguistics could only be a *normalizing quasi-science* that cannot describe authentic data but only the data it has expressly normalized, thereby rendering them empirically undecidable.
>
> (Beaugrande 1997: 35)

Carr maintains a commitment – which, significantly, we do not share (as will become evident in Chapters 4 and 8) – to falsifiable hypotheses as a basic criterion of science. It is crucial for him, then, that linguists have a methodological tool which is at least consistent, if not identical, with the methods used to test hypotheses in other branches of science. Carr's approach adopts grammaticality judgements as its data, or evidential base, and adheres to a belief in the primacy of sentences ('abstract objects which do not exist in a context', 1990: 43) over utterances (spatio-temporal events). Utterances, what speakers actually say, with their notorious 'imperfections', exist, as we have explained, at the level of the empirical. Carr's position here is analogous to that of the realist social theorists Keat and Urry (1982), whose argument, we feel, runs the risk of placing so much emphasis on the unobservable layer of reality that the empirical is demoted out of the picture. Carr defends his position by an appeal to 'the knowledge which allows us to make this crucial distinction' – that is, that between well-formed and ill-formed expressions. On the basis of that knowledge, he claims, 'we are able to dispense with much of what is given in a corpus; it is clear that corpora play little or no part in strictly theoretical linguistics' (Carr 1990: 99). Devitt and Sterelny, by contrast, give much greater weight to speakers' meanings. It is these, they say, that '... create the conventional written and spoken forms of the language. But it is because we have learned those conventions that we are able to have the rich variety of thoughts, and hence produce the rich variety of speaker meanings, that we do' (Devitt and Sterelny 1999: 155).

The domain of the real, then, in relation to language, includes **both** the mechanisms internal to the human organism which make language processing possible **and** those properties and powers of language which enable intersubjective communication. The significance of this second property of language will be considered more extensively below. At this point, however, we simply want to emphasize the claim that what is real about language includes its intersubjective as well as its intrasubjective properties.

The actual

This, then, is what we intend to convey when we refer to what is 'real' about language, while we trust that we have already made it clear what we mean by 'the empirical' in relation to language – those aspects of language which are capable of perception by the human senses. So do we need to introduce a third domain of reality? We think so. Bhaskar's claim allows us to distinguish between what causes things to happen in the world, which we often cannot observe (the real), and the instances of experience of which we are immediately aware (the empirical). The intervening domain, the actual, is that part of reality – events – which actually happen, as distinct from all those things which might have happened but did not. The reasons why the real does not inevitably coincide with the actual are attributable to the fact that the world is an 'open system', and the social world, in particular, 'is not a mechanism with fixed, indispensable parts and determinate relations between parts, pre-set preferred states and pre-programmed homeostatic mechanisms' (Archer 1995: 165). Outside of the laboratory, even the 'governing laws' of the physical sciences are often overridden by contingent variations: this is the very reason why scientists are obliged to exercise control in their experiments, and to contrive to make certain things happen which might never occur without their interventions (cf. Pawson 1989, Chapter 7). In the social world, the distinctive properties and powers of human beings, and of society itself, make it inevitable that underlying realities will not necessarily materialize into actual events.

Thus by 'the actual' in this context, we mean those linguistic phenomena which 'actualize' the powers and properties of language, some of which may not become manifest at the level of the empirical.

Our first example of this level of reality is, somewhat controversially, the different languages of the human population as it exists across the globe and throughout time. For Chomsky, languages in this sense are sociopolitical constructs, and the differences between them are of less interest to the scientist than their underlying similarities. It is customary for linguists to point out that lay classifications of languages, while adequate for everyday use, bypass a problem which is much more acute for the scientist, which is that the boundaries of varieties are notoriously difficult to establish. A typical example is that although 'Dutch' and 'German' are thought of as two distinct languages, 'the variety of German spoken near the Dutch border can be understood by speakers of Dutch who live nearby, though not by speakers of German who live in more remote areas' (Chomsky 1988: 37). The 'commonsense' conception of languages – what the lay speaker thinks of as 'French', 'Russian' or 'Swahili', for example – is rejected by linguists in this tradition partly because it is so difficult to specify precisely what 'knowledge of' a language in this sense could mean. Yet the same theoretical approach proceeds entirely *as though* this problem did not exist. Thus Chomsky writes:

> The grammar of English will generate, for each sentence, a deep structure, and will contain rules showing how this deep structure is related to a surface structure. ... A person who has acquired knowledge of English has internalized these rules.
>
> (p.106)

Statements such as these seem to us to rely on an independent existence for an entity which can be labelled 'English' – even if for this aspect of the linguistic enterprise the primary focus is on its underlying rather than its surface structure. Lightfoot (1991: 162) maintains that when linguists use an expression such as 'a change in the grammar of Language X', they are using 'a convenient fiction permitting the statement of certain generalizations and ignoring certain types of variation' (cited in Hopper and Traugott 1993: 36), but this approach seems to sidestep a paradox in the argument. For it is inconsistent to claim, on the one hand, that 'Japanese' or 'English' are simply 'convenient fictions' while yet appealing to the native speaker **of** 'Japanese' or 'English' for grammaticality judgements to aid in the process of identifying features of the underlying grammar.

71

Reliance on what speakers themselves believe when they say 'I speak Language X' is undoubtedly fraught with difficulties, some of them analogous to the problems of relying on respondents' self-classifications in respect of 'ethnic identity', as we discuss in Chapter 5 (cf. Carr 1990). Nevertheless, for language learners it is the differences between languages that are the most salient, in the sense that what is to be learned, the 'target language', differs from what is known, the 'mother tongue'. In this context, the motivation to learn to speak 'English' or 'Chinese' is much more relevant, practically, than the concept of universal grammar. Learners enrol, and teachers are employed to teach, in 'French classes' or at a 'School of English'; learners' progress towards becoming speakers of these languages is assessed and may be formally certificated. Economic and social opportunities, on the one hand, or barriers, on the other, may well follow from the results obtained in these language tests: is everyone involved in these processes deluded to believe that different 'languages', in this specific sense, are 'real'?

The approach we are putting forward allows for a middle way between confining the concept of a language variety to something which exists exclusively inside each speaker's head, and granting a fully discrete and separate status to different languages. It suggests that it is the interaction between human practices and linguistic properties which may account over time for the separation of some varieties and the merging of others. These human practices include both the use of a variety for communication (where the emphasis is on agency) and sociopolitical regulation (with an emphasis on structure). Complexity theory provides a means of visualizing the process of such language change, as Nettle explains:

> Consider a many-dimensional space with every dimension representing a different linguistic parameter. Thus, one dimension might be the size of the phonological inventory, another, some aspect of constituent order, another the level of morphological complexity, and so on. Different languages can be seen as occupying points in this space. Each point in the space has a fitness value, representing the extent to which a language at that point in the space will be effective at being learned and used by speakers. Under functional selection, languages should be expected to evolve towards the points with the highest fitness values. ... [However,] in such a complex space, there is unlikely to be just one optimum position to which one can smoothly ascend from anywhere in the space. Instead there may be a number of positions that are locally optimal and onto which languages may settle. ... [S]mall random changes, arising from random variations or social selection, are

sufficient to push different languages off into different parts of the
state space.

(Nettle 1999: 34)

Note that there is no need to invoke any teleological argument here (cf.
Lass 1980). Languages are not organisms, and have no genetic
imperative to 'seek' survival, despite the fact that some chains of
changes observed by historical linguists give the appearance of a language, for example, ' "trying" to keep its phonemes apart' (*ibid.*: 51).
Furthermore, our position here is emphatically not one which seeks to
reify language varieties. They are not natural kinds, their boundaries
are porous, their codification is indeed often a matter of politics rather
than linguistics; nevertheless languages as actualized variants do have
an existence as cultural emergent properties. '[T]he existence of blur-
red boundaries and transitional varieties between languages', as Nettle
(*ibid.*: 65) observes, 'does not undermine the identification of the
languages themselves. It merely means that we cannot place the
boundaries precisely in those cases.' On our account, then, language
varieties – 'languages' – are examples of the domain of the actual. The
issue of naming and accurately classifying varieties is a different
matter from recognizing and acknowledging their existence.

If movements of human groups across the globe had taken slightly
different courses from those they *actually* did in history, if natural
disasters, diseases or technological developments in weaponry had
obliterated speakers of this language rather than that, if the development of cultural institutions had occurred here rather than there, then
the *actual* languages in existence might look rather different from the
collection we have now. In our account, all actual *languages* are connected in meaningful and significant ways to the generic human
capacity for *language*, and both of these domains are similarly connected to the empirical products of the language capacity and actual
language varieties, that is, utterances and texts. Once again, however, a
concept of emergence is necessary to demonstrate the nature of such
connections.

Our second example of what we mean by 'the actual' domain of
'real language' takes us back to the question of attested linguistic
products, and the implications of developments in corpus linguistics.
Our key claim here is that one function of a corpus is to make manifest
the intersubjective properties of language.

As we have seen, for some linguists, the 'corpus' is of little
interest. (Note that by 'corpus' is often meant any collection of attested
utterances or written sentences, and not necessarily the macro, electronic corpora which are our focus in this section.) As Halliday (1991:

30) notes, Chomsky's theory of competence and performance drove 'a massive wedge between the system and the instance, making it impossible by definition that analysis of actual texts could play any part in explaining the grammar of a language'. As should be clear by now, our own interpretation of realism is quite different from that which disregards empirical data, or language behaviour, and for us corpora have an important ontological significance. The conceptualization of corpora as evidence for language at the level of the actual is suggested by Beaugrande (1997), who posits language as a complex system, that '... runs on a dialectic between the *virtual control* that *specifies constraints* and the *actual control* that *manifests constraints*' (p.127).

We develop these ideas in Chapter 7. However, of at least as much importance in the present discussion as theoretical linguists' objections to corpora is the criticism from within applied linguistics of their pedagogic role, and probably the best-known critique from this position comes from Widdowson. (See also the debate between Owen 1993 and Francis and Sinclair 1994.) Widdowson's criticisms are important, because he provides a persuasive account of why applied linguistics finds so little support for its enterprise in theoretical linguistics. This is because the pedagogic purpose of applied linguistics inevitably requires an understanding of language not limited to '... linguistics applied [which] is, in effect, misapplied linguistics' (Widdowson 2000: 6). His objection to corpus studies is that, while they may well be valuable, surprising and important, they are contributions to descriptions of language, rather than to language learning. As a description of language, a corpus is a 'static abstraction', underpinning a 'linguistics of the attested [which] is just as partial as the linguistics of the possible' (*ibid.*: 7). The corpus does not, of course – in itself – instruct the language teacher as to how language can best be learned, but it is important to note that many applied linguists are demonstrating what the possibilities seem to be. (See, for example, Burnard and McEnery 2000; Hunston 1995, 2002; McEnery and Wilson 1996; Wichmann *et al.* 1997). Widdowson is sceptical of its pedagogic value partly because corpus data, especially when presented as the recurring patterns illustrated in concordance lines, take communication out of its ethnographic context. In direct contrast to the objection raised by many theoretical linguists, that the attested language behaviour collected in a corpus is too tightly connected to the particular, Widdowson's objection is that it is not tightly connected enough. Corpus studies, he says, show 'only ... the textual traces of the processes whereby meaning is achieved' (2000: 7). In our view, empirical 'traces' are critically important in understanding both social and linguistic processes, and while we would agree with Widdowson that pedagogical issues are not resolved merely by having access to a corpus from which to draw examples of language use, we find in corpora, and the traces they reveal, some important facts about the nature of language.

As a body of attested language behaviour, the corpus points both towards the unobservable but nevertheless real structures underlying that behaviour, and towards the equally real, but not exhaustive, empirical experience of language in use which we can observe everywhere around us. The most significant feature of a corpus, for the present discussion, is its demonstration of the intersubjective properties of language. Recent developments in corpus semantics (Teubert 1999; Stubbs 2001a) have added to the evidence on which this orientation towards language is based. As Stubbs puts it, '[c]orpus linguists think they have identified a layer of order in these data where none was previously suspected' (Stubbs 2001b: 169), and one of the findings from within this relatively newly visible 'layer' is that 'repeated instances of collocations across a corpus show that meanings are not personal and idiosyncratic, but widely shared' (*ibid.*: 168).

It is probably worth noting at this point two other features of the corpus linguistic enterprise which are consistent with the realist ontology we are outlining, and the epistemological and methodological implications which we develop elsewhere in the book. The first point is a general one which recurs throughout the literature on corpus linguistics, and it is the recognition that the traditional division of language into syntax and lexis is threatened by corpus findings. As Sinclair (1991: 108) expresses it:

> The model of a highly generalized formal syntax, with slots into which fall neat lists of words, is suitable only in rare uses and specialized texts. By far the majority of text is made of the occurrence of common words in common patterns, or in slight variations of those common patterns.

Halliday takes an even stronger position: 'I have always seen lexico-grammar as a unified phenomenon, a single level of "wording", of which lexis is the "most delicate" resolution' (Halliday 1991: 32). (We return in Chapter 7 to the issue of whether there are different levels of language which are related to each other, or simply different manifestations of a single level.) Finally Stubbs, again, suggests how the newly revised distribution of labour between lexis and syntax points to the intersubjective status of language:

> If all words have predictable collocates, then lexical meaning is distributed over several words, the meaning of an individual word is influenced by these collocates, and the balance between

> propositional and connotational meaning shifts towards the latter.
> Many more words have evaluative connotations and discourse
> prosodies than previously recognized.
>
> (Stubbs 2001a: 242–3)

In the following section, we shall investigate these propositions in more detail, with reference to the concept of emergence.

The second point, about method in corpus work, is made repeatedly by Stubbs, who, like Brumfit, engages with the responsibility of the language analyst to be in some sense 'objective'. Stubbs avoids quite explicitly any claims to naïve objectivity which would merely rely on the computer to bypass human interpretation. He does, however, claim that 'computers make it more difficult to overlook inconvenient instances' (1996: 154), and sets some store by the 'publicly accessible observational data' (2001b: 163) used in corpus studies, whose statements 'can be replicated and corroborated – or of course questioned and refuted – on independent data' (*ibid.*). Issues of method in applied linguistic research, and of the claims to a modest epistemic authority which we believe realism makes possible, will be discussed at greater length in Chapters 4 and 8.

In concluding this discussion of different orders of the reality of language, we should point out that there is no rigid distinction to be drawn between the domains of the real, the actual and the empirical. Corpus studies provide a good illustration of the way in which certain features of language which were once not empirically observable migrate into the empirical domain as technology develops. Hence Stubbs' analogy between the technical resources of computing hardware, concordance software and large corpora, in language description, and the telescope or microscope in descriptions of the physical world (1996: 231). Meanwhile, the development of new language varieties (such as creoles), on the one hand, and the 'death' of others, on the other, represent actualizations of the human capacity for language which may be present in one historical period and absent in another. The processes involved, we would claim, are emergent – from properties of language, properties of social structures and properties of human agency – and it is to the topic of emergence that we now turn.

Language, emergence and complexity

One of our claims in this book is that linear, additive models and descriptions of people using language are unsatisfactory, especially in accounting for the complex ecology of the world outside the laboratory. 'Emergence', as we explained in Chapter 1, refers to the generation of features which are not reducible to their constituent elements and must therefore be regarded as distinct from them. 'Complexity' refers to the property of nonlinear systems whereby small changes in particular aspects can lead to large changes in the system as a whole, changes which are not time-reversible. The two ideas are glossed in a popularizing science book (Johnson 2001) as follows. '[T]he most elemental form of *complex* behavior', the author explains, involves 'a system with multiple agents dynamically interacting in multiple ways, following local rules and oblivious to any higher-level instructions.' This system 'wouldn't truly be considered *emergent* until those local interactions resulted in some kind of discernible macrobehavior' (p.19). *Emergence*, as we argued in Chapter 1, refers to the generation of new entities or phenomena from the combination of other entities or phenomena. Because the new entity is emergent from this combination, it possesses certain distinct features, namely: irreducibility to any of its constituent elements; autonomy from any of its constituent elements; the ability to interact with any of its constituent elements.

There are those in the human and social disciplines who view the adoption there of the discourse of emergence and complexity with scepticism, because of its origins in the physical and natural sciences. Critics doubt the extent to which these concepts and processes, deployed in explanations of phenomena such as earthquakes and ant colonies, can be applied in the social world. Stewart (2001), for example, argues that the complexity and particularity of social processes make them unsuitable for mathematical modelling, as does the involvement in social action of ongoing interpretation by participants themselves. We share such reservations, and indeed our position relies on a recognition of the distinctive properties and powers of entities in the *social* world. The writers on whose work we draw are concerned with the engagement of human beings in social interaction, and, like us, are unpersuaded by mechanistic accounts of these processes. However, we believe that the concepts of emergence and complexity are crucial to explaining social action, including social actors' use of language, which is the topic of this book. We also believe that explanations of socially situated language use entail a recognition of natural phenomena, such as the biological endowment of human beings with particular kinds of vocal, aural and visual apparatus and particular kinds of brains, and that speakers' language use is partly a product of various kinds of interaction between nature and culture.

Language as emergent in the species

The link between the natural and the social is most obvious at the level of human biology. No-one knows exactly what happened in the chain of evolution which led the capacity for language to become the defining property of the human species which it is now widely recognized to be, but several accounts draw heavily on the insights of complexity and emergence theories for potential explanations (Knight *et al.* 2000a; Wray 2002). For example, the notion of adaptive, evolutionary change as comprising long periods of equilibrium punctuated by catastrophic changes is cited by Bickerton (1996) as a likely scenario for the sudden evolution of the linguistic species, in support of which theory he refers to both the fossil record and the claims made by evolutionary scientists such as Gould. Elman holds to the familiar complexity-theory position that 'small alterations in developmental pathways can lead to very large differences in outcome' (1999: 22). Both these writers prefer an explanation which allows for some continuity between humans and other species exhibiting communicative behaviour. Thus Bickerton, who makes a strong case for the qualitative difference between humans and other species, nevertheless summarizes its source thus: 'We have language grafted onto a primate brain, and that's it' (1996: 156). And Elman maintains that 'Language is simply the result of a number of tweaks and twiddles, each of which may be quite minor, but which in the aggregate and through interaction yield what appears to be a radically new behavior' (1999: 24–5).

That emergentism features in explanations of the evolution of human language at this foundational level is not critical to our argument about social and applied linguistics, but such claims are certainly consistent with it.

Language as emergent in the individual

Some recent work on language acquisition challenges nativist claims for a large degree of 'hard-wiring' to create the language faculty, proposing instead that the biological endowment of the linguistic capacity and the individual child's experience are interactively engaged in the process. Alternative approaches

> ... emphasize the ways in which the formal structures of language emerge from the interaction of social patterns, patterns implicit in the input, and pressures arising from the biology of the cognitive system. The emergentist approach to language acquisition views language as a structure arising from interacting constraints.
>
> (MacWhinney 1998: 200; see also MacWhinney 1999; Seidenberg 1997)

Where direct empirical evidence is not available, computer modelling is used to simulate the ways in which children might learn language (e.g. Steels 2000). Research involving simulations which 'teach' computers 'languages' has given rise to some counter-intuitive explanations for it. Experimenters have found that the imposition of constraints in their modelling equivalent to maturational limitations seems to enhance the ability of the program to compute 'linguistic' input. Thus Elman (1999) suggests that 'the ability which children have for learning language derives not from a special mechanism which they possess and adults do not, but just the reverse. It is children's *lack* of resources which enables them to learn languages fluently' (p.16). In other words, this kind of research (which, we should point out, is not central to our concerns, but illustrates interesting parallel arguments) suggests that language in the individual may be the emergent outcome of the engagement of the embodied human being with physical and cultural resources operating within particular constraints, including temporal ones. (See also Kramsch 2002a.)

In applied linguistics, these propositions have begun to be discussed in the context of second language acquisition, notably by Larsen-Freeman (1997, 2002), who concludes that language meets the criteria for complexity. It is, she argues, 'composed of many different subsystems: phonology, morphology, lexicon, syntax, semantics, pragmatics', and 'the subsystems are interdependent. ... [T]he behavior of the whole emerges out of the interaction of the subsystems' (1997: 149). Larsen-Freeman also proposes that second language acquisition is a complex process, and that the interaction between different aspects of it (the L1, personality, age, etc.) may be of greater significance than any one factor in isolation. Her third proposition is that the interlanguage system, constructed by learners of a second language in the context of their facility with their first, is self-organizing, and what learners do provides evidence of the feedback and adaptability which are also characteristics of complex systems. We think these lines of speculation are likely to prove fruitful, and in Chapters 4 and 8 we explore their implications for research in applied linguistics. Of greater interest here, however, is the issue of emergence in the context of socially situated language use.

Language as a cultural emergent property

Reference to 'culture' entails a departure from the physical and natural science orientations which have contributed most to explanations of phenomena in terms of complexity and emergence. The distinctions between the domains of reality identified by Bhaskar, for example, are illustrated with reference to the properties of a gemstone: what we can observe *empirically* is the way it glitters as it reflects light of a certain wavelength; the atomic structure of the crystal is *real*, existing as it does whether or not human beings are aware of it; the *actual* is exemplified by scientists acting on substances, causing events to occur in the process of their investigations. The properties of culture, and of language, are different in significant ways from the properties of crystals, so let us now state what we mean by emergent properties in this context. As we have seen, the capacity to process grammar may be conceptualized as existing within each human organism, but the products generated by that individual property are not reducible to individuals. If Bickerton is correct, the capacity for language which facilitated distinctive kinds of cognition in the human species also made possible self-consciousness and 'off-line' thinking – thinking, that is, which is not tied to the present time or location, the 'disengaged awareness' which Taylor (1985) alludes to: 'To be able to talk about things is to be potentially aware of them outside of any particular transaction with them' (p.151). This linguistic ability turned the human brain 'into an inference engine powerful enough to make possible the totally unprecedented cultural explosion of the last fifty millennia' (Bickerton 1996: 84). It is the ability of members of our species both to entertain 'off-line' thoughts, and, crucially, to share them with others, that represents the qualitative difference which language makes, and which makes culture possible: 'Human thinking possesses capacities wholly outside the range of nonhuman thinking; it changes the world, while the latter does not even change the individual' (*ibid.*: 112–13).

These thoughts, externalized in utterances, are the 'intelligibilia' which Archer (1988: vxi) glosses as 'any item which has the dispositional capacity of being understood by someone', and which culture as a whole is said to comprise. Linguistic products – language behaviour, utterances, discourse, texts – have an externality from the individual mind, and this is the source of some of the properties and powers of language which we see as critical to a social science of (applied) linguistics. These claims are hardly original, having been debated within philosophy for centuries. The contributions of Herder, Humboldt and Heidegger are discussed by Taylor (1985), for example, in a review which considers both constitutive and expressive theories of meaning. He concludes that language has the power not only to 'bring to explicit awareness what we formerly only had an implicit sense of' (p.256), but also that it 'serves to place some matter out in the open between interlocutors. ... [It] enables us to put things in public space' (p.259). Or, as Carr puts it: '... the grammar which constitutes the language is a public object, whereas the HSPM [human speech parsing mechanism] is a part of human psychology', and further, '[l]anguage ... exists in an intersubjective space, and in this sense we literally do not "stop at our skins": it is precisely language, subsisting intersubjectively, which allows us to reach beyond our private existence' (Carr 1990: 44). Volosinov (1973: 86) expresses a comparable idea: 'I give myself verbal shape from another's point of view, ultimately from the point of view of the community to which I belong'. It is only in this speaker-external public space that linguistic symbols such as the deictic pronouns *I* and *you* have meaning (Halliday 1978; Searle 1995; Taylor 1985).

Such a 'public space' is also invoked in Popper's notion of 'World 3', whose distinction between subjective and objective knowledge we referred to in Chapter 1. World 3 could not exist without language, and it is where propositions about all aspects of human knowledge (and imagination) are located:

> By World 3 I mean the world of the products of the human mind, such as stories, explanatory myths, tools, scientific theories (whether true or false), scientific problems, social institutions, and works of art. ...
>
> Many World 3 objects exist in the form of material bodies, and belong in a sense to both World 1 and World 3. Examples are sculptures, paintings, and books, whether devoted to a scientific subject or to literature. A book is a physical object, and it therefore belongs to World 1; but what makes it a significant production of the human mind is its *content*; that which remains invariant in the various copies and editions. And this content belongs to World 3.
>
> One of my main theses is that World 3 objects can be real, ... not only in their World 1 materializations or embodiments, but also in their World 3 aspects. As World 3 objects, they may induce men to produce other World 3 objects and, thereby, to act on World 1; and interaction with World 1 – even indirect interaction – I regard as a decisive argument for calling a thing real.
>
> (Popper and Eccles 1977: 38–9)

Of course it is challenging to operationalize these ideas in this particular context because language is both topic and medium. So there is debate even between the various exponents of Popperian and realist claims about science as to whether the 'World 3' status of propositions about intersubjective understanding are claims about language; an alternative position is that 'linguistic facts', while available as propositions in a World 3 space, are facts exclusively about the language faculty and not about language as any kind of intersubjective entity. Pateman (1987), for example, posits two conceptions of language, distinguishing the nativist characteristics of language from its sociocultural instantiations, and reserving for propositions about the former the label of 'linguistic facts', while the latter can, for him, only be 'social facts'. A different position is adopted by Searle (1995: 228), who is willing to identify language as 'a kind of institutional structure', and who proposes that it is the symbolic medium which makes culture possible. Only through language can material objects come to be assigned functional values, such as the marks on paper which signify that it is to count as money, for example, or the system of beliefs which makes possible the idea of 'scoring points' when a person physically crosses a visible line carrying a material object such as a ball. Wittgenstein's arguments against the possibility of a private language are cited as evidence for language as an essentially social phenomenon by Itkonen (1978), who claims that 'use of language is logically interdependent with public use of language' (p.119), and who builds on the intentionalist theories of Grice, Searle and others to identify language with social action.

The distinctiveness of a conception which is emergentist, stratified, and which recognizes the importance of complexity explanations, is that it allows for an interplay between the language processing capacity of the individual and the products of that capacity as World 3 entities. The intersubjective actualizations of language are, as we have claimed, the 6000 or so human languages extant in the world today – and the epistemological and methodological difficulties inherent in demarcating the boundaries between those which are spatially proximate does nothing to diminish their reality as both social and linguistic entities.

The claim that languages are cultural emergent properties owes much to the recent work of Archer (1988, 1995, 2000). She asserts that it is human practice, the business of being in the world, which is the source and origin of social life and the social world. The logical and substantive priority of practice implies that language needs to be viewed as a practical activity, a means by which the working relationship between human beings and the world about them is accomplished (Archer 2000). Since practical, embodied activity in the natural world 'comes first', as it were, languages must be seen as emergent from this engagement between human practice and the natural environment. One implication of this is that the practical order and the linguistic order are not co-extensive: we can do or experience things that we cannot express in language, that reach beyond our discursive abilities or understandings.

We are proposing, then, that languages are emergent products of the engagement of human practice with the material world. They qualify as emergent, as defined above, on several counts. Firstly, they are not reducible to their material embodiment as sound waves (or written marks), nor to processes taking place entirely within individual human minds, nor yet to sets of internal relationships between linguistic symbols.

Secondly, languages have a partial autonomy both from human beings and from the material world. The practices of children developing creoles from the under-grammaticalized pidgin varieties of their parents are sometimes cited to counter the claim that language is essentially social. However, while these practices may indicate the involvement of the innate capacities of human beings to develop new actualizations of linguistic potential, it is also the case that even these practices are intersubjective, and give rise to emergent language varieties that are not reducible to their constituents. Meanwhile, most people learn one or more of the human languages that existed before they were born and will be in existence after they die: the existence of languages is attributable to human beings, but not only to those human beings currently speaking them. Each generation changes the language varieties it inherits, but it is a property of languages that some features are accommodated while others are not. Thus languages may facilitate or constrain what people seek to do, and it is the recognition of language and practice as distinct which allows for the investigation of their mutual interplay, whilst the recognition of language as emergent from embodied practice within the world maintains the crucial connection between language and reality. Our language about reality is thus constrained in important ways by how the world is, even though what we do with language and how ably we deploy it remain a matter of human practice. This is why, as Devitt and Sterelny put it, '... a theory of language belongs within a theory of people' (Devitt and Sterelny 1987: 192).

It is important to emphasize that it is human beings – and not languages – which do things in the social world. In seeking to accomplish things in the world, social actors must use language. Whenever they do so, however, there is an engagement with the linguistic resources available or accessible to them. Through this engagement they experience these resources in enabling and constraining ways.

Thirdly, languages possess an ability to interact with their constituent elements. That is, there is feedback between people, the material world and the languages which are emergent products of the interaction between these. Bates and Goodman (1999: 35) suggest that, 'once it finally appeared on the planet, it is quite likely that language itself began to apply adaptive pressure to the organization of the human brain'. Language enables us to reflect upon, interpret and make judgements about ourselves and others. As Austin, Searle and other 'natural language' philosophers have pointed out, the things we do with language, those ways of acting upon and modifying the world which are performed through linguistic acts, are examples of interactions between languages and people.

Conclusion

This chapter has sought to locate some of the concerns of applied linguistics within wider debates in linguistics and the philosophy of language, suggesting that it is not only 'theoretical linguistics' which must be concerned with theory, and that not only applied linguists ought to be concerned with the empirical evidence of what language is. Having explored some of the different senses in which 'real' is used by writers from across the spectrum of philosophy, linguistics and applied linguistics, we went on to explore how the concepts of complexity and emergence are indispensable to a realist conception of language and social action. We noted that emergentist theories are being deployed in explanations of language development, both phylogenetically and ontogenetically, but explained why we see emergence as crucial additionally to accounts of language as social practice.

Chapter 7 will illustrate how language as cultural emergent property interacts with human agency and social structure, with reference to some specific examples from applied linguistics. Before that, however, we turn to a core area of applied linguistic research to examine various ways in which language, language learners and the language teaching enterprise are understood within the discipline.

4 Researching language learning: theories, evidence, claims

Introduction

So far in this book we have interpreted applied linguistics very broadly. In our dual purpose – of developing and describing a social realist theory of language use, and of illustrating its relevance to applied linguistics – we draw throughout on examples of applied linguistic 'problems' of various kinds. These problems include questions such as what is meant by 'real' language, or by 'real' English; the political consequences of classifying Ebonics as a language; how linguistic, cultural and national boundaries are interrelated; how the concept of ethnicity is deployed in linguistic practice and in social research, and many others besides. In the current chapter, we focus on another core applied linguistic 'problem', using it to probe questions about epistemology and methodology in a research field which involves a significant proportion of the people who are identified as applied linguists. This problem is the one identified, in an overview of the subject (Schmitt and Celce-Murcia 2002) in a recent introductory volume (Schmitt 2002), as 'the dominant application' from among the 'numerous areas' with which applied linguistics is concerned: 'Traditionally, the primary concern of applied linguistics has been second language acquisition theory, second language pedagogy and the interface between the two' (p.2). Another survey of the subject, entitled comprehensively *The Encyclopedic Dictionary of Applied Linguistics*, has as its subtitle, 'a handbook for *language teaching*' (Johnson and Johnson 1999, emphasis added), and the entry here for 'applied linguistics' observes that for a long time the term 'has been used to refer somewhat exclusively to the field of language teaching and learning, rather than to any field where language is a relevant consideration'. Thus, although applied linguistics is clearly expanding its scope, for many people it is still the process of coming to use one or more languages other than the first that is perceived as its core concern.

Accordingly, the goal of this chapter is to continue to develop our account of social realism by exploring how the kind of empirical research familiar to those involved in the teaching of additional languages relates to the key ideas about structure, culture, agency and emergence which we have introduced so far. In particular, we examine the issue of causality, since the problem of how learners can best be helped to make progress in the language they are learning entails an interest in how pedagogy and outcomes are related. Thus we begin the chapter by drawing out some of the implications of our realist position for social research, in particular for research in applied linguistics, and specifically for research in instructed language learning (ILL). This position implies a distinctive view of empirical research, which in the second section we compare with the epistemological assumptions underlying various forms of ILL research. Such an enterprise raises the troublesome issue of what counts as research in applied linguistics. What sorts of claims can be made about languages, cultures, human agency and social relations? What sorts of evidence are adduced in support of these claims? What count as warrants for these claims? These questions are considered in the third part of the chapter. Our aim here is not to provide a comprehensive overview of this very extensive field, but rather to identify some of the persistent issues in ILL research, and to highlight the influence on them of how different research traditions have understood the process of doing research.

It is necessary at this point to include a note about terminology. For want of an unambiguous label for the area of applied linguistics focused on in this chapter, we have adopted the phrase 'instructed language learning' research, which Mitchell and Myles (2001) link to Ellis (1990, 1994).[1] We are referring to that substantial enterprise which investigates the detail of institution-based instruction in languages which students are learning after they have become speakers of one or more first languages in infancy. This choice of term, in preference to the broader 'Second Language Acquisition', aims to accommodate the fact that many SLA scholars explicitly distance themselves from pedagogy and practice, identifying 'the task of SLA research' as not particularly to evaluate teaching strategies, but rather 'to determine whether or not learners have access to universal principles of language and to determine what the nature of grammatical knowledge is' (Gass 2000: 53). In subsequent chapters we develop more fully our proposals for a realist approach to research, taking account of the fact that while the field of instructed language learning is a very significant one in applied linguistics, it is far from the only one. In Chapter 8, in particular, we explore a broader range of research studies from applied linguistics and across the social sciences.

Social realism and empirical research

It is probably fair to say that the longest-established and still dominant tradition in ILL research (Lazaraton 1995) involves the following kind of approach, as summarized by Lightbown (2000: 438) in her review of SLA research between 1985 and 2000:

> The specific goals of the various research projects differ, but there is a unifying desire to identify and better understand the roles of the different participants in classroom interaction, the impact that certain types of instruction may have on FL/SL learning, and the factors which promote or inhibit learning.

Much of what constitutes this kind of research tends to be consistent with conventional, successionist models of causality. Successionist models usually take the form of identifying a dependent and an independent variable and then proposing a hypothesis which suggests that they will vary inversely or conversely, thus enabling some form of causal inference to be drawn. Ellis (1990: 199) summarizes this approach thus:

> The L2 classroom researcher seeks to show how instructional events cause or impede the acquisition of a second language. In order to achieve this, it is necessary to (1) identify which instructional events are significant, (2) find valid and reliable measures of the L2 learning that takes place and (3) be able to demonstrate that the relationship between instructional events and learning is in some ways causal.

Although critiques of the successionist concept of causality have been made in the ILL literature (e.g. Block 1996; van Lier 1990), and we discuss alternatives later in the chapter, it remains a dominant assumption in a significant proportion of the literature.

ILL research, then, like most research in both natural and social science, explores why things happen. Our own position in response to this question is a 'modified materialist naturalist' one. Therefore our starting point in understanding why things happen is a belief that the world consists of phenomena – including human beings and social structures – which have distinctive properties and powers. These objects exist independently of our understandings of them. (This points to a significant limitation in the purely interpretivist research which is often seen as the alternative to successionist accounts of causality, as we explain below.) It is the combination of the powers and properties of human beings and social structures which generates the experienced empirical world. The attribution of these properties and powers is not arbitrary, but is given in what phenomena are: it is given in the nature of human beings, for example, that they are mortal, that they have the biological attributes which enable them to use language, and so on; social structures are emergent, durable, and have the facility to frustrate or further the projects of people both individually and collectively.

This implies a radically different view of causality and therefore of research from that found in both successionist and interpretivist traditions. From a realist point of view, rather than merely cataloguing repetitions of regularly occurring co-events, science should seek to understand and identify the causal relations or mechanisms which produce the observed, empirical regularities. Sayer (2001) summarizes the key components of a realist view of causality:

> Causes – that is whatever produces change – should be understood as causal powers possessed by objects (including individuals and social structures) that may or may not be activated. Whether they are depends on contingently related conditions, and if and when they are activated, what results also depends on contingently related conditions.
>
> (p.968)

So what are the things in the social world which have these properties and powers? As we noted in Chapter 1, the components of the social world, from a realist perspective, are human beings and the products of their social interaction, including social structures and culture. It is the interaction between these components of the social world, and the realization of their properties and powers in particular settings and combinations, that give rise to the problems with which social research – including applied linguistic research – is concerned. This account of 'why things happen' allows for the occurrence of patterns and regularities, without entailing a commitment to a nomothetic perspective of 'governing laws'. Regularities – such as, say, tendencies for groups of students with certain characteristics to outperform groups of students with different characteristics on particular tests of L2 performance – may be indicative of causal relations, and establishing such patterns therefore often entails undertaking quantitative research. The account also allows for a recognition of the powers of human agency, including the reflexivity which can act as a 'confounding variable' in traditional process-product studies. The position is also marked by seeking to distinguish between necessity and contingency in causal relations. Research of this type will not discover 'universal laws', because the actualization of the properties and powers of the objects in the world is context-dependent, but it will aim to generalize beyond the individual case of the single ethnographic study, by drawing on particular conceptualizations of propensity and probability. These ideas are developed in detail in Chapter 8.

We can now turn to a richer image of 'complexity' than that suggested when the term is used, as it sometimes is, as a synonym for 'complicated'. It is common to make reference to the 'complexity' of the process of using different languages in different social contexts, and of learning how to do so. For example, Lightbown and Spada (2001: 42) identify a number of 'variables' which 'have been found to influence second language learning'. These include 'intelligence, aptitude, personality and motivational characteristics, learner preferences, and age'. Some of the difficulties for researchers, they suggest, arise because 'these learner characteristics are not independent of one another: learner variables interact in complex ways. So far, researchers know very little about the nature of these complex interactions.' Similarly, Cook (1986: 13) characterizes 'the real world' as 'a complex bundle of many things', but concludes that the researcher's task is therefore to – as it were – untie this bundle and extract separate 'things' to measure.

However, recognizing that variables interact is not the same as recognizing that in their interaction they generate emergent, irreducible phenomena, which are themselves capable of interacting back on their constituent elements. In this view of complexity, there is an emphasis on the fact that 'the behavior of complex systems arises from the *interaction* of its components or agents' (Larsen-Freeman 1997: 143, emphasis added). Larsen-Freeman is one of the few researchers who have begun to explore more fully the implications of rejecting successionist accounts of causation, in characterizing SLA as a complex nonlinear process. If this is what it is, she argues, 'we will never be able to identify, let alone measure, all of the factors accurately. And even if we could, we would still be unable to predict the outcome of their combination' (*ibid.*: 157). As she points out, researchers in the domain of neuroscience are now modelling the brain as an example of a complex nonlinear system, and developments in this area contribute to explanations of extremely sophisticated mental processes. Features of the brain which qualify it to be thought of in this way include its 'decentralized' character, and its feedback systems which contribute to growth and self-regulation (Johnson 2001). As we saw in Chapter 3, the characterization of language itself as a cultural emergent property entails a recognition of its complex and emergent features (Beaugrande 1997, 1999). And language acquisition is also recognized as an emergent phenomenon by researchers who concentrate on the internal cognitive dimension of the process. As Ellis (1998) puts it:

> Emergentists believe that simple learning mechanisms, operating in and across the human systems for perception, motor-action and cognition as they are exposed to language data as part of a communicatively-rich human social environment by an organism eager to exploit the functionality of language, suffice to drive the emergence of complex language representations.
>
> (p.657)

Ellis and Larsen-Freeman both advocate studying language and language learning in relation to other areas of enquiry, and both point to the need for researchers to pool resources across disciplines, since complex problems are unlikely to be solved by simple techniques. However, we are so far not aware of very much applied linguistic research which has taken on these developments to the point of recognizing emergence and complexity across the full strata of the 'domains' of the social world, although we shall discuss in Chapter 8 the work of some who are contributing to such developments.

Epistemological assumptions and ILL research

Perhaps because of the heterogeneity of the discipline, many theories and epistemological assumptions are drawn on in applied linguistic research. In this section, we discuss some recent theoretical debates which have a bearing on this area of it (i.e. instructed language learning), in the context of the realist social theory we have been developing. Since the world does not speak to us directly, nor instruct us as to which categories we are to employ in understanding it, knowledge of this world, as Layder has pointed out, 'is impossible without the use of conceptual instruments, which, more often than not, derive from, or are connected with, wider theoretical parameters or discourses' (Layder 1985: 255). This entails both a rejection of naïve, or direct, realism – whereby the world is apprehended in a straightforwardly transparent manner – and, accordingly, a recognition of the role of theory in both the determination of social ontologies and the apprehension of the empirical world.

'Untying the bundle': the 'variables' approach in ILL research

These insights have implications for research in the variable analysis tradition, so at this point we examine claims which are made for 'the variable' as an important component in traditional ILL research. Hatch and Farhady (1982), for example, explain that '[h]eight, sex, nationality, and language group membership are all variables commonly assigned to people' (p.12), going on to distinguish between attributes like these, which are 'of the all-or-nothing type', because 'the *Ss* [subjects] either are or they aren't foreign students; they are or they aren't speakers of French ...', and other variables which are suscep- tible to gradation and quantification: 'In other cases we can measure very accurately how much of the variable subjects possess' (*ibid.*). (See similarly Hatch and Lazaraton 1991.) Although this approach is by no means ubiquitous in ILL research, significant numbers of studies continue to be published which appear to be heavily influenced by a variable analysis perspective, and as an illustration of this broad orientation we have selected the specific research questions from just three recently published examples.

1. What are the relationships between a range of language learner variables (e.g. previous language proficiency, motivation, beliefs about and strategies for language learning) and the language achievement of advanced Chinese EFL learners at tertiary level; and
2. What differences relating to these variables exist between rela- tively successful and unsuccessful learners?

(Wen and Johnson 1997: 28)

This study is principally an attempt to provide more detailed basic descriptive data on language proficiency, language behaviour, and language attitudes as a function of the immigration background for a small sample ... of high-school students in a rural community in Northern California.

(Hakuta and D'Andrea 1992: 73)

The objective of this investigation was to determine the influence of supplementary mother-tongue instruction, self-esteem, length of residence, and *schools*, on the French second language perfor- mance of first generation immigrant children.

(Fazio and Stevens 1994: 433–4)

In each case, a language learning 'problem' is identified, and a number of factors are considered as potentially having a bearing on that pro- blem. Investigations take the form of measurements of these factors and identification of their respective significance. The expression of each problem incorporates a fairly precise delineation of who is involved ('advanced Chinese EFL learners at tertiary level', 'a small sample ... of high-school students in a rural community in Northern California', 'first generation immigrant children'), and what the language learning enterprise is ('French second language performance', '[English] lan- guage achievement'). The specificity is consistent with the prescription outlined by Cook (1986), who demonstrates how an 'overall, untestable proposition about speech and writing' such as 'Is speech more important than writing?' is progressively 'narrow[ed] down ... so that it can receive a reliable answer'. The 'precise, answerable question' he devises is: 'Are the scores on the EPVT of a group of educated French adult learners of English in technical schools in France who are taught orally significantly better than those of an otherwise identical group who are taught through writing?' (p.19). The gap between these two questions offers us a preliminary indication of one of the reasons why, in our view, variables-based ILL research has so far not delivered on its promise of progress towards consistent, aggregated findings. Byrne (2002: 20) puts the realist position well when he points out that:

> ... the implications of localism/context as expressed in interaction, mean that no single hypothesis can be generalized beyond the exact conditions under which it is tested. If there is any non-linearity then no covering law is ever possible. In this frame of reference experiments merely describe local and unique conjunctions. Hypotheses cannot be somehow summed into a general overarching account.

'Governing laws': the problem of generalizability

So we would agree fully with Cook's rejection of an 'unanswerable' question such as whether speech or writing is more important [in learners' progress towards an additional language], but we also sympathize with impatient practitioners or policy-makers who want to know where to invest their resources with a *different* group of learners working in different social and educational circumstances. Can the findings of a study based on a much more tightly specified research question such as the one Cook supplies be anything other than trivial? Are there any 'covering laws' or generalizable findings to be gleaned from ILL research? It is hard not to conclude that aggregated findings from studies of this kind seem not to produce very much consensus. This point is made baldly by Wardhaugh (1998) in an overview on the topic: 'Given all the thought and effort that has gone into so many years of such [SLA] research, one might well wonder ... why researchers still have such a poor understanding of how people learn a second language' (p.585). Other commentators are perhaps less damning, but recognition of divergent and often even contradictory findings is inescapable. In some commentaries, the problem is characterized as at least partially methodological, with inconsistencies represented as matters of technique, specificity or rigour, arising 'partly because of the lack of clear definitions and methods for the individual characteristics'

(Lightbown and Spada 2001: 42). Chaudron (1988), in an overview of research conducted in 'second language classrooms', claims:

> Since a number of the features reviewed here had conflicting findings across studies, and factors such as the identity of the speakers and listeners were not consistently controlled, it is evident that greater rigor and a well-defined research agenda are needed for future studies of L2 teacher talk.
>
> (p.89)

and:

> ... there has been little consistency throughout the classroom-oriented research in the choice of descriptors of task and activity types. Research in classrooms has been limited by not having an agreed-upon set of activity types ... , so little comparison was possible among studies. ... Until there is greater uniformity, the research will be difficult to consolidate into immediate implications.
>
> (p.187)

More recent overviews of research in specific areas come to similar conclusions. In relation to research about input-based approaches to teaching grammar, Ellis (1999: 64, 73) states:

> ... it is becoming increasingly difficult to draw clear conclusions given the sheer amount of research now available, the problems of comparing results across studies, and the interactivity of the variables involved. ... Design differences make it difficult to compare the results of these studies.

And in an overview of studies about the teaching of grammar in foreign language classrooms Mitchell (2000) concedes that '... it seems that we still lack a set of generally agreed principles, with clear empirical support, for the selection of grammar items which may merit explicit treatment in any "what works" programme' (p.293); and 'applied linguists are not at present in a position to make firm research-based prescriptions about the detail of "what works" in FL grammar pedagogy' (p.296). Again, although mindful of the variations in contexts of teaching and learning, and therefore with somewhat more ambivalence than Chaudron displays, Mitchell calls for moves '... to increase agreement among researchers on what kinds of tests and resulting data will count as providing evidence of L2 learning' (pp.298–9). Other solutions often proposed are larger and/or longer studies (Wardhaugh 1998), more replication studies (Lightbown 2000), more detailed applications of sophisticated statistical procedures and so on.

In response to the inconclusiveness of findings, then, there are both calls for more studies and replications of existing ones, and depictions of the challenge of identifying and coping with large numbers of variables as largely technical matters. The summary by McDonough and McDonough (1997: 45) on this point questions whether all the factors involved in the areas to be researched can be taken into account: '[I]n most educational situations the list of possible confounding variables is so large, with some systematic and some unsystematic ones, that realistic and satisfactory control and counterbalance are nearly impossible'.

The issue goes deeper than this, however, and at this point we must introduce another objection to the importing of techniques developed principally for investigating inanimate objects into social domains. As social realists, we adhere to an essential distinction between *people* and *things*. This is expressed cogently by Hacking (1997: 15) (who has researched socio-medical problems such as schizophrenia), when he points out that:

> while phenomena in the natural world are 'indifferent' to how they are labelled, human and social phenomena may be affected by the discussions of what they do, how they are labelled – they are thus of 'interactive' kind, and there is a 'looping' back into the object itself of how those involved understand it.

The 'variable' of a learner's first language is much less stable than a variable such as temperature in a chemical experiment. This does not go unacknowledged in traditional approaches, as this observation by Long (1993: 235) illustrates: 'It will be important ... to be aware of the dangers inherent in importing criteria from the natural to the social sciences, since we are dealing with people, who can affect the systems and processes SLA theories seek to explain in ways physicists, for example, needed not worry about.' However, the implications are more far-reaching than this might suggest.

To the extent that 'subjects' have an active role in deciding how 'French' they wish to be, they may frustrate the quantifier's efforts to place them into the correct category, which points to a twofold problem. On the one hand is measurement of the language variety, and 'the tendency in SLA ... to reify language so that French, English and so on are treated unproblematically as homogenised "target languages" ' (Roberts 2001: 109–10). On the other hand is social group membership. Rampton (2000: 101), for example, suggests that, in the light of developments in social theory 'whether it is age- or ethnicity-based, belonging to a group now seems a great deal less clear, less permanent and less omni-relevant than it did 15 years ago', and a similar point about age categories is made by Coupland (1997).

Discrepancies in how the researchers and the researched under-stand categories seem to have arisen in one of the studies cited above, when a proportion of the high-school students studied claimed greater proficiency in Spanish than was demonstrated in the tests they took, apparently because of their affective 'orientation towards maintenance of Spanish' (Hakuta and D'Andrea 1992: 77). This problem is reported as a methodological one: '... it appears that attitudinal orientation contaminates self-reported proficiency ... to a substantial degree' (p.95). The discourse in which such statements are made works to suggest similarities in the properties of the objects studied in the natural sciences, where one substance may be found to have 'con-taminated' another in the laboratory, and the human subjects studied in social science, where people's values and aspirations 'contaminate' their assessment of their own language proficiency. Nevertheless, despite a discursively implied equation between human 'subjects' and physical objects ('[a] variable can be defined as *an attribute of a person or of an object which "varies" from person to person or from object to object'* (Hatch and Farhady 1982: 12, additional emphasis added), certain kinds of measurability turn out to be altogether more prob-lematic – for what turn out to be sound theoretical reasons – than these methods textbooks would have us believe.

Critics of traditional ILL research have likewise problematized the way in which people are classified as Native Speakers and Non-native Speakers, as though these too were given, absolute categories (e.g. Davies 1991; Firth and Wagner 1997; Rampton 1990), and similar problems inevitably recur in variables research which is designed in accordance with the dominant approach we have been describing. For example, in our own experience as supervisors of graduate students, we have had to respond to queries about whether a study of cross-cultural linguistic behaviour (such as apologizing, for example) can include subjects who are 'English' on some criteria (such as nationality and place of birth), but seem to be untypical on others (such as skin colour or residence outside the UK). Dilemmas such as these point to the danger of what Pawson (1989: 24) identifies as 'selective meas-urement due to the impregnation of observational categories by theoretical notions': in other words, the researcher has a preconceived concept, perhaps adequate for 'everyday' purposes (of 'Nonnative Speaker', or of 'Englishness'), but the process of scientific measure-ment is compromised by deploying this category as a variable without specifying the theoretical basis on which it rests.

> Treating the world as though it comes in monadic, discrete, sin-gular lumps omits consideration of the role of theory and

conceptualization in the perceptual distinctions we make. ... The
reason why empiricist measurement is captured in such a critical
loop is the lack of any notion of the role theory plays in understanding and justifying a particular regularity or model or law.

(ibid.: 70–1)

The challenge of theorizing social categories is explored in more detail
in the next chapter.

Researchers with a more holistic orientation raise the possibility
that this 'untying of the bundle' can never be achieved, although we
believe that the full implications of this warrant further exploration.
Lazaraton (1995: 465), for example, doubts whether the dominant
approach to ILL research can ever generate the generalizations many
see as desirable: 'Quantification of any set of data does not ensure
generalizability to other contexts, nor does a large sample size. ... In
other words, generalizability is a serious problem in nearly all the
research conducted in our field', while van Lier (1990: 38) claims that
'[m]ost of our efforts at doing experiments or quasi-experiments, with
all the attempted controls of variables and randomisations of treatment, may be doomed to failure (especially given the complexity of
language learning processes)'.

Incorporating the social: interpretivist alternatives

Commentators such as these have contributed to ILL research which
sees its object as extending beyond the 'factors' which vary across
teaching practices, learners and languages, and there is undoubtedly a
healthy and growing literature focusing on ILL in its broader social
context. Critics of the dominant approach have written of the 'imposition of an orthodox social psychological hegemony on SLA ...
[which] gives preeminence to the research practice of coding, quantifying data, and replicating results. ... At best it marginalises, and at
worst ignores, the social and the contextual dimensions of language'
(Firth and Wagner 1997: 288). These authors propose that sociocultural
contexts should be afforded much greater recognition in ILL research,
and they and others have suggested research programmes capable of
doing this.

We would not want to suggest that there is an absolute divide
between what we are presenting, for the purposes of our particular
argument, as two very broad approaches, or traditions. The debates in
the literature clearly indicate some fundamental points of difference
among the protagonists: see, for example, responses to Firth and
Wagner by Long (1997), Kasper (1997), Poulisse (1997); or the

exchanges among Beretta and Crookes (1993), Gregg (1993), Long (1993), Schumann (1993), Block (1996) and Gregg *et al.* (1997). Nevertheless, several of these authors are at pains to identify areas of shared assumptions, and there have been a number of calls for complementary approaches in ILL research, or 'hybrid' research, as Ellis (1990: 202) calls it, commenting on 'the old controversy between those who favour an experimental approach and those who favour ethnographic enquiry or the use of introspective methods' which he sees as 'a sterile and unnecessary debate'.

However, for some of those who reject the dominant tradition, the epistemological differences are too profound to ignore, or to overcome by simply mixing methods. Van Lier (2001: 90), for example, commenting on the implications of conceptualizing language learning settings as complex systems, observes:

> It is of the utmost importance to realize how different the job of researching language learning becomes once we decide that the social context is central. To continue looking for operationally defined, discretely measured, statistically manipulated, and causally predictive variables would be to approach one job with tools that belong to another.

As McGroarty (1998: 600) recognizes, '[a]t issue is the matter of description of the appropriate unit or units of analysis'. Discussing whether 'motivation', for example, can legitimately be conceptualized as a quality residing within each individual, as traditional research has tended to assume, she speculates whether groups (classes, companies) could perhaps '... be called learning organizations, capable of demonstrating inquisitiveness or motivation as an aggregate, not only as a collection of individuals' (p.601). Those who are dissatisfied with approaches which use experimentation and variables are usually committed to embracing a much more comprehensive 'unit of analysis'.

Thus in relation to language itself, Wardhaugh (1998), for example, is particularly outspoken about the shortcomings of what he identifies as 'the psycholinguistic approach, which ... ignores most of language and all of society' (p.589). Beaugrande repudiates any conception of 'language by itself' as a basis for investigating communication, including processes of teaching and learning language(s). In relation to learning, '[f]rom the sociocultural stance', according to Lantolf and Pavlenko (1995: 110), 'acquiring a second language entails more than simple mastery of the linguistic properties of the L2. It encompasses the dialectic interaction of two ways of creating meaning in the world (interpersonally and intrapersonally)'.

Constructivists such as McGroarty (1998) call for a recognition that '... the activity of L2 students and teachers is simultaneously linguistic, affective, and social; theory and investigation must acknowledge all three domains to render the picture complete' (p.604), and advocates of qualitative methods such as Davis (1995) see them as:

> an alternative to mainstream SLA studies in viewing acquisition not only as a mental individualistic process, but one that is also embedded in the sociocultural contexts in which it occurs. From this point of view, mental processes are not unimportant, but they are situated in a larger sociocultural context that is equally important. In other words, ethnographers and other qualitative researchers take a holistic perspective in conducting research.
>
> (p.432)

ILL research which develops different 'tools for the job' from those outlined in preceding sections includes studies focusing particularly on learners as active social agents, those exploring the contribution of sociocultural theory to this field, those developing the 'ecological' metaphor, which connotes language learning as an organic, rather than mechanistic, process (Kramsch 2002b), and those whose critique of the dominant tradition is explicitly political. These are by no means discrete sub-fields: there is much cross-fertilization among these perspectives, which – certainly if considered together – appear to be gaining ground in ILL research.

Associated particularly with the first of these four broad trends is Breen, who, as early as 1985, observed, 'We need a metaphor for the classroom through which teacher and earners [*sic*] can be viewed as thinking social actors and not reduced to generators of input-output nor analyzed as dualities of either conceptual or social beings' (Breen 2001 [1985]: 127). In a recent edited collection of studies about 'learner contributions to language learning', he argues that '... language learning is, in essence, cultural action towards meaning within context' (2001: 182). One illustration of the way in which such an orientation contrasts with that of the three example studies summarized on page 91 above is provided by Norton (2001). She undertook an extensive ethnography of immigrant language learners in Canada, and in the findings reported here she contrasts the responses of one student from Poland and another from Peru to their ESOL (English for speakers of other languages) course. Norton posits the notion of these learners as positioning themselves in relation to 'imagined communities', a concept which could not readily be accommodated within the 'variables' stance outlined above.

Another recent collection brings together studies influenced by the theories of Vygotsky and the sociocultural tradition, associated in ILL research particularly with Lantolf (Lantolf 1996, 2000a; Lantolf and Pavlenko 1995). Echoing some of the claims about learners' contributions discussed in the previous paragraph, Donato (2000) comments, '... sociocultural theory is about language classrooms where *agency* matters. That is, learners bring to interactions their own personal histories replete with values, assumptions, beliefs, rights, duties, and obligations' (p.46). He continues, '[w]here mentalist theories assume that language learning can be understood without taking into account the active and purposeful agent, sociocultural theory maintains that no amount of experimental or instructional manipulation ... can deflect the overpowering and transformative agency embodied in the learner' (p.47). Donato's research contrasts with that of the dominant tradition in that it does not assume that pedagogical 'tasks' are the stable, invariant 'recipes' which some of the versions of ILL research discussed in previous sections might suggest. Instead, they are perceived as 'emergent interactions' (Lantolf 2000b: 20), irreducible to their constituents.

A third challenge to successionist, variables-based models, overlapping significantly with the previous two, has been given the label 'ecological perspectives'. This is glossed by the editor of a recent collection as 'a convenient shorthand for the poststructuralist realization that learning is a nonlinear, relational human activity, co-constructed between humans and their environment, contingent upon their position in space and history, and a site of struggle for the control of social power and cultural memory' (Kramsch 2002a: 5). Contributors to this development in applied linguistic research are by no means confined to ILL, and we return in later chapters to some of the other aspects of their work.

Our illustrative example here is an 'in-depth analysis – on an incremental, almost moment-by-moment basis – of what takes place in the course of a first English as a foreign language (EFL) lesson in a Dutch secondary school, on the first day of the academic year' (van Dam 2002: 237). Like much of the research discussed in this section, this study is presented partly in opposition to the dominant paradigm: 'Since my concern was with the emergence of a classroom *culture*, not with any specific teacher or student behaviors in terms of a communicative (or other) SLA orthodoxy, I adopted an approach that is multidisciplinary and *ecological*' (*ibid.*). One of the questions guiding this research – despite the (metaphorical) use of the measurement term 'degree' – will illustrate how different the approach is from that of the studies whose questions we quoted earlier: 'To what degree does speaking in another language entail a reframing of the self?' (p.252).

Finally in this very brief review of challenges to the dominant tradition in ILL research we move on to the critiques which engage with the politics of the enterprise on a more macro scale. According to Roberts (2001), SLA studies in the past few decades have not ignored social context. However, 'often the references to socio-cultural context give it only a marginal role in the process of language development' (p.108). Unsurprisingly, then, ILL is often represented as relatively 'neutral' politically: teachers have the progress of all their students at heart, and research which can identify effective practices thus has a benign potential. But as Roberts continues, 'there is relatively little concern with the social import of second language development', by which she means '[t]he transformation of many cities in Western and Northern Europe from monolingual to multilingual environments' (p.109), and the effects of this on individuals, relationships and groups.

A 'critical' viewpoint characterizes mainstream ILL research questions as inevitably far from value-free, and raises further questions such as 'who decides what counts as "better" practice and outcomes?'; 'how has the language being taught come to be a "target"?' Critics of dominant approaches in applied linguistics draw attention to the political implications of the prominence of English worldwide (e.g. Auerbach 1995; Phillipson 1992, Phillipson and Skutnabb-Kangas 1999). McGroarty (1998: 612) points out that language learning is a process which is heavily influenced by government policies and people's interpretations of those policies, and that learners' social locations and 'local socioeconomic niches' are bound to frame the value and use of particular varieties in particular contexts. Curriculum decisions, similarly, are inevitably constrained by considerations of financial resources, market priorities (which influence which text-books get published and distributed) and so on (Pennycook 2001). The 'critical realist' position adopted by Corson (1997) calls for a recognition of these cultural contexts: '... the historic power differentials maintained in the (non-linguistic) discourses of wider social formations, which provide the real social context, still sit outside the concerns of applied linguistics. And when they are included, they turn up in a rather untheorized way' (p.181).

In the light of these ideas, the research question which asks 'what works?' must also be seen as a political one. Policy-makers, as well as practitioners, may look to research to help in the identification of more successful practice in the language classroom. The question 'what works?' is a legitimate one to address to researchers, and it lies behind the calls for evidence-based practice across a range of publicly-funded areas of social life. (See Mitchell 2000 for a call for applied linguistic researchers to adapt to this changing context.) However, this too is an area where epistemological and political questions are inevitably enmeshed with issues of research method. Research in the natural sciences sometimes comes to public attention for being compromised by the priorities of its funders (such as drug companies, for example). Yet the influence of interest groups other than 'scientists' may compromise social scientific research too, as academics struggle to establish and maintain their career positions by attracting research grants from prestigious sources, and publishing their findings so as to gain maximum ratings in the Research Assessment Exercise or its equivalents. It is thus quite plausible that the identification of knowledge and theoretical understanding will be at least partly at odds with the priorities of policy-makers commissioning ILL research.

Evidence and ILL research: claims and warrants

As we try to demonstrate in this book, issues of ontology, epistemology and methodology are inevitably interrelated, whether explicitly or not. A number of reviews of ILL research methods have been published, and it is not our aim to summarize such a large topic here. Rather, through some observations about methods in ILL research, we aim to consider their relevance for our core arguments. It is customary to map this area along a continuum, from those which centralize the question of how the human organism, on the intra-individual scale, acquires additional languages, through to those which use ethnographic techniques to investigate intersubjective discursive practices, and classrooms as cultural systems, so we shall follow this approach in these remarks.

Experimentation, comparative method and classroom interaction studies

In the context of advocating a 'culling' of proliferating SLA theories, with a view to establishing SLA as a 'normal science', Long (1993) addresses the kinds of methods which research should employ, and he identifies the experiment as 'the highest form' of the 'scientific' approach, and 'third-party replication of experiments' as 'one of the most crucial safety measures for protecting the integrity of a field' (p.233). In our area of interest, it is psychometric investigations in particular which make use of experimental methods, and ILL research may draw on this approach to inform pedagogical practice, even though the research may take place outside any actual classroom (Nunan 1991, cited in Ellis 1994: 566). Thus issues of cognitive processing, such as whether automatic recognition of spelling errors is linked with learners' general ability in the L2, for example, may generate experiments in laboratory conditions. Learners are tested on their performance in the target language, and then, in a 'controlled' environment such as a computer laboratory, they are presented with stimuli such as specific words to which a response is required. Measurements are taken – of each subject's response times, for example – and the results compared either across groups of subjects or for correlations with test results, and so on.

In practice, many ILL studies are necessarily *quasi*-experimental, obliged 'to sacrifice some controls because of real-world constraints' (McDonough and McDonough 1997: 160). Gregg (1993) argues that experimental intervention is necessary in research, so that underlying mechanisms may be identified and the construal of laws as nothing more than empirical regularities can be avoided. Whilst we share his view of the importance of distinguishing causal connections from empirical regularities, we are at odds with his optimism that experimental methods can be relied on to do this, for two reasons. Firstly, the conditions for experimental research in the social world are exceedingly difficult to bring about and sustain (not to mention the fact that they are likely to be ethically dubious). Secondly, our view of language as a cultural emergent property would entail a very particular role for experimental research, one which '... should take the form of examining the single empirical relationships in a great many contexts rather than the current practice of examining a great many relationships in a single context' (Pawson 1989: 202). However, this approach is challenging to operationalize, as we discuss in Chapter 8.

Comparative method studies aim to establish which of two or more methods of language teaching 'is most effective in terms of the actual learning (the "product") that is achieved after a given period of time' (Ellis 1994: 569). Classroom interaction research focuses on the characteristics of the interactions between teachers and learners (including learner–learner interactions), using various techniques of observation. Such studies may involve pre-coded schedules and the quantification of the occurrence of types of interaction or utterances; it may focus on any number of kinds of discourse produced in the classroom, on error correction or the processes of small group work and so on. ILL evidence derived from the observation of classroom interaction may be collected with the goal of generating 'understanding' rather than 'proof' (van Lier 1988), seeking to be 'interpretive' as opposed to 'normative'. On the other hand, some classroom interaction research 'manipulate[s] instructional variables such as participant (as in studies of small group work) and task (as in studies of different types of pedagogic tasks) experimentally' (Ellis

1994: 573). Evidence resulting from this approach is vulnerable to the critiques of variables-based epistemologies and successionist models of causality which we have discussed above, so we will not repeat those arguments here.

Ethnographic evidence in ILL research

The method most typically contrasted with variables-based studies is ethnography: extended research involving interviews, observations and some participation by the researcher in the lives of those being studied. Again, it is neither feasible nor appropriate to review in detail here the characteristics of the ethnographic method, but it is relevant to our discussion to consider one of the claims often made for its epistemic authority. It is something of a truism that context-specific case studies, ethnographies and actors' own accounts receive criticism at the methodological level, failing to persuade sceptical readers because of the reliance 'on the vividness and logic of their descriptions and inferences as confirmation of the validity of the descriptions ... [which] can hardly be justified merely by asserting the "interpretive" or subjective nature of the qualitative endeavour' (Chaudron 1988: 23). As we have noted, dialogue on this issue is unlikely to be productive if the epistemological positions of the protagonists are incommensurable. Van Lier (1990: 42) identifies 'two basic principles that are generally agreed to underlie ethnographic enquiry'. One of these is 'a *holistic* treatment of cultural factors, or, in other words, a concern with context', a point which relates to the 'bundle' metaphor and the question of the size and nature of the unit of analysis, both of which we have discussed above. But it is the other core principle on which we focus now, namely 'an *emic* viewpoint', glossed as 'the rules, concepts, beliefs and meanings of the people themselves, functioning within their own group' (p.43).

Paradoxically, there is a strand in 'qualitative' and 'interpretivist' research approaches which could lead to the replacement of one kind of empiricism with another, an approach we might label 'experiential empiricism'. By this we mean that there are potential dangers for research in relying too heavily on people's accounts of their experience. Quite apart from the technical difficulties inherent in accessing people's experience by means of recording what they say about that experience, we need to be clear how far a respondent's claim to 'be', say, 'a Spanish speaker' can illuminate our understanding of, say, the learning of Spanish among a particular social group. Now, as we saw in Chapter 2, some theorists claim that participants' discourses are the very stuff of social reality. Thus Shotter (1993: 21), for example, believes that '... new ways of talking "about" social relations, new forms of debate, work to constitute and to establish the very relations to which the words uttered within those ways seem to refer'. While there may be some truth in this, we find it unconvincing that social relations can be *only* the products of discourse, so that although, as Pawson recognizes, in the everyday world we all engage in the practice of 'get[ting] hold of a bit of the world and assign[ing] it a value' (Pawson 1989: 70), and although research must take account of 'the significance of, and the variation in, cultural meanings and natural discourse' (*ibid.*: 20), the social scientific interpretation of the world, and the classification of its constituents, demands some explicit theorizing. As Byrne puts it, '... classification is perhaps the most important way in which we can understand a complex non linear world' (2002: 5). To be sure, conventional analytic categories may be inadequate or inaccurate, as some of the critics we cite have claimed, but the use of participants' categories will not necessarily serve us any better.

This is why we view with some scepticism claims such as those made by Norton (2000: 58) in her presentation of her informants' accounts of their experiences as adult immigrants to Canada learning and using English there in differentiated social contexts. 'It is important to note', she says:

> ... that the stories these women have told are *their* stories. I have taken seriously their interpretations of events and their understanding of cultural practices in Canadian society. I have sought to understand the world as they have understood it, and have not questioned whether their interpretation of events was the correct or true interpretation.

Our point is not that researchers should reject participants' own accounts of their experiences, but there is no intrinsic reason why these accounts should be assumed to provide reliable information about, for example, the social structures which may be constraining or facilitating language learning processes. Indeed, Norton herself provides some highly theorized sociological commentary on the experiences of her informants, in addition to the extensive extracts she reproduces from their diaries and interviews. This in itself, together with the fact that the extracts appear, edited, in an academic monograph, recontextualizes these 'authentic' accounts, and suggests that the analyst has, quite properly in our view, brought to bear on her interpretation of the topic being researched (adult immigrants' experiences of language learning) knowledge and understanding additional to that of the participants themselves.

This is not to argue that respondents' accounts are in some way 'inferior' but rather that they are inescapably partial, and this in two senses: the purpose of everyday understandings is practical adequacy in the context of daily life and not the practice of social scientific enquiry; respondent accounts, insofar as they remain grounded in this practical adequacy, also remain tied to a less objective view of the social world than that sought by the researcher. It is the very opacity of social life that requires us to develop theoretical accounts if we are to grasp those features of it that are not given in our everyday, phenomenal experiences. If the way the social world appeared to us was the way the social world was, then there would be no need for social science and no basis for claims to epistemic privilege (and far fewer human errors!). It is partly because the social world is not transparent in this way that we experience its force in the form of constraints – and its power in the form of enablements – and that we need to develop novel, frequently counter-intuitive, theories about what it consists of and how it works. As Brumfit (1997) acknowledges, theory-making is a social practice, to be sure; however, as he puts it, if 'the claim is made that theory-making is *merely* a social practice, with an implication that it can make no claims to privileged usefulness', then it is both unconvincing and somewhat disingenuous. Researchers lay claim to epistemic privilege even as they write to champion the perspectives of the researched. As Brumfit continues, '... publishing a book or an article is a claim to have ideas worthy of consideration and is precisely the same kind of claim that any "expert" may make' (p.93).

Rejecting the scientist's variable categories only to embrace the 'emic' categories used by those who participate in the processes we are researching can thus lead to a different set of epistemological problems, which suggests that interpretation of complex, nonlinear, emergent systems and processes cannot be achieved simply through thick description and holistic accounts.

Conclusion

In this chapter, we have sketched out some of the influential perspectives taken by researchers engaged with just one kind of applied linguistic 'problem', which we labelled 'instructed language learning'. We began by suggesting that variables-based research rests (however implicitly) on a *successionist* theory of causality. A *generative* theory of causality, we proposed, opens the way for more dynamic accounts of the phenomena with which we are concerned. We argued that research – including applied linguistic research – needs to go further than merely acknowledging that the real world of human interaction is complex (a term used often merely as a synonym for 'complicated'), and should take fuller account of complexity, of emergence and of the implications of the stratified nature of the social world.

We noted that the theoretical and methodological orientations adopted by ILL researchers are heterogeneous, but we argued that these can nevertheless be seen to cluster around certain themes. Where the focus is on how teaching 'input' relates to learning 'output', researchers prioritize generalizability, often seeking law-like patterns which may account for regularities in learner characteristics, teaching styles and language-learning achievement. We provided a brief indication of some attempts to review the aggregated findings of ILL research as a step towards identifying 'what works' in language teaching, and concluded that there is very little consensus from the vast literature of studies in the variables tradition.

Where the focus is on the social context in which learners experience second or foreign language teaching and use, the field has clearly been influenced by sociocultural theory, the attractions of holistic descriptions and a critical perspective. Contributors to the more descriptive, ethnographic tradition, we noted, query the desirability of generalized claims, and privilege learners' own accounts of their experiences. An additional influence on which kind of research is undertaken was identified as the political and economic climate, affecting funding and the biographical experiences of researchers themselves.

It will be evident from these observations that we think there is scope for each of these broad perspectives to benefit the other, and that contemporary developments in social theory have an additional potential application in this kind of applied linguistic research. In the next chapter we begin to extend and develop these ideas by considering one of the most fundamental aspects of a research programme, namely the theoretical descriptions and categories by means of which we come to have knowledge of the social world.

Note

1. Even this term is potentially ambiguous, but we are not concerned here with the detail of debates about 'formal' versus 'informal' instruction.

5 Social categories and theoretical descriptions

One implication of the argument we have been exploring is that empirical descriptions of the world will always be incomplete, since that world is not fully or directly intelligible to its inhabitants (including, of course, social theorists and language researchers). This raises directly an important epistemological issue to do with the status of the theoretical accounts we produce about this world. If our empirical measure of the world is inescapably partial, how are we to develop theories which remain empirically grounded whilst yet seeking to provide a social scientific account of social reality? And in what ways do the accounts produced by social researchers differ from those produced by other inhabitants of the social world?

This chapter will explore some of the implications of these questions for concept formation and methodology in applied linguistics. Our examples in this case will be drawn from research in sociolinguistics: the distinctions between sociolinguistics and applied linguistics are not central to our argument, but as this chapter is chiefly concerned with the identification of social groups and the varieties of language they use, its orientation is as much towards 'socio' as 'applied' linguistics. We will consider how both sociological and sociolinguistic research can take account of actors' own understandings and mobilizations of such categories whilst also embedding these within a realist theoretical description of the social world.

It's all a matter of variables ...

Correlating linguistic variation as the dependent variable with independent variables such as linguistic environment, style or social categories, is the primary empirical task of sociolinguistics.

(Chambers 1995: 17)

[S]ocial variables generally, including ethnicity, are usually untheorised or undertheorised and used in whatever way is convenient for the linguistic analytic purpose at hand.

(Milroy 2001: 237)

This claim by Chambers, which we quoted in Chapter 1, articulates a well-established position in sociolinguistics, and there are two aspects of it that we want to address. Firstly, we wish to argue that the constitution of independent variables based on social categories is itself a task of theoretical description. Thus the identification of such categories as 'independent' becomes immediately problematic. Secondly, and in line with the view of the stratified social ontology that we have elaborated in earlier chapters, it implies that the linear variable correlations often adduced in sociolinguistic research provide an insufficient description of social reality. Where such models are useful, we want to suggest, is in indicating empirically the 'traces' of causal relations. We shall explore this idea in the context of beginning to suggest how a realist epistemology can inform methodology in sociolinguistic research.

Of the 'independent variables' listed by Chambers, it is the group identified as 'social categories' that will be our main concern. As any introductory text on sociolinguistics will explain, the social categories which are most often the concern of sociolinguistic research include age, sex (or gender), social class and ethnic or racial group. These categories, not surprisingly, coincide with those that are used in many other areas of research across the social sciences, but in recent years social scientists have begun to question their validity. One line of critique has come from those writing within a postmodernist tradition, where the challenge to a notion of objective social categories is part of a larger attack on any concept of objective truth and scientific rationality. Another source of objection is from those writers, influenced by social constructionism, who are wary of accepting *a priori* categories in the social world, preferring to explore how it – and everything in it – is constructed in texts and talk (e.g. Potter 2000 and Chapter 2 above).

The approach we are proposing may perhaps be seen as steering a middle course between the empiricist ontology that underlies many conventional quantitative studies – if only implicitly – and the strong relativism implied in full-blown constructionism. While we do wish to defend a modest notion of objectivity in social research, we also recognize the limitations of empirical research based on correlations of variables, and we are critical of its tendency to hypostasize social categories, and of its linear view of variation. Our perspective is consistent with that of a number of social scientists researching a range of issues in the social world, who have turned to realism and complexity theory to provide answers to the question of how we can know that the variables we name and use represent reality (Archer 1995; Layder 1997, 1990; Sayer 1992; Williams 2000).

Social categories such as 'class' or 'ethnic group' are not, of course, brute facts (Searle 1995). Take, for example, the categories listed on the 'equal opportunities' forms issued by employers to prospective employees. These categories are relatively recent: they did not exist until they were devised by particular people for specific purposes. This is one reason why debates about ethnic monitoring have proved so durable (and inconclusive): they are about who has the power to define whom and for what purposes, and the resulting categories carry within them a network of implicit propositions about what is salient for these purposes. For instance, the ethnic monitoring forms currently in widespread use by public service employers in England today distinguish ethnicity in terms of heterogeneous criteria: 'White', 'Black other' (skin colour); 'Indian', 'Pakistani', 'Bangladeshi', 'Chinese' (belonging to a nation-state – although it is unclear whether this is meant to imply affiliation to, birth in, or parents' birth in, one of these states); 'Black African', 'Black Caribbean' (skin colour plus compound geographical regions).

The process of monitoring employment patterns in relation to the responses selected from this list presents a number of problems: Is membership of these groups ascribed by others or self-chosen? If people are given the opportunity not to answer, how valid can the exercise be as a measure of patterns of job selection? Since the categories are not of like kind, how can they serve as the basis for a single categorization? We shall return below to the theoretical incoherence of ethnic categories for the purposes of social research, but we introduce some of these problems here because they provide a particularly striking example of the fact that social categories cannot be regarded as given, independent variables to be deployed in the way that correlative models imply.

Of course, it is not only social categories based on ethnicity that are permeated by interconnected – and often implicit – propositions. Another widely used social category in both research and policy is age. Legislation and social practices pertaining to the rights and responsibilities of people at specific ages vary widely, historically and geographically. (We are witnessing one such variation at the time of writing, when there is debate within the UK about whether or not the age of consent to intercourse should be the same for a homosexual as a heterosexual act.) Although there is an unavoidable physical, biological dimension to the ageing process, the significance attached to this is not determined by it. Attaining the age of 50 means many different things in different parts of the world and does not automatically entail any of them. In other words, all categories rest on propositions. In the instances cited, for example, these include implicit claims about correlations between geographical origin or skin colour with way of life, or cultural attachments; and between chronological age, emotional maturity and responsibility (and that this correlates differentially with different sexual orientation).

All social categories, then, are forms of description. Those employed by social scientists need to be 'theoretical descriptions' (Layder 1990; Pawson 1989). Thus the challenge facing social researchers is, at the least, to be conscious of the claims embedded in the social categories they use, and, preferably, to form their categories on the basis of a coherent theory. When the theoretical basis of social categories is made explicit in this way, they can be seen as 'theoretical descriptions'.

Two kinds of social category

Few social researchers, including sociolinguists, would dispute the claim that the social categories used in research cannot be taken as presented to us by the social world, and are therefore dependent on theories about it. Our argument will start by drawing a distinction between two kinds of social category: those constituted by involuntaristic characteristics, and those characterized by some degree of choice on the part of the people who belong to them.

We should note here that the distinction we are drawing is not the same as that often made in social psychology between ascribed and achieved – or chosen – identities. This theory derives from the structural functionalism of Parsons, which (as we noted in Chapter 2) is concerned with patterns of norms into which people are socialized, through the occupation of particular social roles. In pre-industrial societies, according to this approach, social roles are largely ascribed, that is, fixed and largely unalterable, whereas in modern industrial societies, social roles are achieved. The distinction drawn here is less concerned with 'roles', but is, rather, about the way in which researchers' descriptions of the social world are theoretically informed. Our distinction is thus between those forms of social category which are based on objective features which people happen to have in common, and those which presume some common understanding on the part of those grouped within the category.

Following Greenwood's useful distinction (1994), we shall refer to the first kind of category as 'social aggregates'. These are groups – such as the poor, the unemployed, women over 50 – whose only common feature is the property identified as salient by whoever is employing the category – such as those responsible for benefits policy or for selling insurance to over-50s. Aggregates do not imply shared conventions and norms to which people can be party. Of course, it is undeniably the case that being poor or unemployed may induce some common habits, forms of recreation, states of health and so on, but this cannot be taken as a commitment to a shared culture of being poor or unemployed. And again, although the feature in question has an objective quality – lack of a job or lack of income or having lived for a certain number of years – the grouping of people having this feature in common is a consequence of a particular description, one that realizes some purpose in aggregating people in this particular way. It is important to note that 'aggregate' in this sense is not equivalent to 'average': it is used in the mathematical sense of 'a collection of elements having a common property that identifies the collection' (Chambers Dictionary).

The extent to which the poor or the unemployed or those over 50 wish to identify with such a definition of themselves, the extent to which belonging to such an aggregate is seen as expressive of what they are, cannot be determined from membership of the category itself. There are no shared rules and conventions about how to belong to the culture of the poor or the unemployed. Nevertheless, the objective features of people's situations that are the basis of their ascription to the category (low income or no job) may seriously constrain potential efforts to be described in terms of other categories (as 'upper class', say, or as 'wealthy').

The second approach to categorizing groups of people identified by Greenwood is with reference to their membership of 'social collectives'. These are descriptions of those groups in which members must be party to sets of conventions and norms in order to belong to the group in the first place. There are two implications that follow from the use of the term 'party to'.

Firstly, it signals that membership of such groups is indicated by an awareness of, and therefore some kind of commitment to, the conventions that constitute the group in the first place. As we suggested in Chapter 1, a social institution such as marriage entails an understanding of what it is in order to undertake it (or to reject it). Marriage is, properly speaking, a conventional arrangement. It is used by Greenwood (1994) as an example of a collective category, whose membership involves understanding certain rules about it, performing a recognized ceremony, having a spouse and so on. Being unemployed or over 50, by contrast, are not conventional arrangements, although there may well be all manner of conventional ways of responding to the fact of being unemployed or over 50.

Secondly, the term 'social collective' avoids what Archer (1988) has called 'the myth of cultural integration'. We explore the significance of this further in Chapter 6, but we may note here that it is possible to employ the social category 'married people' without reading back from it, as it were, that all those falling into this category share an *identical* commitment to the meaning of 'being married'. This conflationary impulse is particularly marked in the discussion of groups based on notions of race or ethnicity (Carter 2000) as we shall see.

The distinction between the social categories of aggregates and collectives that we are advocating is one grounded squarely in the notion of emergence. Social reality, we have noted, is made up of more than the sum of the individuals who comprise it. This 'more' consists of those features of social reality, such as legal and political institutions, property relations, belief systems and cultural mores, that are the emergent product of (arise out of and are irreducible to) social interaction. Some of these products of social interaction possess emergent properties of their own and so are able to exert systematic causal effects on subsequent interaction. Our distinction between social aggregates and social collectives seeks to reflect the emergent nature of the social world. Social aggregates, as Greenwood has noted, have no structural features (social or otherwise) that ensure their maintenance throughout changes in membership, and they are not constituted by joint commitments by members to arrangements, conventions and agreements. Social collectives, on the other hand, as emergent entities, possess the conceptual and practical resources for the formation and maintenance of identity over time.

Aggregates, collectives and sociolinguistic research

Age-based categories

Let us now consider the relevance of these two kinds of social category for research in sociolinguistics, taking age-based categories as a first example. One well-researched topic is the occurrence of distinctive features in the speech of adolescents (e.g. Cheshire 1982; Eckert 1988; Kerswill 1996a; Romaine 1984). Studies on this topic usually start with the researcher identifying as salient the property of falling into a given age-range. From this perspective, 'adolescents' constitute an aggregate category, since there is no entailment (logical necessity) involved in belonging to the category 'adolescent' and engaging in any particular kind of behaviour, including speech behaviour. Aggregating people on the basis of a feature such as age is the choice of the researcher, and having that feature neither rests upon nor implies a common cultural understanding of what is involved in having it. In other words, people who just happen to be, say, 15 years old at a particular date are constituted as a group by the process of categorizing them as such. They do not have to understand what being an adolescent is in order to be categorized as an adolescent, but will become a member of the category involuntaristically. So they have nothing in common which is a direct product of being 'an adolescent', other than the contingent fact of being a certain age. This is the force of Chambers' argument, which Coupland summarizes as suggesting '... that age is not a truly *social* dimension at all, if by this we mean one that is socially negotiable' (Coupland 2001b: 188). As Coupland notes, however, this is a partial and unsatisfactory position for explanations of patterned linguistic behaviour, and we suggest below how it might be modified in terms of the distinction between aggregates and collectives.

Research into the speech of members of the category 'adolescent' usually proceeds by analysing variables at the levels of phonology, lexis or syntax, and establishing correlations between membership of the category and the tendency to use one of the variants. A finding that often emerges is of 'adolescence [as] the focal point for linguistic innovation and change' (Chambers 1995: 176). Kerswill (1996b), for instance, reports a tendency for adolescents to use /t/ rather than /?/, even when style and context are accounted for. However, while the majority of speakers in the group studied display this tendency, there are invariably counter-examples. These findings often point to significant patterns, but they remain *descriptions*, as opposed to *explanations*, of the correlations found. We would suggest that it is at this point that the aggregate category 'adolescent' ceases to be useful in the process of looking for *explanations* of sociolinguistic phenomena, precisely because it is simply an aggregate of contingent features.

If we want to explain *why* many adolescents are in the vanguard of linguistic change, and why some are not, we need to introduce a strong notion of social agency – an acknowledgement that people have some degree of choice over what they do, including how they speak. This in turn requires the use of social categories that recognize the relevance of actors' own understandings. Those findings that appear at first to be anomalies in the statistical correlations become more explicable if the researcher can reconstitute the theoretical descriptions of social categories as collectives rather than aggregates. How 'adolescents' manage and negotiate an adolescent identity is quite another matter from how they get to be members of this category in its aggregate sense. If its members do behave in similar ways, as well they may, this is the result of cultural patterns and mores that influence 'doing being an adolescent', and not of their chronological age. Thus, especially if this social category is one which is meaningful to its members (if, for example, they have eagerly awaited the arrival of their thirteenth birthday and initiation into 'teenage' status, with the right to participate in activities deemed inappropriate for younger children, and so on), then they may behave as they think adolescents should. But any such similarities in behaviour, values, or attitudes are not attributable to the 'common property that identifies the collection' – its aggregate status. Adolescents who subscribe to the value systems of either 'Jocks' or 'Burnouts', for example (Eckert 1988), do so on the basis of their own decisions (even if there is not an infinite range of options from which they can choose, and even if they see these as the only options available).

As research produces descriptions that are based on collective (as opposed to aggregate) social categories, it reveals properties of the interaction between structure, culture and agency. Thus, an investigation of why some young people use marked variants while others do not entails recognizing the role of the speakers themselves in this variation. However, moving away from an aggregative view of social categories presents the researcher with a different order of epistemological problem (which may be one reason why people frequently opt for an aggregative approach). The core of this problem is that the identification of collective categories involves the researcher in making judgements about who is 'party to' the norms and rules that constitute the category in question.

Such judgements will be less difficult in some cases than in others. To return to Greenwood's example, cited earlier, it is reasonable to assume that those people who are married have some understanding of what this description means (although, as we also pointed out earlier, this by no means entails that they will all have the same understanding). Constituting 'married people' as a collective category in this way does not preclude its deployment by researchers as a social aggregate category. Regardless of whatever meanings marriage has for the couples studied, once they become married they are bound by the legislation applying to married people – including certain financial benefits or restrictions, for example. A researcher who is interested in a question such as whether there is any sort of correlation between being married and having a mortgage would use the category of 'married' as though it were an aggregate category; on the other hand, another researcher, interested perhaps in the causes of divorce, would be obliged to attend to marriage as a collective category, and ask people about their commitment to it as an institution. We are advocating methodological relativism here: which sort of category we employ will depend on what it is we are trying to find out.

Thus it should be clear that in defining aggregate categories, less attention is paid to actors' own understandings. The feature defining membership of an aggregate category must be one that is contingent, external and measurable. You may see yourself as the youthful Adonis, but you've still been around for 50 years, and the researcher (or the insurance salesperson) will go by the birth certificate rather than rely on the personal PR. Analytically, then, with aggregate categories, priority is given to the analyst's own depiction of that category.

'Ethnicity'-based categories

Whilst some social categories can therefore be constituted by researchers as both social aggregates and social collectives, others are more troublesome. This is particularly the case when we are dealing with aspects of social reality that do not lend themselves readily to empirical measurement and where, moreover, actors' interpretations are critical. Adolescents may be defined aggregatively by the researcher as all individuals between the ages of 13 and 18. Researchers may take the decision to focus on this age-group because of a belief (derived from previous research) that adolescents tend to use language in particular ways. However, using language in these ways is not simply an irresistible stage in 'sociolinguistic maturation' (Kerswill 1996b); it involves a degree of choice. This is why actors' understandings are a central element in the theoretical description of social collectives. 'Jocks' and 'Burnouts' are descriptions that rely on social actors' adoption, and maintenance, of distinct linguistic features. Their adoption of this form of social action suggests that the individual is not only 'party to' the norms and rules relevant to being a member of the group, but has also made some assessment of the potential benefits and losses attaching to group membership.

It is considerably more difficult to disentangle aggregate and collective categories when we use descriptions such as 'racial' or 'ethnic' groups. On the whole, 'ethnic' is preferred to 'racial' as the term for these kinds of categories when they are used in sociolinguistic studies, although some appear to use the terms interchangeably (e.g. Rampton 1995b). Milroy (2001) draws some distinction between the two by an appeal to the learned, cultural components of ethnicity and the physical characteristics of race. However, the distinction is elided by her claim that race denotes those physical characteristics 'which are treated as ethnically significant' (p.237), and she is quick to note the salience of discrimination by majority groups against minorities for the identification of both racial and ethnic groups. Similarly, Fought (2002) suggests that '... ethnicity is not about what one *is*, but rather about what one *does*', and points out that '... the category of race itself has historically been socially constructed, and is extremely difficult to delimit scientifically' (p.444). Nevertheless, we find her use of the concept of ethnicity ambiguous and inconsistent, and the argument we develop here is equally applicable to 'race' and 'ethnicity' as a basis for a researcher's social classifications (cf. Carter 2000).

How are people to be placed in 'ethnic' categories when ethnicity is not an empirically observable feature of human beings? If this is done by skin colour (which is problematic, as it is not a categorical variable), or place of parents' birth, 'ethnic group' is being employed as an aggregate category. It therefore implies nothing about commitment to sets of norms or conventions (of language, dress, custom or habit, although all or some of these may be observable amongst many members of a particular category). If people are classified into 'ethnic groups' with reference to some notion of identity or culture, then the term is being employed as a collective category. The researcher then faces the familiar problem of making judgements about who is party to which sets of norms and conventions, and who is not.

We would claim that this problem arises because it is not possible to distinguish between ethnic groups as aggregate categories and ethnic groups as collective categories, and that this inevitably leads to confusion about what it is that is actually being measured. Researchers are then unlikely to be able to operationalize concepts with the precision that they need. They may seek to side-step the issue by simply adopting commonsense terms and definitions, or by deploying the self-definitions used by their informants, but, as we argue below, such a move raises a number of problems for the analysis of any findings.

To take one recent example, Fought (1999), in her study of 'Chicano English', is concerned with a sound change which is taking place in both the 'minority' and 'majority' communities of California. Her article classifies speakers with reference to ethnic categories – as it must do, given her commitment to 'the need to analyze variation within the context of those social categories that are of particular significance to the specific community being studied' (p.5). These categories, like those from the UK discussed above, are of several kinds and are resistant to empirical verification. They include: 'speakers of Anglo ethnicity', 'Anglos', 'Anglo speakers', 'the majority Anglo community', 'the California Anglo community', 'Puerto Ricans', 'Puerto Rican speakers', 'a Latino community', 'Latino young adults', 'Los Angeles Chicanos', 'the minority Mexican-American community', 'speakers of other ethnicities', 'minority communities', 'minority groups', 'minority speakers', 'African-Americans', 'African-American local communities', 'the black and white communities'.

Our disagreement with Fought is not about her study as a whole, but rather with the use of ethnic categories in this kind of research, of which her study is but one example. In order to establish correlations between use of a specific linguistic feature (in this case, /u/-fronting) and membership of a social group, the researcher identifies the group – and those groups with which it contrasts – *a priori*. Since the membership qualifications of 'ethnic' categories are notoriously difficult to pin down, as we have argued, the boundaries of the categories to be compared are inherently unstable.

For speakers themselves, this analytical problem may be of very little significance. In order to go about one's social business on a daily basis, it is quite satisfactory to define oneself and others – when it is relevant for particular types of interaction – in terms such as 'Anglo', 'black', 'Puerto Rican' or 'Latino'. And indeed such self-definitions are important for the analyst in interpreting such phenomena as strong identification with one social group – and the language associated with membership of it – rather than another. However, from our perspective, it is quite clear that there can be no logical necessity between belonging to such an imprecise category as 'Anglo' or 'Chicano' and using language in particular ways. Firstly, the category is inherently imprecise. It is not clear whose definition of it is to be authoritative, nor which attribute(s) of the category are to count as definitive. Secondly, speakers are not bound by their membership of any social category to use one set of language features rather than another. Coming from a Puerto Rican background may predispose speakers to use one pronunciation rather than another, but there is no logical or necessary entailment for them to do so. For us, the concept of 'ethnicity' is conflationary, in that it fails to distinguish between culture, structure and agency.

Class-based categories

People are routinely classified by institutions, such as government agencies, and by social actors in routine interactions, as belonging to particular groups. There are clearly identifiable patterns in the way membership of these groups correlates with opportunities for employment, housing, health-care and so on, and the concept of 'social class' is a familiar one to invoke when discussing such correlations. In sociolinguistics, correlations are identified between membership of a particular social class and the use of particular variants within a language, though the definitions of class used within the discipline are controversial. Williams (1992), for example, points out that Labov's conception seems to rely on both subjective and objective aspects, and he is critical both of Labov's deployment of a subjective, social psychological concept of class and of his emphasis on '... the manner in which differences exist between objective groups rather than on the nature of the power relations that exist between them' (p.81). Despite some attempts in the sociolinguistic literature to accommodate less consensual conceptions of social class (e.g. Erickson 2001; Milroy 2001; Milroy and Milroy 1992), recent textbooks (e.g. Hudson 1996) appear to perpetuate the conflation of status and class. Holmes (2001) explains that '[t]he term social class is used here as a shorthand term for differences between people which are associated with differences in social prestige, wealth and education. ... [C]lass is used here as a convenient label for groups of people who share similarities in economic and social status' (p.135). Class then continues to be treated as an attribute possessed by individuals, which can be correlated with other 'variables' in studies from within a whole range of social scientific disciplines. It is common for social class to be deemed to have an existence which is not observable, or therefore knowable, except as a statistical variable.

An alternative conception is prompted by the recognition that patterns of structured social relations tend to be stable and persistent, providing the contextual social conditions into which individuals are born. Structural inequalities are then understood as the *necessary* product of class *relations*. The empirical traces of these relations, such as disparities of wealth and income, are just that: traces of a larger set of social relations whose complex combinations generate, amongst other things, persistent and measurable outcomes. These relational patterns are logically antecedent and temporally prior to the individual, generating anterior distributions of resources within which individuals are involuntaristically placed by the accident of birth. Being born poor in a capitalist society will profoundly affect your chances of one day becoming a millionaire or the Vice Chancellor of a major university.

The claim here is that socially sustained and structurally reproduced distinctions among people are generated by social class processes. These distinctions are the categorical ones of social relations rather than aggregated individual attributes; that is, they derive from the powers and liabilities of class agency. All of these powers and liabilities are profoundly social and relational: they are properties of agency in an involuntaristic, collective sense. Amongst such powers are those for collective organization and social solidarity (in, for example, trade unions, social movements and political parties) and for the use of particular cultural resources (texts, symbols, dialects, histories and so forth). Class agency also entails liabilities. In the case of working-class agency these include: comparative political powerlessness, in terms of restricted access to the central points of political and economic decision-making; employment insecurity; and low opportunities to legitimately acquire income. These propensities are thus irreducible to individual attributes, not only because they are social and relational, but also because they are temporally prior to individuals themselves: they are amongst the structuring features of the contexts in which individuals seek to manage and negotiate a personal trajectory.

Culture, structure and agency

Structured social relations, then, make certain outcomes more likely than others for the occupants of different class positions. These probabilities, however, are always conditioning rather than determining, and each individual has some degree of choice about how to respond to the contexts in which she finds herself (Layder 1997; Carter and Sealey 2000). One of the areas in which a degree of choice is exercised is in relation to the cultural resources that are a feature of the context of social existence. Language is pre-eminent amongst these cultural resources, being not only the means of accessing these resources, but also a resource in its own right. As a cultural resource and a 'World 3' entity (see Chapter 3), one of the properties which language possesses, we have argued, is an objective existence. What makes a theory, a book, an idea – or indeed, a language variety – objective knowledge is its 'possibility or potentiality of being understood, its dispositional character of being understood or interpreted, or misunderstood or misinterpreted' (Popper 1972: 116).

World 3 knowledge therefore has an independence from individual users; it does not have a colour or a gender; it does not belong to one social class or another. Its elements can be used by any individual or group possessing the appropriate symbolic code. This is a significant constraint. People's structural location may mean that they do not have access to the symbolic code necessary to access parts of World 3, and their geographical location will influence their access to different language varieties.

There are other constraints on people's access to linguistic resources. An individual who seeks to become a fluent speaker of a language not widely used in the locality faces obvious practical difficulties, while adopting the speech style of those who are widely seen as members of a different social category is likely to be viewed as a form of 'crossing' (Rampton 1995b), which may attract social censure. Nevertheless, such deviations from the supposed norms are possible, because language has properties which make it *potentially* available to any human speaker.

Furthermore, language as a system constrains its speakers in various ways, pointing to its partial autonomy from its speakers. Beaugrande (1999: 131) describes the interplay between language and agency thus:

> The *standing constraints* persisting on the plane of the system (e.g. the English article going before the noun) interact with *emergent constraints* being only decided on the plane of the discourse (e.g. the lexical choices appropriate for a job interview).

Reducing language to simply what speakers say (as in various forms of constructionism) eliminates its World 3 structural features, namely its relations of coherence and logicality, its grammatical, syntactical and lexical patterns and relations. Reducing language to its systemic, logical features (as in various forms of structuralism) eliminates its World 3 emergent features, namely that language change is brought about by the engagement of human purpose with an independent and antecedent body of linguistic resources.

In both cases the conflationary impulse results in the neglect of the interplay between linguistic and other cultural resources, and the processes by means of which human beings, in seeking to modify or maintain aspects of their social worlds, modify or maintain those resources. When this interplay is overlooked (or squeezed out) the outcome is often too close an association, in the researcher's account, between language and its most typical speaker. Cultural coherence is then assumed by the researcher on the basis of typical speech use and typical speech use is adduced as the basis for a claim for cultural coherence (Archer 1996).

Ethnicity and language varieties

A particularly striking example of this kind of conflation is provided in the various labels that have been assigned to a variety of American English, namely 'Black English', 'African-American Vernacular English' and, latterly, 'Ebonics'.[1] Wardhaugh (1992), for example, claims, '. . . we can be sure that there is such a variety of English as Black English in the United States' (p.326). In the preceding passage, he has described the linguistic features that contrast with standard English, providing empirical evidence for his claim that the variety exists. He continues, 'Those who speak it recognize that what they speak is something different from the varieties employed by most non-blacks' (pp.336–7).

This sentence provides examples of two of the problems we have been discussing. Firstly, the perceptions of the speakers themselves are presented as equivalent to the theoretical description of the variety by the linguist. As we have said, we believe speakers' perceptions to be important sources of sociolinguistic evidence (Preston 1999; Niedzielski and Preston 2000), but we would wish to distinguish speakers' own accounts from those of the analyst, since the two kinds of description serve different purposes. The second problem is signalled by the need for Wardhaugh to qualify 'non-blacks' by the word 'most'. The passage continues:

> Most Americans are prepared to categorize someone who contacts them by telephone as either black or non-black using speech alone as the criterion, and most such categorizations are correct. In cases of mis-categorization, it is usually because of special circumstances: a black person has been brought up very closely with non-blacks, or a non-black has been brought up very closely with blacks.
>
> (Wardhaugh 1992: 337)

Now, from our perspective, the alarm bells should begin to ring for the researcher, prompting a re-evaluation of the categories 'blacks' and 'non-blacks'. If the variety really is 'Black English', then *all* those speakers and *only* those speakers who belong to the category 'black' will use that variety. However, as both Wardhaugh and any number of studies and personal experiences will testify, there are exceptions in both directions (black speakers who don't use the variety and non-black speakers who do). Fought (2002), for example, cites a study by Hall (1995) which 'found that some European-American women were more successful at performing a stereotyped "Black identity" on the phone than African-American women', while a manager told Hall that ' "the best white woman we ever had here was Black" ' (Fought 2002: 456). Such discrepancies mean that it behoves the researcher to analytically detach the variety from the speakers, and to seek a more satisfactory theoretical description of the relationship between agency (speakers) and culture (language varieties).

Let us be clear about this. Our objection to Wardhaugh's use of the term 'Black English' is not that it imperfectly captures the empirical usage of the language form denoted by the term. Few descriptive terms will have a nil leakage of this sort (Bell pers. comm.). Our objection, rather, is to some specific characteristics claimed for this kind of variety. Naming a variety 'Black English' ties together the terms 'Black' and 'English', thus defining a particular, empirically identifiable, language variety in terms of its use by a group of speakers. One problem with this is that the empirical identification of this group is not straightforward, in the way that, say, 'New Zealand English' could be defined by classifying the population of speakers to be investigated as 'every English speaker born in, and currently resident in, New Zealand'. A further problem is that the relationship between 'being black' and the empirical distribution of the language variety is unclear. Are 'black people' those who speak 'Black English'? No, because many of them do not speak it. Is 'Black English' defined as that language variety spoken by 'black people'? No, because many 'non-blacks' use it (witness the rap musician Eminem, for instance).

Part of the difficulty with 'speakers of Black English' as a social category for research purposes – social or linguistic – is that it conflates aggregative features (the number of people who happen to share particular somatic features, including skin colour) and collective features (the extent to which individuals using the variation are 'party to' norms and conventions which define membership of that group).

In a colour-racist society, to be dark-skinned may mean being predisposed towards using those distinctive language forms which are expressive – and constitutive – of particular forms of social solidarity (see Gilroy 1993). These include identification with various symbolic forms, such as music, for example, as well as ways of speaking. But, as we have said, predisposition is not entailment, so the researcher needs to identify the circumstances in which this mechanism (these structural conditions interacting with these cultural resources) is triggered to produce this particular outcome (these speakers utilizing this variety). The claim that 'Black English' is a description derived from the use by a majority of 'blacks' of a determinate language variety implies *a priori* a particular causal relationship between being 'black' and speaking in a particular way. 'Black English' is defined as the language variety that (most) 'black' people speak, but this does not take us far beyond empirical description. What we want to know is why this is the case and, more interestingly perhaps, why some 'blacks' do not use it whilst some 'non-blacks' do. Clearly it is not the 'blackness' of the language that is the causal mechanism. We need, in other words, social categories that allow an exploration of the relationship between language variety, human agency and social relations (being of a certain skin colour in a society in which this is perceived in certain, derogatory ways, for example).

One significant study in which these issues have been explicitly addressed is the research into Creoles in the Caribbean by Le Page and Tabouret-Keller (1985). These authors do distinguish between language and speaker, claiming, 'We should constantly remind ourselves that languages do not do things; people do things; languages are abstractions from what people do' (p.188). Le Page and Tabouret-Keller found that their informants were likely to hold stereotypical views about the various 'communities' found in their locality, and that their beliefs about both ethnic categories and language varieties were influential on their behaviour. However, from the researchers' point of view, these beliefs were highly problematic, for many of the reasons we have outlined above (such as the variable salience given by different informants to skin colour, family descent, religious affiliation and so on). Le Page and Tabouret-Keller's account, in contrast with the traditional correlational studies that they criticize, emphasizes the role of agency:

> the individual creates for himself the patterns of his linguistic behaviour so as to resemble those of the group or groups with which from time to time he wishes to be identified, or so as to be unlike those from whom he wishes to be distinguished.
>
> (p.181)

These 'acts of identity' assume a high priority, and individual agency is paramount: 'A community, its rules, and its language only exist in so far as its members perceive them to exist' (p.205). Now although we are sympathetic to several aspects of Le Page and Tabouret-Keller's account of 'acts of identity', we would wish to take issue with this particular claim on two counts. Firstly, it would appear to deny the World 3 status of language itself, by asserting that the existence of languages is dependent on the perceptions of their extant speakers. Yet, as World 3 objects, languages possess properties – such as their syntactical relations – which are independent of particular speakers. If this were not the case, the hermeneutic recovery of 'dead' texts would be impossible. Although exclusively oral languages do not leave the traces on which researchers must subsequently rely, there is no reason to assume that such languages lack the properties which would allow them to be 'recovered' if, for example, aural recordings were available after the deaths of all their speakers.

Our second objection to Le Page and Tabouret-Keller's claim is related to the first. To insist that languages only exist insofar as their 'members perceive them to exist' is to subject languages to 'the tyranny of the present tense' (Archer 1995). The corollary of their claim would seem to be that the structures of languages are the effect of members' beliefs about languages, of contemporary action and perception. It then becomes difficult, on both counts, to explore the interplay of language with agency, with the efforts of people to modify or maintain some aspect of social reality. To reiterate, we regard it as essential both to recognize and to maintain a distinction between a) social actors' own purposes and choices from among linguistic varieties, and how they perceive these from their own experience (agency); b) the structural

123

enablements and constraints which condition the choices open to them (social structure); and c) the properties of language itself (culture).

Conclusion

This chapter has adduced three main claims. Firstly, since the social world is not directly accessible to individuals, the social categories that we employ to understand it do not present themselves directly to us. Our second point is that social researchers must therefore provide a defence of the theoretical descriptions they employ. Finally, we want to suggest the basis for a realist approach to methodology that incorporates these two claims.

a) Social categories as theoretical descriptions

The claim that the social categories that we employ do not present themselves directly to us means that such categories are fashioned out of theoretical networks, and are devised for particular purposes. The positing of social categories is not the exclusive preserve of researchers: the social categories that we all use in our everyday interactions are often matters of unexamined convention and tacit agreement. These categories may conceal the assumptions about social reality on which they rest. Any uncritical use of them in social research will import these hidden assumptions, which makes problematic any efforts to define, for research purposes, social categories like 'adolescents', or 'the Latino community', or 'lower working-class speakers' in such a way that they can function as 'independent variables'.

Some theoretical descriptions of these phenomena locate individual speakers at the centre of a nest of concentric circles. Speakers then voluntaristically proclaim their identification with certain social groups rather than others, subject to the pressures exerted on them by immediate peer groups – the gangs to which they belong, the tight social networks of which they are members (Milroy and Milroy 1992) – and the more remote contextual influences such as social class. Chambers (1995) summarizes aspects of this idea as follows: '... the difference between social networks and social classes as norm-enforcement mechanisms has to do with their proximity to the individual, or the immediacy of their influence' (p.68), and '... the difference between class and network seems to be one of degree rather than kind' (p.71).

The problem with such accounts, from our perspective, is the linear model on which they are implicitly based. In this, the linguistic practices adopted by actual speakers are regarded as deviations or deflections from the probabilistic patterns identified by the correlations of independent variables. Actual speech that does not conform to the pattern predicted by the correlated variables becomes a remaindered leftover, to be explained by factors exogenous to the variables originally considered, such as local networks, political attachments and so on.

b) Discriminating between theoretical descriptions

The recognition that all social categories are theoretical descriptions, or, as Pawson (1989: 287) puts it, that 'all measurement is an act of translation', also raises the question of how to discriminate between the often competing accounts provided by these descriptions. Our second claim is that social researchers must provide a defence – involving an explicit and conscious scrutiny – of the theoretical descriptions they employ. (We assume at the very least that researchers believe that what they produce offers a different understanding from the understandings of participants, as non-researchers, of whatever aspect of the social world is being investigated. They may, in the end, produce understandings that turn out to be similar to those of non-researchers, of course, but this would still be for different reasons.) In other words, as we argued earlier, researchers must at least claim some form of epistemic authority.

Theoretical descriptions necessarily draw on other theoretical descriptions, and these other descriptions, as World 3 entities, are necessarily independent of the people who deploy them, in the important sense that they did not produce them. As propositions about reality, these descriptions can be assessed in terms of their truth or falsity, their consistency, their evidence and so forth. The importance of a realist ontology is critical here. It provides us with a firm view of the reality to which our theoretical descriptions refer; our descriptions are descriptions of *something*. Indeed, along with Devitt and Sterelny (1987: 190), we would argue that one cannot theorize about anything, least of all language, without implicit commitment to a view of the world. How things seem to us, in other words, depends *both* on the world *and* on our descriptions of it.

Combining a World 3 view of knowledge as theoretical descriptions produced by other minds, and upon which subsequent descriptions to some extent rest, with a robust recognition that entities do not depend for their existence or nature on our theories about them, allows for the defence of a modest notion of objectivity within the social sciences.

c) A realist approach to theoretical descriptions

The epistemology we are advocating offers one way of defending a notion of social science without excluding the perspectives of the researched. This is because, and this is our third point, it is not methodologically prescriptive and will always seek to account for the interplay between people and the world in which they live. This entails acknowledging that a narrow sense of objective reality, one in which the irreducible subjective realities of human consciousness and being are left behind, is likely to be deficient. The tension this generates between the efforts to achieve an objective standpoint by leaving a more subjective one behind involves a considerable epistemic risk (see Nagel 1986: 7), but in our view it is one worth taking.

One important methodological implication for sociolinguistic research seems to us to be as follows. Rather than defining the problem as the correlation of linguistic variation with variations in speakers' membership of (theoretically defined) social categories, researchers might start from the case. That is, the initial focus is on the language produced by speakers, and 'investigation becomes case not variable driven' (Williams 2000: 11). This kind of approach was adopted by Le Page and Tabouret-Keller when they collected data from a random sample of children who had immigrated to Britain from the Caribbean. They identified a series of linguistic variables and did not correlate these with pre-selected social categories, but subjected their findings to cluster analysis. Byrne (1998: 170) defines clusters as 'types, qualitative sets, which "emerge" from the application of computation to large multi-variate data sets'. From their results, Le Page and Tabouret-Keller inferred varying self-identifications by the children with others in their 'multidimensional social space' (1985: 127).

Now as we have already explained, this account runs the risk of giving too great a weight to self-definition, although for some research purposes self-defined social categories may be the most appropriate. Alternatively, the researcher can follow Williams' (2000: 11) suggestions for those engaged in survey research, and defer the identification of categories until a later stage of the analysis:

> The conjectural character of the data collection leads to a flexibility about both the definition and the measurement of 'variables', indeed the variables themselves are simply outcomes, or 'traces' (Byrne 2000) of yet unidentified (though possibly hypothesised) mechanisms. The only thing that we know is 'real' is the case itself and the operationalisation of the variables is deferred to the identification of antecedent case characteristics.

Of course, the notion of a 'case' suggests that the researcher has already identified a phenomenon of which the object under scrutiny is itself an instance – or case – and this might seem to imply that the suspension of classification to a later stage of analysis is illusory. To be consistent in our argument, we would have to acknowledge that even the collection of instances of speakers using language, and the identification of differences in the speech they produce – in other words, data collection approaches based on cases – are acts of interpretation and rely on some prior theorizing. This is why no director of a sociolinguistic project would be likely to send untrained researchers out with an instruction simply to 'record people talking': a lot of theoretically informed planning would underpin the collection of data. However, there is a difference between collecting 'cases' of linguistic production, on the one hand, and, on the other, deciding in advance which 'variables' are relevant, and which apply to each speaker.

In this chapter we have highlighted some of the problems with social categories based on notions such as 'ethnicity', and suggested how a distinction between aggregates and collectives could be used in research into language variation. In the next chapter, we explore a further dimension of social identity and group identification, taking the applied linguistic topic of intercultural communication as our example. In this, together with the following chapter, we continue to develop the implications of our argument for approaches to research. In relation to the sociolinguistic issues discussed in this chapter, we shall suggest that analysts could allow for the possibilities not only that neither commonsense social categories, nor social scientific ones, will correlate categorically with the linguistic variables they have identified, but also that the mechanisms bringing about linguistic variation and change may be complex and multiplicative, rather than linear and additive.

Note

1. For extended discussion of this variety, see Rickford 1999a, and on the controversy about Ebonics in education, to which we referred in Chapter 1, see for example Rickford 1999b.

6 Social domain theory: interpreting intercultural communication

Introduction

In our earlier discussion of what applied linguistics is, we have cited Brumfit's (1997: 93) definition: 'the investigation of real-world problems in which language is a central issue'. One such problem is that people can often fail to understand each other even when, on narrowly defined linguistic criteria, they have access to a shared language variety. Even within a context familiar to all the participants, knowledge of grammar and vocabulary alone does not guarantee the 'communicative competence' identified by Hymes (1972) as the knowledge of 'when to speak, when not, and ... what to talk about with whom, when, where, in what manner' (p.277).

An increase in the movement of people internationally – as a result of the 'globalizing' of the economy and of forced migration – has led to a considerable increase in contact between people of different social and linguistic backgrounds, compounding the potential for communicative failures. Considerable resources are expended on ensuring that interlocutors do have a shared linguistic code in their repertoires, and commercial enterprises value employees who are fluent in several languages. However, there is a growing recognition that access to a common language variety does not necessarily lead to shared understanding. The applied linguistic problem to be explored in this chapter, then, is that which has come to be labelled 'intercultural communication'.

This area features as a component of language courses, but its significance extends beyond the pedagogical dimension of applied linguistics. As we have indicated, commercial organizations may have an interest in offering 'training' in intercultural communication to their employees (Mead 1994), and 'the workplace' is one site of applied linguistic research in this field (e.g. Candlin 2002; Clyne 1996; Roberts and Sarangi 1999). Studies have been conducted of 'interethnic service encounters' (Bailey 1997), while interactions in health settings have also received extensive attention (e.g. Cameron and Williams 1997;

Candlin and Candlin 2003; Frank 2000; Teschendorff 1994). Encounters in courtrooms and police stations, as well as other aspects of the legal process, have also been studied from this perspective (e.g. Beach 1991; Bhatia *et al.* 2003a; Bhatia *et al.* 2003b; Krouglov 1999). Moreover, this is an aspect of communication in social life where applied linguists have contributed directly to the amelioration of a recognized problem, by providing not only analysis but suggestions for improved practice to professionals such as healthcare workers and interpreters (e.g. Candlin *et al.* 2002; Cass *et al.* 2002; Roberts *et al.* 2000).

Intercultural communication involves speakers' communicative – not merely linguistic – competence, and those problems which occur are often variations on the pragmatic misunderstandings which can arise between speakers in any sociocultural interaction. For example, a speaker may assume a greater degree of shared knowledge with an interlocutor than is actually the case, and therefore say less than is required to be understood, thus flouting the 'maxim of quantity' (Grice 1975). The additional layer of potential problems identified in the literature on intercultural communication includes contrasting expectations about *what counts* as an adequate, relevant or appropriate contribution to an interaction. Illustrations are often provided of 'critical incidents', where these contrasts give rise to problems in communication. Here is an extract from one such example:

> Mrs Jane Simpson enjoyed her job as a departmental secretary in a large, well-respected university in the United States. She enjoyed trying to be helpful to students as they worked their way through department and university regulations on their way toward earning their bachelor's, master's, and doctoral degrees. One day, a student from India entered the department office and began demanding attention to his various problems with his visa, low course grades, and his thesis adviser. He never said 'please' or 'thank you,' talked in a tone of voice reminiscent of a superior talking to subordinates, and gave orders to Mrs Simpson.
>
> (Cushner and Brislin 1996: 198)

The intended audience for this text, as listed on the book's cover, includes 'professionals in multicultural settings and business people around the world'. Readers are invited, often in the context of a course of training in intercultural communication, to consider the source of such problems, and the subsequent discussion sections encourage them to recognize the unstated assumptions made by both parties. This example is used to illustrate, among other things, 'a big problem in cross-cultural encounters – figuring out which behaviors directed toward one are role-based and which should be interpreted personally' (*ibid.*: 221). This approach represents an instrumentally focused strand in intercultural communication studies. The goal is for those involved to 'develop broader vocabularies and conceptual bases about intercultural interactions that will empower them to understand and solve their own cross-cultural problems more efficiently' (*ibid.*: 2).

This is not the only perspective from which intercultural communication has been studied, however. As with many other areas of applied linguistics, various disciplines have made contributions. These include management training such as that illustrated in the example above, where patterns of difference in cultural practices are taught in order to reduce the risk of mutual misunderstanding (e.g. Hall and Hall 1990). In addition, the area has been discussed in: social psychology, where there is an emphasis on how the individual accommodates to unfamiliar social settings and learns to manage the concomitant stress (e.g. Gudykunst 1995); language teaching, where writers seek to emphasize that problems in communication are rarely simple matters of linguistic translation (e.g. Byram 1997; Kramsch 1993); and discourse analysis, where the insights from ethnographies of speaking are brought to bear on intercultural encounters (e.g. Gumperz 1982). Obviously, these different perspectives derive from different academic traditions and have different goals, with varying degrees of emphasis on analysis and application.

In this chapter, we aim to demonstrate how the theoretical approach we are presenting can help to clarify the concepts involved in the study of intercultural communication. We shall draw on these different disciplinary traditions listed, while suggesting that sociological realism brings an additional dimension by making plain the respective contributions of language, structure and agency to intercultural communication.

Different meanings of 'culture'

The term 'intercultural communication' invites some definition. According to Blommaert (1998), '[f]ew fields are as fuzzy as that of the study of intercultural communication', and indeed most texts on the subject include at the very least a definition of 'culture', recognizing that a shared understanding of the word cannot be relied on. Meanwhile, from a social theoretical perspective, Archer (1988: 1) claims that culture 'has displayed the weakest analytical development of any key concept in sociology and it has played the most wildly vacillating role within sociological theory'. (For a review of the contributions to the concept as used in pragmatics, from a range of perspectives, see Sarangi 2000.)

In the intercultural communication literature it is customary to distinguish 'high culture' from 'anthropological culture' (Scollon and Scollon 2001), and to make clear that intercultural communication is not particularly concerned with the art, literature and other enduring products of a society. Rather, it responds to 'the customs, worldview, language, kinship system, social organization, and other taken-for-granted day-to-day practices of a people which set that group apart as a distinctive group' (*ibid.*: 139). From a more psychologically oriented position, Brislin (1993) identifies 'culture's features' as those 'ideals, values, and assumptions about life that guide specific behaviours' (p.23). In other words, internalized 'cultural' norms influence observable practices. Both perspectives emphasize routine behaviour ('anthropological culture') rather than the artefacts of an elite ('high culture').

These two senses of the word are, however, related to each other: there must surely be some link between those phenomena which can be identified as somehow exemplifying, say, 'Japanese art' and 'Japanese manners', or 'English literature' and the English language. It is not always possible to classify a particular cultural artefact as belonging to either 'high' culture, with the elitist connotations of that term, or popular culture. Yet many people would have a sense that they can detect American sensibilities in both the routine exchanges expected in an American diner and in an American film or crime novel. (The reason for the scare quotes around some of these phrases will become apparent below.) Moreover, the quite extensive list of features which comprise the 'anthropological' sense identified by Scollon and Scollon requires further exploration before we can deploy the concept of 'culture' in any explanation of what happens in ***inter-cultural*** communication.

Culture and cultures

The starting point for this kind of definition is, implicitly, a claim that human beings can be classified into 'distinctive groups', and that these cultural groups are recognizable by the practices of those who belong to them. As we saw with 'ethnicity', discussed in the previous chapter, there is a persistent danger that the categorization of people into groups of this kind will do violence to the complexity of human experience. In the singular, 'culture' denotes something which is common to the experience of all human beings; yet the plural form 'cultures' denotes categories by which to distinguish groups from each other. Even when hedged with a rejection of generalizations and stereotypes, definitions almost invariably imply a degree of homogenizing

131

of 'culture' within a group, and a demarcation of separate 'cultures' between groups.

A further conceptual problem with the term is that of circularity. When 'culture' is used in the classification of groups of people, the implicit argument usually runs along the following lines. People can be identified as members of 'Culture A' because they come from one of the territories associated with 'A' people, and engage in certain practices. What are these practices? They are whatever people from Territory A are held to do. The argument is a closed one, in that it supposes that all people of Culture A must do these things, and anybody from Territory A who does things differently becomes an anomaly, simply because they have flouted the *a priori* definition of what being a person of Culture A entails. As Blommaert (1998) points out, it is common to associate a 'culture' with a group of people bearing a name, such as 'the Japanese', despite the fact that 'there is no way in which nationality or ethnic membership would guarantee the salience, the relevance or indeed the presence of "culture" or "ethnicity" in communication'.

The defining practices of each culture, moreover, are very wide in scope. Scollon and Scollon (2001: 139) group together such potentially disparate elements as 'customs, worldview, language, kinship system, [and] social organization'. It is quite possible to participate in, and reproduce, some of these elements and not others. In such cases, it becomes very difficult to determine whether or not an individual continues to qualify as a member of Culture A. On the one hand, anything he or she does should by definition constitute a Culture A practice; on the other hand, deviation from the dominant norms of behaviour identified with members of the culture identifies the person as somehow not a full or typical member.

Our position calls for an explicit recognition that conventional conceptions of culture in the tradition, for example, of Parsons and structural functionalism tend to assume that social homogeneity is brought about by cultural homogeneity. Such conceptions contain two questionable assumptions. The first of these is 'the notion of a *cultural pattern* with an underlying unity and a fundamental notion of coherence'. That is to say, what makes Culture A distinct from Cultures B, C and so on, is that each exists as a separate and consistent entity. The second dubious assumption is 'the notion of *uniform action* ... produc[ing] social homogeneity' (Archer 1988: 4). That is, when people belonging to Culture A follow its practices, they act in accordance with its normative patterns, which is what produces the social homogeneity of Culture A. Archer continues: '... to view culture as "a community of shared meanings" mean[s] eliding the community with the meanings'.

Whether we focus primarily on practices or on worldview, or on the one as determined by the other, we are likely to take the circularity problem with us, along with what Archer terms 'the Myth of cultural consistency' (*ibid.*), unless we disentangle some of these elements from each other.

This problem applies as much to 'small cultures' (Holliday 1999), such as institutions (schools, universities, commercial organizations, the police force), as to 'national cultures'. That is to say, institutions, strictly speaking, cannot possess cultures, since the term 'institutions' refers to relatively stable and bounded social spaces, elements of social structures, whereas to possess culture means to possess the understandings that are available only to human beings. This is not to say that we reject outright the informal use of the idea of an 'institutional culture'. We recognize that persistent, stable social interactions clearly do generate interaction orders (Goffman 1983), which are not reducible to individual interactants or interactions. Such interaction orders lead to particular kinds of expectation about how interactions within the institution are to be conducted, and subsequent interactants do what they do and say what they say within the constraints affecting these contexts. Thus it is that human decision-making shapes institutional practices, often reinforcing socially dominant beliefs and patterns of behaviour such as, for example, racism and discrimination. Nevertheless, we would insist that culture is an emergent human product, constituted by and through human meanings, which are therefore not available to 'nations' or 'institutions'.

Culture as a system of propositions

Let us put aside for the moment the problem of identifying different 'cultures', and what people have to do to qualify as members of Culture A rather than Culture B, although we shall return to this issue below. Assuming that we have identified a recognizable, single culture, we would advocate drawing a distinction between the *propositions*, or 'ideational elements', of knowledge, belief and norms, accessible to this group of people, and the *practices* in which they participate. As Archer (1996: 682) points out:

> When we examine a kinship structure, for example, we are not just investigating how that 'group' *does* intermarry, transmit property, have specific obligations towards specific others and so on, but what rules govern their inter-marriage etc. Comparison of kinship structures is to compare different rules not different groups, for the rules regulate what the members do.

This distinction makes it possible to explore the properties of the 'rules' themselves (although, as discussed below, there are further issues to be considered in respect of the ways people respond to such rules). Groups of ideas, components of the 'Cultural System' (Archer 1988), may be more or less internally consistent, and people will always have access to various beliefs, about which they will make choices. Thus a citizen of the United Kingdom, for example, who might be classified as belonging to 'British culture', may be more persuaded by the commitments, values and claims about the future which are to be found in the manifesto of the Labour Party than that of the Conservatives. This manifesto will need to demonstrate at least a degree of internal consistency in respect of claims about, say, public spending and taxation: opponents from other political parties will seek to expose any inconsistency. However, the two groups of views – those which hold that the state should spend significantly on public services, and those which prioritize individual responsibility, for example – can, despite being mutually inconsistent, co-exist as elements within 'British' culture.

When human beings interact, however, two further components are involved, beyond the nature of the Cultural System itself. Firstly, each person has to respond to the propositions and beliefs available in the culture. They may exhibit inconsistency in their views (espousing high public spending, let's say, while resenting high personal taxation) because of 'intellectual idleness, patches of ignorance, nostalgia or closing the emotional shutters' (Archer 1988: 5). Yet for any individual too great a degree of logical inconsistency within their beliefs and values will almost certainly become untenable, and may provoke a crisis. Those MPs who 'cross the floor' because of differences between crucial aspects of their own beliefs and those of the party they are supposed to represent, or the bishop who finds himself no longer able to accept an article of faith such as the resurrection, may become celebrated examples of the cost to an individual of trying to subscribe to ideas from the Cultural System which are internally incompatible.

The second component to be distinguished from the ideas themselves, alongside whatever individuals make of these ideas, is how people choose to *act*. Actions and practices may *derive from* the ideas and propositions of the Cultural System, but they are not synonymous with them. So, I may be persuaded by the arguments of the political party which promises high public spending, but decide for any number of reasons, including apathy, pessimism or cynicism, not to go out and vote on election day. Or I may be a convinced atheist, and yet have any number of reasons – from a general desire to conform to social expectations, to fearing harsh political and maybe even physical sanctions – for being seen to attend church (or mosque or synagogue) and to visibly engage in acts of worship alongside true believers. In other words, none of these three elements: the consistency of ideas within a Cultural System, nor the beliefs of an individual living in that culture, nor the observable practices of the people of the culture, can be 'read off' unproblematically from any of the others. This is one aspect of what Archer (1988) terms the 'Myth of Cultural Integration'.

There is yet a further distinction to be drawn, which is that between the ideational cultural system and the degree of social uniformity which it produces. The issue here is how, and to what degree, people come to act in accordance with the propositions of the cultural system. Those writers on intercultural communication who draw on social psychology often rely on theories of socialization, including claiming a key role for identification with some groups in contrast to others. Traditionally, this process is portrayed as a predominantly one-way influence from adults to children, who participate in behaviour '... that allows them to become valued members of their culture' (Brislin 1993: 127). 'Socialization', he continues, 'includes activities in which children are *guided away from* certain behaviors and are strongly encouraged to engage in others. ... Children learn which of these behaviors are appropriate and which are inappropriate, depending on their culture' (*ibid.*). One element in coming to recognize what is valued in one's own culture is a concomitant rejection of its obverse, which may, of course, be highly valued by members of some other culture. (One example would be children's learning about the degree to which it is acceptable to show and talk about one's emotions. Behaviour that some people interpret as frankness and warmth, others may perceive as an embarrassing display or an intrusion on privacy.) To some extent, intercultural communication training consists in a process of re-socialization, to allow for the valuing, respecting – or at least tolerating – of a wider range of behaviour than people were 'socialized' into as children.

It will probably be evident by now that this account depends on one of the elisions we have already rejected, between beliefs and behaviour. It also depends on an identification of groups of people *as* groups, an identification which is required of the participants themselves, and some explanation for why people should make such identifications. Thus Gudykunst (1995: 9), for example, posits the need for a 'linking concept' in order to explain interpersonal and intergroup communication. He continues, 'I use the concept of the stranger to accomplish this', while Cushner and Brislin (1996: 325) claim:

> In people's interpersonal relationships, one of the major reasons for
> both categorization and differentiation is the basic human need to
> form in-groups and out-groups. In-groups consist of people who
> can be trusted, whereas out-group people should be kept at a dis-
> tance.

We do not find this claim a particularly convincing one, for several
reasons. It classifies as a 'basic human need' something whose status
as such is difficult (if not impossible) to demonstrate empirically,
except insofar as there is evidence that people do constitute themselves into groups of various kinds, some of which are in conflict with
other groups. However, there are many counter-examples, including
people who choose to defy these notional group boundaries and
interact with members of some other group: if this did not happen,
then presumably there could never be any intercultural communication! Furthermore, stating the issue in these terms relies on the use of
internal, psychological states to account for external, sociological
phenomena. As we suggested in Chapter 5, we see such issues as
involving aspects of the social world which go beyond the innate
endowments of humankind.

Culture in relation to structure and agency

The realist account of how cultures are constituted thus differs from
this social psychological one in several respects. It maintains a clear
distinction between ideas, social structures and human agency, as
explained above, and it suggests that the process of 'socialization' is
not one of consensus among people who arrange themselves into
simply identifiable groups. As Archer (1988: 5) says:

> Power relations are the causal element in cultural consensus
> building and, far from unproblematically guaranteeing behavioural
> conformity, they can provoke anything from ritualistic acceptance
> to outright rejection of the culture imposed.

In other words, the process of seeking to build cultural consensus can
be thought of as the 'politics of legitimation' (Habermas 1987). The
powerful engage in this process in order to effect their own political
purposes or consolidate their positions of power, but there is no
guarantee that the desired uniformity will result: indeed people may
reject the culture outright. The presence of consensus at the level of
observable behaviour does not permit a direct reading of people's
commitment to the culture at the level of beliefs.

Thus we can distinguish between the members of any given
'culture' and the relationships between: these people as contemporary

human actors; the propositions, 'rules' and knowledge that make up the cultural system; and the enduring social relations which structure the context within which the people act. These distinctions can be illustrated with reference to the 'critical incident' quoted on page 129, whose authors want readers to be aware of a distinction between 'which behaviors directed toward one are role-based and which should be interpreted personally' (Cushner and Brislin 1996: 220). 'Mrs Simpson', they continue, 'was playing a role that could have been played by any of a hundred people.' This is a distinction which many social theorists would also wish to make, and not only in relation to intercultural interactions. In our account, individuals are confronted by pre-existing social relations, which include an array of social roles, including that of 'university department secretary'.

> Roles ... are more important for understanding what is going on between landlords and tenants or bank cashiers and customers than their relations as persons. Moreover the role has to be granted some autonomy from its occupant or how else do we explain the similar actions of a succession of incumbents, or that when pro-moted to bank manager our original cashier now acts quite differently?
>
> (Archer 1996: 682)

Inherent in this description is a notion of change, but it is important to recognize that the time-scales involved in change are different for structure and for agency. During the time that 'Mrs Jane Simpson' spends working in university administration, many structural changes may take place in the education system, including, for example, changes in legislation, in processes of accountability between employer and employee, in levels of investment in the public and private sectors respectively, and so on. So there are changes in the nature of her 'role', changes which would have taken place whoever occupied that position. Over the same period, she is responding per-sonally to changes in the nature of her role, but is also gaining in experience, and interpreting that experience in the light of her indi-vidual priorities and values. Perhaps there is very little change in the role during her career at the university, with a consistent and stable level of 'system integration' (Lockwood 1964), whereas perhaps Mrs Simpson and the other actors participating in interactions in the department change a great deal. Antagonisms between her and her colleagues may develop without any threat to the organization of the university at all. Or, conversely, there may be considerable turmoil at the system level, but relatively smooth 'social integration' among this group of people. Thus the 'cultural' context within which the Indian student enacts his exchange with Jane Simpson is likely to be changing across a number of dimensions. Each participant may bring to bear in this encounter different propositions (explicitly formulated, or as unexamined assumptions) about the distinction – or lack of one – between a person and his/her institutional role. In addition to recognizing the part played by culture and agency, our theoretical position also gives weight to the influence of social structures. The authors of the incident have this to say in their commentary about the dimension which we would identify as structured social relations:

> Another role aspect of this incident is that Indians from wealthy families often have had servants. An unfortunate fact is that often only wealthy families can afford to send sons and daughters overseas for their schooling, as scholarships are not easily available and are highly competitive. These wealthy students may adopt role-based behaviors in their interactions with others, taking on the role of superior when interacting with those they perceive to be fulfilling servantlike roles (as Mrs Simpson was perceived by this student in her role of secretary).
>
> (Cushner and Brislin 1996: 221)

From our position, these 'unfortunate facts' are the product of large-scale historical, political and economic processes which go beyond the interpretation by individuals of their respective social roles. The distribution of wealth and of educational opportunities, at both national and international levels, is a social fact over which neither Mrs Simpson nor this student has any direct personal control. Remembering the observations about different time-scales which were made above, it is important to recognize that the social structures which constrain and enable the actions of present agents '... are the effects of *past actions*, often by long dead people' (Archer 1995: 148). These two actors occupy positions which are anterior to either of them, which stand in a necessary relationship to each other (university student and university employee), and which exist in a context where material resources are critically involved (availability of student places, fees to access them, and so on). This is not to say that there is no scope for differential or progressive *interpretations* of these realities. As Archer (*ibid.*: 70) says:

> ... whatever social structures are examined, they are only operative in and through the world of people which props the door permanently open because human action is typified by innovativeness, a capacity for interpreting the same material conditions, cultural elements, circumstances and situations in different ways and

hence for introducing novel patterns or courses of action in response to them.

Analytically, then, there is a gain from recognizing this incident as involving culture *and* structure *and* agency, while consistently maintaining the conceptual distinctions between, and the specific characteristics of, each. This would preclude representing the incident as a manifestation of a clash between two reified entities such as 'Indian' and 'American' cultures. Scollon and Scollon (2001: 138) go some way towards recognizing this danger when they point out that '[c]ultures do not talk to each other; individuals do. In that sense, all communication is interpersonal communication and can never be intercultural communication', while Scollon (2002) finds the phrases 'cross-cultural' and 'intercultural' 'particularly problematical', because 'they tend to imply closely bounded social groups' (p.136). Similarly, Byram (1997) is wary of 'the dangers of presenting "a culture" as if it were unchanging over time or as if there were only one set of beliefs, meanings and behaviours in any given country' (p.39). He continues, '... we should not think in terms of encounters between different languages and culture systems, but rather of encounters between individuals with their own meanings and cultural capital' (p.40). And likewise Holliday (1999) explains clearly the fallacy of imagining that 'a culture' could be a causative agent, which follows from the reification of cultures: 'After reification, culture appears large and essentialist, and indicates concrete, separate, behaviour-defining ethnic, national and international groups with material permanence and clear boundaries' (p.242).

So how are we to understand the connections between the set of propositions we have labelled the cultural system, the roles and relationships identified as social structures, and the people with the power actually to do things in the world, human agents? An approach which we have found useful here is that developed by Layder to describe the social world as interlinked 'domains'.

Domain theory

Layder's model attempts to capture the social and temporal distancing of social relations from lived experience, while recognizing that, at the same time, every lived experience is embedded within the other domains.

The first of these social domains is that of 'psychobiography'. All human beings develop unique biographies in which 'personal feelings, attitudes and predispositions' contribute to a continuing selfhood, which is 'embedded in their daily routines and experiences' (Layder 1997: 2–3). Thus 'the notion of "psychobiography" points to the development of the self as a linked series of evolutionary transitions, or transformations in identity and personality at various significant junctures in the lives of individuals' (*ibid.*: 47).

The second social domain, which also focuses on human agency, is that of 'situated activity'. Despite the unique quality of our psychobiographies, human beings are pre-eminently *social* actors, much of whose life involves the negotiation of face-to-face interaction. 'Situated activity' refers to these experiences of social life.

The situated activity of face-to-face conduct, however, is itself embedded within what Layder identifies as the domain of 'social settings'. Here the focus shifts from agency – that is, what actors do and experience – to structures – the social context within which these interactions are situated. These are the physical and social contexts 'of social activities and specific social practices' (*ibid.*: 87), such as workplaces, schools or places of worship, and their routinized ways of doing things. Here, the resources of the cultural system are drawn on as actors interpret contexts, but, as discussed above, the practices they engage in will not be fully determined by the typical or predominant beliefs held in the society concerned.

This brings us to the domain which is most distant from actors' experiences. 'Contextual resources' refers to the anterior distributions of material and cultural capital which social actors inherit as a consequence of being born in a particular place at a particular time. While individuals have no choice about this, the distributions of these resources are systematically reproduced. This again entails a particular view of the relation between agency and structure, one in which each is regarded as possessing distinct properties, while they are also mutually influential.

We are not, of course, claiming that we experience these domains in this stratified way, as we live from moment to moment and day to day, but we nevertheless do want to insist that our lives are constantly shaped by all of them, and the relations between them, and that we are more aware of some of them than others. Structural domains involve institutional constraints and enablements that are themselves partly the product of the distribution and allocation of economic, political and cultural resources, which means that they may be more opaque to actors' knowledgeability. Actor knowledge is greater at the level of interaction. For example, 'Mrs Simpson' and the 'Indian student' are likely to be more aware of the choice of words each has used in their encounter than they are of the possible connections between their respective careers and the diplomatic or trading arrangements negotiated between politicians representing the United States and India in previous decades, which are themselves conditioned by long histories of imperialism, colonialism, conflict and conflict resolution.

'Culture', in this framework, infuses all of the domains, which are, in any case, 'completely interdependent' (Layder 1997: 77). Ideas available in the cultural system are known and responded to by individuals (psychobiography); utilized in interactions (situated activity); reinforced through routinized practices, whether explicitly articulated or not (social settings); and differentially available to different groups of people, both in themselves and as a result of inequitable distributions of material goods (contextual resources). As this is rather a dense presentation of these concepts, we shall attempt to exemplify them with reference to some actual experience.

An empirical example

In this section, we shall test the utility of this stratified account of culture, structure and agency for the area of applied linguistics identified as intercultural communication by applying it in detail to another empirical example. This time, the illustration is an authentic one, described in an account by Boas (2001). It has been pointed out (Blommaert 1998) that much of the literature on intercultural communication relies on invented examples. We have already discussed the role of empirical data in language study, and are persuaded of the need for an authentic example to illustrate our approach to analysis.

As part of an assignment for a course in intercultural communication, Boas reproduced an email message from an 18-year-old Australian exchange student of her acquaintance, 'Joanne', sent when the latter had been in Germany for three months. The message lists several of Joanne's quite negative experiences as a visitor to Germany, all of which Boas analyses with reference to various theories about intercultural communication. We too will refer to these ideas, but we shall use the lens of Archer's analytical dualism and Layder's domain theory in seeking to demonstrate the explanatory gain which is afforded by this approach.

In her message, Joanne complains that she 'can never get a straight answer' from the Germans she encounters, and that none of her fellow students have explained to her some of the basic information she needs, such as where to find out which periods on the timetable are sometimes free: 'They aren't very specific, or helpful for that matter'. She has not managed to make friends, because:

> I have got no idea how to start a conversation with these people, they are so short in their answers and questions it is impossible to get to know somebody (well I'm finding it impossible, and I made friends easily in Australia).

In contrast with what she is used to, Joanne finds that she is not invited to meet up outside the classroom with fellow students, or informed about their plans for socializing, so that 'I usually am left standing by myself'. She is also discomfited by the confounding of her para-linguistic expectations:

> They never smile. I would be sitting in the classroom and I would look up to see a person staring at me, so of course I smile, they don't smile back they simply look away. I don't feel very welcome in this country. When I smile at friends of mine that are guys (in particular) they shrug their shoulders, and go 'What?'. A friend of mine who is also from Australia and living in Germany this year has observed that the only people that smile back in the street are the mentally retarded.

Joanne finds Germans generally 'impatient' and 'pushy in the street, shopping etc. . . . Didn't their mothers teach them manners! . . . I think I'm trying to say that they lack common courtesy.' Finally, Joanne describes with some feeling a particular incident, which occurred just three weeks after her arrival in Germany. The class was to be divided into groups, but 'eventually I was left sitting completely alone, while the others all had a group'. The teacher noticed and, 'half way through asking me where I wanted to go, I burst into tears (I was homesick, and had pms)'. He assigned her to a group, one of whose members objected, 'It will be too boring for her; put her in another group'. She describes feeling excluded when this group organized itself to go and get coffee, puzzled by their behaviour – 'they had no reason not to like me' – to the extent that 'they sure made me feel like dirt'.

The domain of situated activity

In her analysis of this situation, Boas draws on the concepts and theories of several commentators on intercultural communication and miscommunication. One area of research which is often used to explicate the source of dissatisfaction such as that described by Joanne is cross-cultural pragmatics. This is most helpful within the domain of situated activity, where human beings draw on their 'practical knowledge of how to go on in social situations' (Layder 1997: 52), and where 'collective agreements and shared understandings are created during the encounter that influence the subsequent proceedings' (*ibid*.: 85). Several writers point out that, although this practical knowledge may be a resource which is – in a generic sense – shared by all human societies, the forms it takes may be different. Thus 'intercultural communicative competence', according to Byram (1997: 51), involves developing the procedural knowledge '... of social groups and their products and practices in one's own and in one's interlocutor's country, and of the general processes of societal and individual interaction'. 'Reading' and practising competently this kind of procedural knowledge involves handling highly context-specific variables. As Meier (1997: 24) puts it:

> What is perceived as a formal context in one culture may be seen as informal in another. What is considered in one culture to be a normal amount of complimenting may seem excessive in another. What may be viewed as accepted topics of phatic communion (i.e. small talk) in one culture may be perceived negatively in another.

In relation to our current example, Boas, who has herself lived in Germany for several years, suggests that the directness displayed by the student who thought Joanne would be bored in her group may have been an indication, not of any intention to reject or offend Joanne, but rather of truthfulness and sincerity.

This example illustrates an aspect of intercultural communication which relates to the propositions of the cultural system as they are realized in specific instances of communication. Early work on the idea of 'politeness' and 'face' suggested that there is a tension between human beings' need to feel 'separate' (unimpeded, individual, private), and their need to feel 'connected' (approved of, involved, social) which is universal (Brown and Levinson 1978; Goffman 1971). Later critics have pointed out the danger of ethnocentrism if this claim is interpreted with reference to the ways in which the tension is managed only in certain societies or 'speech communities' (principally anglophone societies). In particular, the suggestion that 'politeness' equates with 'indirectness' has been questioned, to leave room for the possibility that speakers who eschew hedges and oblique indications of their desires (when making requests, for example) may be demonstrating politeness (in the sense of respect for the other's face), valorizing directness as honest and open (Meier 1997; Wierzbicka 1985, 1991). House (1989, 1996) proposes that one aspect of what we would designate 'procedural knowledge' in the 'domain of situated activity' which is likely to differ between native speakers of German and of English is the relative weight given to the proposition under discussion (the ideational aspect of the interaction) and the face of the addressee (the interpersonal aspect). She also maintains that Germans are likely to give greater weight to the protection of negative than of positive face. In other words, Joanne's colleagues might be expected to show consideration for her by avoiding imposing on her and her right to self-determination in her free time. This would account for the German students smiling less than Joanne expects them to.

In this section, we have sketched out some aspects of how Joanne and her fellow students negotiate the domain of situated activity, and have drawn attention to points of similarity and difference between the kinds of knowledge, particularly procedural knowledge, on which people from two different parts of the world might draw in order to do this. We see this as only a partial explanation, however, of what happened to these particular social actors.

The domain of social settings

As Layder (1998: 95) explains:

> social reality is not simply composed of people's meanings, experiences and subjective understanding, but ... is in large part constituted by systemic features that are relatively impersonal, inert and which represent the standing conditions confronting people in their everyday lives.

When Joanne set off for her visit to Germany, many social actors, the majority of them no longer living, had already shaped the social settings within which she would experience her student exchange. As we have seen, she brings her store of interpretive resources (that is, schemas, frames and scripts) to settings such as the shopping queue or the classroom, and her peers bring theirs. Layder's account emphasizes that there are differences in the degree to which participants are free to make their own decisions about how to 'go on' in these social settings. He is not particularly concerned with constraints deriving from differences in the 'cultures' of social settings as they are found in different parts of the world, but points out that within any given society there is variation in the degree to which people are free to make their own decisions about how to proceed, depending on factors such as the weight of institutional constraints, explicit differentials in power among participants, and so on. The more 'sedimented in time and space' the patterns of social relations are, the more 'demanding' are the practices expected. For example:

> The bureaucratic rules and regulations that inform and shape the working practices in many employing organizations ... are good

examples of the demanding or mandatory character of reproduced relations and practices. Workers <u>must</u> take account of established practices or risk censure (a reprimand), some kind of deprivation such as the withholding of certain rewards (such as promotion, a pay increase or better working conditions) or even a more serious penalty (such as being fired).

(Layder 1997: 111–12)

Now there are, once again, generic similarities across different countries in respect of matters such as the requirement for employees to abide by regulations demanded by employers, or students by those demanded by teachers, but the research carried out in intercultural communication highlights differences in the manifestation of these common requirements at the level of what we would term 'social settings'. Thus international business travellers are as likely as Joanne to have their expectations confounded about such matters as the amount of autonomy in negotiating on behalf of the company afforded to employees of similar rank from, say, the USA or Japan (Scollon and Scollon 2001), or the appropriateness of revealing personal information in the context of what may be seen as a principally commercial interaction.

A number of researchers have sought to distil from various sources sustainable and generalizable claims about differences among countries in respect of the 'sedimented social relations' with which we are concerned here. There is a methodological difficulty with such research, however. By definition, the phenomenon as we have identified it, namely 'sedimented social relations', is not empirically observable. As we discussed above, there is a distinction between people's beliefs about what they should do and what they actually do, while their knowledge of how social relations are structured may be very partial. Thus, while it may be the case that the literature on 'cultural categories' and 'cultural dimensions' may tell us something about the contrasts in the properties of social settings in different parts of the world, we would counsel caution about the social theory on which these findings are implicitly based.

As will be clear by now, we take the view that human beings the world over and throughout time share certain properties in common. These include self-consciousness, embodied physical existence, and an 'ineluctable interaction with an equally material world' (Archer 2000: 318). Given the fact that we are 'made as we are', we are 'inescapably concern[ed]' with 'our physical well-being, our performative competence and our self-worth' (*ibid.*). The universality of the human condition necessarily poses a challenge to any essentialist notion of a plurality of cultures, since it entails an engagement by all human

145

beings with inevitable tensions, such as that between separateness and connectedness referred to above. Commentators on intercultural communication have listed collections of such tensions, with a suggestion that, while the tension, or continuum, is common to all individuals and the groups to which they belong, different groups veer to varying degrees towards one end or the other of these continua. Thus White (1999), for example, summarizes a scheme proposed by Kluckhohn and Strodtbeck (1961), which contrasts different perceptions of such core concepts as: human nature (as good, evil, neutral or mixed; as changeable or unchangeable); human relationships (as individual, collective or hierarchical); and space orientation (as public, private or mixed). One important area of variation among different groups of people is that held to be prevalent in their attitudes towards social interaction.

Trompenaars (1993: 29) identifies 'dimensions' of the way people relate to each other, which include universalism versus particularism; collectivism versus individualism; and achievement versus ascription (how status is accorded). These dimensions are strikingly similar to the 'pattern variables' identified by Parsons, whose conception of social relations we discussed in Chapter 2. Trompenaars' research method was to present respondents with scenarios, somewhat similar to the critical incident we cited at the beginning of this chapter. These scenarios, however, involve some kind of dilemma, and the choices for which respondents opted were taken as an indication of their priorities along the kind of continua sketched above. Thus those who choose to get a friend out of trouble even if it means lying to the authorities, for example, are held to be demonstrating a 'particularist' orientation, while those who say they would act in accordance with respect for the law, irrespective of personal consequences (to themselves or a friend), would be taken to have given a 'universalist' response. White (1999) summarizes this research thus:

> Having used this and other problems with management trainees from over fifty nationalities, Trompenaars concludes that some countries are more universalistic than others, that is, people abide by the rules – formal or codified, while others are more particularistic, that is, specific personal relationships will influence behaviour rather than observation of impersonal rules. He suggests that nations have different starting points for dealing with such dilemmas, and that they may be more or less universalistic, depending on what the rules are about.

From our own position, these conclusions are conflationary, in that they attribute to 'countries' properties and powers which can only belong to human agents. They also elide beliefs, which are part of the cultural system, with behaviour. This kind of account is also potentially deterministic, suggesting that being born in a particular country will lead to an adherence to a particular set of values. However, we would concede that, as constraints operating at the level of social settings, certain routinized and sanctioned expectations about matters such as those investigated may demonstrate a tendency to vary among different societies in accordance with the findings of studies such as these.

The relevance to Joanne's experience thus bridges the domains of situated activity (how her fellow students and others she encountered actually behaved in interactions), and social settings (established practices, many of them institutionalized). The education system is one such social setting, and comparative research in different countries can highlight contrasts in the ways similar overall goals, such as the socialization and education of the next generation, are realized in very different ways. Thus, Alexander (2000: 540), for example, concludes from his study of primary schooling in five democracies that:

> [e]very element of teaching which we explored, from task, activity, organization and routine, to judgement, interaction and discourse, raised questions of value, priority and purpose. Pedagogy connects the apparently self-contained act of teaching with culture, structure and mechanisms of social control.

The countries where Alexander did his research did not include Germany or Australia, but Boas, citing House, claims that the former sets greater store on the transmission of knowledge than on the development of the students' characters. This is consistent with Alexander's finding that teachers in the anglophone classrooms he observed (in England and Michigan, USA) gave a higher priority to pupils' personal and individual development than did those in France or Russia. Attention to distinctions at a national level, however, takes us into a more macro domain, that of contextual resources.

The domain of contextual resources

Those who write about intercultural communication routinely point out that claims about the cultural traits of whole nationalities are very dubious. Blommaert (1998), for example, asserts that 'nationality in itself is a bad index of cultural identity', adding 'as a Belgian, I am rather well placed to make that assertion'! Nevertheless, it is our contention that such a linkage does follow implicitly from research which conflates the elements in the social world that we see as distinct. Only by separating out the respective contributions of structure, culture and agency is it possible to explain what is wrong with the commonsense generalizations such as those found in certain kinds of popular discourse. (Examples include tourist guide-books, such as the following: 'Greeks tend to socialize mostly outside their homes ... Greeks are not big drinkers ... Greeks don't generally eat breakfast.'[1])

Nation-states cannot equate with 'cultures', because they are different kinds of entity. Nation-states have a material reality, insofar as they occupy a physical space. That this space is denoted by a particular name is to some extent a discursive, rather than a material, fact, and obviously the way different areas of land have been named has changed over time as the result of political action. Furthermore, 'resources such as land, food, weapons or factories' (Archer 1995: 175) are not discursive products, and their differential distribution among human beings contributes to the 'contextual resources' with which we are concerned here.

Crucial to this domain are observations about how social relations are structured within any given nation-state, as well as what contrasts are to be found between different countries. Perhaps because of its provenance in industrial training, some of the intercultural communication research takes a particular interest in social inequality, using tolerance of inequality as an index by which to compare different 'cultures'. For example, Hofstede (1991) carried out a questionnaire survey with a large number of respondents (116,000) who were employees of IBM, in 72 of its national subsidiaries. One of the 'cultural dimensions' he identifies as a result of this comparative research is labelled the 'power distance index' (PDI), glossed as 'the extent to which the less powerful members of institutions and organizations within a country expect and accept that power is distributed unequally' (p.28). Hofstede describes how the 'mental software' that children acquire differs along this dimension. In a low PDI culture children are likely to be afforded a status much closer to that of adults, whereas those born in a high PDI culture will be expected to show obedience and respect. These differences are observable at school and in the workplace, so that '[i]n the large power distance situation superiors and subordinates consider each other as existentially unequal; the hierarchical system is felt to be based on this existential inequality' (p.35).

Our contention would be that degrees of inequality within a country (not a 'culture', since systems of ideas cannot themselves demonstrate inequality in this sense) are a product of structured social relations. What is at issue can be seen at the level of social interaction as 'the processes of exchange and power, involv[ing] the use of resources, namely political sanctions, liquid assets and expertise' (Archer 1995: 297). Different social agents are endowed with differential bargaining power, based on the availability to them of these various kinds of resources. (The ability to command a particular language variety is of course a resource in itself.) When resources are concentrated in few hands, there will be a bigger differential between 'haves' and 'have-nots'. Analytical dualism allows for the possibility of heterogeneity among these groups, however, so that those with most expertise are not necessarily those with most political power, nor either of these with most wealth – although they may be.

Furthermore, and this is an important point, there is no necessary connection between culture and structure in these relationships. Hofstede (1991) makes a point of avoiding 'the ecological fallacy' (i.e. 'confusing the level of the individual with the level of the society' p.112), and counsels 'against conceptualising a culture as though it were a personality writ large' (p.255). However, he seems not to distinguish between the existence of inequality and people's tolerance of it, representing culture as 'a set of likely reactions of citizens with common mental programming' (p.112), a metaphor which suggests a relatively inert and predictable range of responses to circumstances such as material inequality. Archer (1995: 175), however, points out the need to maintain the distinction not only between what different individuals may believe, but between these beliefs and the distribution of resources:

> ... material relations may [be] and frequently are legitimated by reference to ideas, but the two should not be elided, for a material relationship can be sustained by coercion and manipulation, thus its legitimation is not a matter of necessity.

Using Hofstede's scores, 'Australia' would be classified as placing a greater stress than 'Germany' on individual achievement and rights, expecting individuals to focus on satisfying their own needs; 'Australia' is characterized as a culture in which social encounters are open to more individual variation than in 'Germany', where people are more comfortable with routine and ritual. However, instead of positing global contrasts between 'Germany' and 'Australia', as places from which Joanne and her interlocutors derive contrasting 'cultures', we might do better to picture two capitalist political economies, with some shared and some specific history of intra-national conflict and negotiation. Both Joanne and her fellow students are structurally located with access to the resources of education and international travel (in the context of the exchange programme), to which large numbers of other citizens in both countries do not have access. In this respect, there may be more in common across sub-groups of national populations than there is between groups within a given country. This, of course, is why it is often in the interest of the powerful to bolster concepts about nationhood from propositions in the cultural system, in the service of sustaining particular political arrangements; but these are always vulnerable to interpretation by the human agents who are exposed to them.

That Joanne expects some areas of commonality to follow from her social position, even if she is unlikely to have articulated it in terms such as these, is implicit in much of what she says. Although, as we have seen, her own frames of reference differ in detail from those of her colleagues, her expectations about her social location are – reasonably enough – that it will be consistent with what she is familiar with from Australia. It is not difficult to imagine a context where, by dint of structured social relations over which she has no control, her location in another country would be considerably different. For example, to be seen in an extremely poor neighbourhood (in either Germany or Australia) with certain clothes and accessories might well invoke a much sharper contrast than the one she describes here, as would seeking an educational exchange with a country where female education is prohibited.

Another charge which can be levelled against some of the mainstream literature on intercultural communication, then, is that it is de-politicized, neglecting to explore the ways in which structured social relations condition the interactions in which it is interested. Blommaert (1998) makes a similar point, reflecting on the fact that, although '[i]f "cultures meet", they usually do so under rather grim socioeconomic circumstances, with a clear societally sanctioned power difference between the various parties involved', yet there is 'a multitude of books and training programs on contact with South East Asian people (notably the Japanese)', but a dearth of such material 'for interactions with the Sudanese, the Angolans or the Samoans'. While employees may – to some extent – share a vested interest in minimizing miscommunication during commercial transactions, other categories of interactant, such as asylum-seekers (Blommaert 2001b) or migrant workers (Roberts *et al.* 1992), may encounter much less goodwill in their efforts to bridge communication problems.

Thus the domain of contextual resources is always and inevitably implicated in interactions in the social world. It is tempting to elide the macro level of 'nation-state' with gross 'cultural' differences, but we would claim that there are very good analytical grounds for refusing to do so.

The psychobiographical domain

The fourth of Layder's social domains is the most individual. Against some of the current claims from postmodernism about selfhood, we would argue that each of us has not only a physical identity which distinguishes us from everything else in the world, but also a continuous sense of self. Psychobiographies are 'the personal feelings, attitudes and predispositions of individuals' (Layder 1997: 2–3). Our existence in the world, which is constantly changing and shaped by different kinds of forces which are separate from us, also means that no two individuals will experience the world in identical ways. One property of 'being human' (Archer 2000) is being able to reflect on ourselves and our experiences. Joanne's email message is other-directed, but there is always the potential for the 'inner conversation' which is an emergent property of the human agent, to be deployed in dialogue.

Let us consider how Joanne's psychobiography may be relevant to the case study we have been discussing in this chapter. We have very little specific information to go on, but we do learn that she 'made friends easily' in Australia. Not everyone makes friends easily, for numerous reasons. Suppose Joanne had arrived in Germany with a history of feeling rejected when trying to become part of a social group. This might have made it more or less easy for her to deal with her failure to make friends in this new context, but it would certainly have been different.

At the point when she was feeling baffled by not being able to find a group to work with, she writes that she 'was homesick and had pms'. Might her reaction have been different if the incident had occurred at a point only slightly different from the time when it did? Her account of this incident is preceded in the message by some background:

> I will describe a particularly horrible morning to you. It was the first time I had to get the bus by myself. I missed it because it was too early. So L. had to drive me to school. I felt like a complete idiot. I couldn't even get the bus. So I wasn't feeling that happy to begin with. We had an information gathering and we had to sit and listen to the teacher (I couldn't understand. 3 weeks after getting here).

In context, this part of the text is represented as illustrative of some general trends in Joanne's experience of intercultural communication. Yet much of this passage is about Joanne herself. The final sentence quoted deals with a cognitive issue, about understanding spoken German in an authentic communicative context. It is possible that another student would have found this less demanding, due to a greater facility with spoken German perhaps (what if Joanne had happened to be born into a family with some German-speaking relatives?), or if she had been taught using a different method (one introduced a year after she started her course, say, or used in the neighbouring school but not hers).

Much of the rest of the content, however, is about the *affective* impact of these experiences. Joanne describes this morning as 'horrible', reports that she 'felt a complete idiot' and that she 'wasn't feeling that happy'. The conclusion to the incident is that her colleagues 'sure made me feel like dirt'. The affective is a crucial strand in the psychobiographical domain: Layder (1997: 62) claims that 'the emotional dimension infiltrates thought and action at every opportunity'. Blommaert (1998) maintains that the affective is also a critical variable in intercultural communication. He found when researching the experiences of Turkish migrants in a refuge for battered women in Belgium that they deployed a particular communicative style, 'Immigrants' Dutch', particularly when telling 'the most painful and sensitive aspects of their story'. Shifts in the choice of language from actors' communicative repertoires may well be as sensitive to the psychobiographical domain as to any supposed 'cultural difference'.

As we have said before, there is a constancy about human beings' contradictory impulses towards both dependence and independence, both intimacy and separation. The access we have to the emotions as depicted in literature from all times and cultures indicates their universality, despite the specificity of the ways they may be understood, represented, or held to be significant (cf. Craib 1998). Archer (2000) identifies emotionality as an emergent property of the interaction between the human being and the natural, practical and discursive orders of reality (p.197), and these connections serve to reinforce the interconnectedness of the domains whose different properties we have sought to elaborate in this account of the area of applied linguistics designated 'intercultural communication'.

Other detailed studies of the experiences of individuals tend to reinforce such insights. For example, the extended ethnographies reported in Bremer *et al.* (1996b) include a number of case studies (Bremer *et al.* 1996a). Berta, from Chile, whose approach to learning French displays a propensity for problem solving and a willingness 'to learn and become involved in French society' (p.123), demonstrates a particular pyschobiographical disposition. Tino, from Italy, living in Germany, is seeking more fulfilling employment; the situated activity of his counselling interview includes such misunderstandings as the reluctance on his part to pay for further training, while the counsellor knows (but fails to make explicit) that funds would be available for this (contextual resources). Santo, an Italian living in England, does not attend language classes, due not to lack of motivation (psychobiography) but to lack of opportunity (contextual resources). His personal resources, however, facilitate a particular kind of negotiation in the situated activities recorded in the social settings of a travel agent and an estate agent. '[T]hrough Santo's interactions we have evidence of a learner who uses his assertiveness to redress the imbalance of power between minority and majority speaker' (p.158). Further examples of what we would identify as the interplay between the different domains of social life are suggested in the 'critical ethnography' produced by Canagarajah (1999, 2001). While his analysis is in many ways at odds with the realist account we have been developing, we would endorse the inclusion, in his description of students learning English in a Sri Lankan university, of the political, economic and historical context of this activity, together with details of the community setting, the classroom setting, and the differentiated ways in which his students interpret and respond to available contextual resources. We continue the discussion of the similarities and differences between our own position and those of 'critical ethnographers' such as Canagarajah in Chapter 8.

Conclusion

This chapter has developed our account of the stratified nature of the social world, illustrating how culture, agency and structure are different kinds of things, with different properties and powers. We have suggested that some of the key concepts used in mainstream studies of intercultural communication are vulnerable to theoretical critique. The approach we are advocating seeks to provide greater conceptual clarity through a fuller appreciation of the importance of a variegated social ontology. We have thus sought to demonstrate the utility of the concept of analytically separable yet experientially linked social domains for this particular branch of applied linguistics.

Social realism conceptualizes culture as an emergent property of the social world, which entails a radical shift in the way it is understood in social research. Culture is frequently presented as though it were an attribute of the individual, a property of – or possession held by – people, as a result of where they live, the religion they practise, the colour of their skin and so on. This view carries the implication that cultures are fixed, limited, bounded and essentially connected to certain people by dint of the place they were born or the language they speak. (Connections between place, language and culture are quite

153

explicit, for example, in the discourse used by the Foundation for Endangered Languages, whose call for conference papers in 2003 invites exploration of whether, on the one hand, 'knowledge of the language of your forebears [can] link you to a place that you have never seen', and, on the other, whether 'widespread languages (national, imperial, commercial) [are] cut off from their roots'.)

Against this, we have argued for a view of culture which regards it as comprising the limitless realm of human resources which we have referred to, following Popper, as World 3. This makes culture inescapably intersubjective. Just as no-one can have a private language (as Wittgenstein has observed), no-one can have a private culture. Since cultural resources are always mediated through agency, people fashion their own ways of being in the world in accordance with those cultural resources that are available to them. This concept of culture is dynamic, highlighting the fact that people move around (and draw from, as well as contributing to) those areas of the cultural realm within which they feel comfortable and 'at home'. (And where one feels at home, the ease one feels in a particular cultural context or milieu is itself partly constituted through that context or milieu itself. An individual's *habitus*, to use Bordieu's term, predisposes them to see themselves as a particular type of person for whom certain pastimes and recreations, ambitions and expectations are appropriate or attainable.)

If culture is an emergent and necessarily open-ended realm, then claims that nation-states can be founded on a singular or unique cultural or linguistic heritage, or that language can function as a simple badge of ethnicity, are highly problematic. Static accounts of culture have to find a way of incorporating into their theories the very large numbers of people who do not fit into a neat correspondence of culture : nation : language. These people are likely to find themselves classified as 'between two cultures', as having 'hybrid' or 'diasporic' identities and so on. There is a strong implication in such formulations that there is an originary, authentic culture from which certain people are displaced or marginalized. A less rigid, less essentialist view of culture, such as we have outlined, might facilitate a more inclusive, cosmopolitan approach to the links between language and culture.

None of this is to deny that access to the resources of World 3 is restricted and unequal, both linguistically and politically. For example, if a proposition has only ever been articulated in one particular language, and has not yet been translated, it is available only to speakers of that variety. In extreme cases, it is possible that shared world-views, expressed through one of the threatened languages found only in very tightly bounded geographical locations, will never become available at all to most of the human population: when a language 'dies', part of World 3 expires with it – unless or until other people restore the code in which it was expressed. If student places in educational establishments are restricted by wealth (or by an ability to speak a particular language), people's mobility in World 3 is correspondingly differentiated. In such ways are language, power and culture intimately related.

In this chapter, using some authentic examples of intercultural communication, we have taken further the account we are aiming to present of the links between language and social action, from both applied linguistic and social theoretical perspectives, and have sought to demonstrate the inherent complexity and multidimensionality of any proposed account of intercultural communication. The next chapter takes up some of the issues raised here with reference to four further areas of relevance to applied linguistics.

Note

1. *Rough Guide to Cephallonia and the Ionian Islands* (2001) Glasgow: Omnia Books Ltd.

7 Language in the world: properties and powers

Introduction

The purpose of this chapter is to demonstrate how the concepts elaborated so far throw light on some areas of policy and practice which are of particular interest to applied linguists. These are presented in order from the most micro, linguistic end to the most macro, social end of a notional continuum, and they include: linguistic autonomy; literacy and the writing system; language and literacy education policy in England; and the struggle over ideas about global and threatened languages. Obviously, each of these topics is very substantial, and we cannot possibly discuss them with the depth of treatment they receive elsewhere, so the chapter will aim to explore how the concepts which are the central concern of the book illuminate debates about these issues in what we hope is a distinctive and constructive way.

However human beings have come to have access to language, as a species or as individuals, the products of linguistic activity can be seen as analytically separable from them, and it is this which points to the partial autonomy of language as a cultural emergent property. Before going on to consider evidence for 'autonomy', let us first deal with the qualifier in this label. In this section we shall be demonstrating some of the ways in which language seems to function in its own right, and we find in the descriptions we cite of sound systems, morphology, syntax and corpus semantics some surprisingly similar discursive moves. Presumably because it is language systems which are the theme of these accounts, they sometimes appear to have agency ascribed to them. When this is no more than metaphorical, it is largely unproblematic. For example, the writers of teaching materials for Linguistics undergraduates at the University of Reading follow a stylistic convention in their presentation of examples of affixation when they write that 'many affixes in English **select** a free stem of a particular word-class'. We assume that this is intended simply to highlight a correlation, and not to suggest that morphemes literally have the capacity to choose between stems and demonstrate an evaluative preference for some above others. When writers (such as de Boer below) explicitly provide explanations for the apparent ability of language to organize itself, we see it as productive. However, when it seems that a serious claim is being made for the agential power of language independent of human beings, we have to insist on a recognition of the limits to what language, as a cultural emergent property, can be claimed to 'do'.

Linguistic autonomy

The autonomy of syntax

Human languages have some features that are peculiar to them, and the feature which is frequently identified as distinguishing human languages from other symbolic systems, including the protolanguages used by other species, is syntax. It is the grammatical dimension of human languages which is their quintessential feature, since it does not correspond to any extralinguistic phenomenon; and it is this which makes possible the expression of relationships and of possibilities beyond what lexical items alone can express. Bickerton (1996: 65) describes syntax as 'the Rubicon between thought as we know it and more primitive ways of thought'. The properties of a grammatical language which are highlighted from this perspective are its compositionality ('the property whereby an expression's meaning is a function of the meanings of parts of that expression and the way they are put together') and recursion (the 'property of languages with finite lexica and rule sets in which some constituents of an expression can contain a constituent of the same category') (Kirby 1999). Although all human languages have these properties, different varieties manifest them in different ways. There is as yet no consensus about the reasons for these variations, but there is some evidence that processes internal to languages themselves may explain them. For example, Nettle (1999) discusses the fact that OV languages, in which the Verb follows the Object, 'favour' morphological marking through suffixes, while VO languages may have suffixes or prefixes. He accounts for this by observing that 'the presence of one item alters the probability of presence (or persistence) of the other items in the suite' (p.133). In this case, the mechanism proposed (as suggested by Hawkins 1994) is ease of parsing for both patterns: speakers experience a general 'harmony' in processing OV order and Noun-Postposition order, both of which place the phrasal category last within the phrase. This is an example of an intra-syntactic property of language, and even at this level the dynamic, emergent and probabilistic qualities of the system are illustrated.

157

The autonomy of language sounds

The same is true at the level of sounds (in spoken languages; the equivalent sub-system in sign languages is gestures). That is, there are limitations on sequences of phonemes: a system of such constraints is universal, but its manifestations differ across different languages, so that, for example, '[t]he sequence /pik/ is not a possible Twi word because it breaks the phonotactic rules of the language, whereas /mba/ is not a possible word in English though it is a word in Twi' (Fromkin *et al.* 2003: 323). Again, some researchers are exploring the possibility that these kinds of intra-language constraints do not require sophisticated inbuilt neural mechanisms to explain them, if the systems are 'self-organizing'. Thus de Boer (2000), for example, identifies probabilistic tendencies for the co-occurrence of certain pairs of vowels and of consonants within specific languages, as well as regularities in the way speech sounds are strung together into syllables. He claims that while functional explanations for these tendencies are plausible, so that speakers optimize sound production on articulatory, perceptual and cognitive criteria, these fail to explain the differences across languages, and it also remains unclear who is carrying out the optimization. His proposition is therefore that:

> If none of the individual speakers carries out an explicit optimisation of their sound system, but (near-)optimal sound systems are nevertheless found more frequently than nonoptimal ones, it is clear that the optimisation must be an emergent property of the interactions in the population.
>
> (p.178)

De Boer has used computer simulations to test this theory, and concludes from these, whose outcomes replicate the patterns of co-occurrence of sounds found in human languages, that 'the characteristics emerge as the result of self-organisation under constraints of perception, production and learning. The systems that are found can be considered attractors of the dynamical system that consists of the agents and their interactions' (pp.193–5). Once a variety has such patterns, they can become partially self-perpetuating as boundaries between varieties, in that either the adoption of items from other varieties will entail modification of them in accordance with 'vowel harmony and other phonological constraints' or 'the difficulty of adaptation leads to the exclusion of foreign words from the phonological or morphological system of the borrowing language' (Thomas 1991: 57).

Interaction between linguistic levels

However, further intralinguistic properties can be identified when the interactions between the different levels of language are taken into account, and this begins to throw doubt on any notion of absolutely autonomous – i.e. separate – levels of the linguistic system.

Poets, humorists and many other creative users of language take advantage of coincidences between the sounds of words and their meanings. Such resources of language play are affordances of the linguistic system itself, as is demonstrated by the fact that both poems and jokes often lose a lot in the process of translation. Written languages afford different kinds of potential for play and creativity in the interaction between sound, visual symbol and meaning. Lewis Carroll's quip in *Alice in Wonderland*, 'Take care of the sense and the sounds will take care of themselves', and the visual poem 'The Mouse's Tail' (*ibid.*) are both examples of interplay between the different levels of language, whose meaning is emergent from this interaction.

Another example of intralinguistic interaction is where speakers of a variety with rich case marking, in the process of many uses over a long time, lose a phonological distinction which also serves as a morphological marker. Nettle (1999) suggests that this small phonological change could in time lead to a 'shift in state space' for this variety, from a highly inflected one to one with increasingly fixed word order. Simulations, using probabilistic modelling, can replicate patterns of change in a language, but it is crucial to maintain the distinction between human beings, who can make choices about language and how to use it, and linguistic systems, whose independence and autonomy from speakers can only ever be limited. Nevertheless, we propose that examples such as these illustrate properties of languages which are, as we would expect of a cultural emergent property, partially autonomous, in that components of the linguistic system interact *with each other* leading to effects on, and changes in, the system itself.

Let us now turn our attention to the interplay between two further levels of the linguistic system, namely grammar and lexis. Echoing some of the themes of Chapter 3, we may start by observing that many scholars of child language development now doubt the existence of an autonomous grammar module, arguing instead for 'a unified lexicalist approach to the processes by which grammar is acquired, used, and represented in the brain' (Bates and Goodman 1999: 37). These authors point out that '... the historical trend in modern linguistics has been to place in the lexicon more and more of the work that was previously carried out in a separate grammatical component' (p.53). Relations

159

internal to the linguistic system which act as constraints on what speakers can do with the linguistic resources available to them may be explored with reference to the empirical evidence of linguistic corpora. Here we are sympathetic to Beaugrande's (1997: 187) proposal that '[o]ur safest recourse is to suspend the project of separating grammar from lexicon and to use a large corpus of authentic data to determine how far the two sides share the "expressive work" in a given language or discourse domain' (cf. Halliday 1978). Corpus research is revealing ever more robust patterns of collocation, colligation, semantic preference and prosody which cannot be accounted for by descriptions of language based on slot-and-filler categories (Clear 2000). As Sinclair (1991: 108) puts it:

> [t]he model of a highly generalized formal syntax, with slots into which fall neat lists of words, is suitable only in rare uses and specialized texts. By far the majority of text is made of the occurrence of common words in common patterns, or in slight variations of those common patterns.

Sinclair discusses, for instance, the word *set*, which frequently occurs in combination with other common words to make phrasal verbs such as *set about, set in, set off* and so on. Corpus evidence reveals that the meaning of the combined 'chunk' is not reducible to either of its constituents (see Carter and Sealey in press). Although neither *set* nor *in* has any particular connotations, either positive or negative, the collocates of *set in* often denote something unpleasant. The kinds of thing which 'set in' are 'drought', 'rain', 'depression', 'rot' and so on. Thus as Sinclair says, '[t]he co-occurrence of two quite common little words can unexpectedly create a fairly subtle new meaning that does not seem to be systematically related to either or both of the original words' (1991: 68) – another example of intralinguistic emergence.

Corpus linguists report their findings in terms which, once again, connote the partial independence of aspects of language. For example, Beaugrande (1997: 209) identifies core items (in this case, the dispositive 'giving to') as 'strong attractors'. Examples from Hunston (2002) include (with agential metaphors highlighted): '... concordances can be used to give very general ideas about **the ways that words behave** and the meanings that can be associated with patterns' (pp.50–1); 'Collocation is **the tendency of words to be biased** in the way they co-occur' (p.68). We would obviously reject any literal implication that words and phrases are choosing how to 'behave', and we do not assume that the authors intend us to draw any such inference, but this attribution of a limited degree of agency to items within the linguistic system, based on quantitative evidence, may be read as a further indication of the emergent properties of language itself.

Interaction between languages and their speakers

However, all these lines of thinking share a common recognition: the *interaction* between language as a system and the human beings who make use of it is of much greater significance than the internal properties of languages themselves.

When writers provide illustrations of a phonological sequence or a syntactic construction that is prohibited in any given language, as is frequently done in linguistics textbooks, they simultaneously demonstrate that speakers can, for particular purposes, disregard or overcome these constraints, as well as stray across linguistic boundaries. The constraint may still be operative within that language, but the speaker can work out, for example, (despite not being a speaker of Twi) how to pronounce /mba/, can create the noun 'friendment' as an alternative to 'friendship', can, as we saw in Chapter 1, generate '*got I have money n't no' (Finch 1998: 3) (if only to exemplify the importance of word order in English) or '?they sowed their isn't they reaped their same' (for poetic effect, as produced by e e cummings), and so on.

Speaker agency is particularly evident in the area of 'corpus semantics' (Stubbs 2001a), where many of the recurrent patterns are not fully determined, as with frozen metaphors and fixed idioms, but are better conceptualized as formulaic frames, amenable to varying degrees of creativity by speakers. These findings serve as a reminder that, although 'collocational facts are linguistic' (*ibid.*: 120), and are indicative of the constraints of the language system, meanings are social, the affordances of agency.

From another angle, in accounting for the origins of linguistic variation, Nettle gives considerable weight to the well-documented sociolinguistic phenomenon of speakers' desire to demonstrate their identification with certain groups in preference to others (Le Page and Tabouret-Keller 1985): 'The social-marking theory ... predicts that linguistic boundaries will form around the core networks of cooperation and exchange in which people are involved in their daily lives' (Nettle 1999: 59).

Recognition of the social character of language is also found in a recent collection (Knight *et al.* 2000a) which presents various approaches to research linking the emergence of language to evolutionary development. The editors retain a modified concept of language as internal to the human individual (I-language) but see a diminished role for its innate inheritance, maintaining that: '[i]t is through others' performance – in other words, through language as embodied in social life – that speakers internalise (and, in turn, contribute to) the language in which they are immersed' (2002b: 11). Language is essential not only for cognition and for the communication of its products, but also, crucially, for the kinds of social contracts which have no material referent. Social facts (Durkheim), institutional facts (Searle), intersubjective knowledge (Popper), are all, as we have repeatedly said, defining features of a social world which is not reducible to individuals. Knight *et al.*'s interpretation of the evolutionary evidence suggests that 'linguistic communication emerges and varies as an expression of distinctively human coalitionary strategies' (*ibid.*: 12). Similar lines of argument are to be found at the ontogenetic level in the emergentist literature (see for example Snow 1999).

Relevance to applied linguistics

Why should these ideas be of interest to applied linguists? As we have noted, the accounts of language developed in the Chomskyan tradition have not proved particularly helpful for their work. It seems that there is currently a rapidly expanding area of common ground between those who are contributing to descriptions of language based on empirical evidence and those whose practical work involves language, as teachers (of first or additional languages, literacy and literature), translators, therapists and so on. There has been much discussion recently about whether applied linguistics should adopt theory from linguistics, or develop theories of its own (Brumfit 1997; Coupland 1997; Davies 1999; Rampton 1997). The theories discussed in this section are, it seems to us, of equal interest to both theoretical and practical linguists. Corpus linguistics, in particular, has an important contribution to make to both language description and language pedagogy, while researchers such as Wray demonstrate persuasively what teachers of additional languages may have to learn from the findings on recent research about the origins of language in the species. Finally, the research techniques used in the fields described here, particularly computer modelling, seem likely to have potential applicability in many areas of social research. Although we are cautious about the adoption of such methods without careful consideration of the theories on which they rest, we see applied linguistics as a research field in which these approaches are very likely to prove useful in the future. We return to this point in Chapter 8.

In the next section, we consider some debates about language in its written form. Again, we pay some attention to the ways in which they are expressed by those who discuss them, but we are mainly concerned to clarify the nature of the properties and powers of people and of language.

Written language and the practice of literacy

Reconsidering 'the great divide' theory of literacy

It is several decades since writers such as Goody and Ong developed claims about the impact and effects of written forms of language on social and cultural practices. One strand of this argument was that the advent of writing transformed the possibilities of social and human development. Critics such as Street have claimed that this view of literacy mistakenly saw it as 'autonomous', detached from ideological and political interests and practices. Furthermore, the critics pointed to the normative assumptions implicit in what they regarded as the exaggeration of the advantages of literacy compared to orality. This identification of the shortcomings of the 'Great Divide' theory of literacy, and the recognition that literacy practices are heterogeneous and context-dependent (Street 1984, 1995), changed the terms of the debate. However, as Gill (2002) points out, the 'autonomous/ideological dichotomy' has in its turn tended to polarize protagonists in 'the literacy debate'. We revisit it here not so much to rehearse the arguments as to explore instead what can be gained by a focus on the distinctive properties and powers of people and language, and on the ways in which the relations between them are modified by the emergence of writing.

Both sides in this debate have made important contributions to our understanding of literacy, and our own perspective seeks to identify what these are without committing us to an outright rejection of either position. It is unfortunate that the whole debate seems inevitably to become entangled with normative and evaluative judgements. Rather as any claim that the human linguistic faculty is distinctive is easily seen as a claim for human superiority, so any position which identifies writing as having properties distinct from those of speech can be criticized for being 'scriptist': valorizing writing and stigmatizing speech (Harris 1980). There is no doubt that these two kinds of idea, distinctiveness, on the one hand, and superiority, on the other, are often found together, but there is no logical reason why they should be. As Bickerton (1996) points out with reference to the human capacity for language, some people object to the claim that this makes humans profoundly different from other species because it seems to chime in with a claim for a God-given right to dominance over those other species. No such inference follows from the first claim, however:

163

language and thought, and the consequences of these, may turn out to be disastrous for the planet and all the species on it, but this does not amount to a refutation of the *difference* language makes. Another of the problems with making claims about orality, as Harris has also noted, is that we do so from the perspective of literacy: to be schooled in literate practices, and to engage in debate by writing books, is to 'speak' from a literate perspective: arguments about orality have to be advanced with caution (see also Linell 2001). It should also be noted, as Street, Barton and others have pointed out, that orality and literacy are typically mixed modes: both are found in most social settings (Barton 1994; Street 1984). Nevertheless, we shall outline the criticisms we have of both positions in the literacy debate, and these involve the components of reality which each appears to eliminate in its description of the phenomenon at issue – literacy. In our terms, the 'autonomists' neglect social practice, while the 'ideologists' fail to give adequate recognition to the distinctiveness of literacy.

Thus the autonomous model is clearly open to the charge of reifying literacy, of treating it as an undifferentiated entity and of failing to connect it as a practice with other sorts of social practices, particularly the pursuit of social and political interests. Street, for example, describes how an autonomous concept of literacy has persisted in the discourse which is used 'to draw public attention to literacy and to encourage both financial and organizational resources into the field', as in campaigns in 1990 for International Literacy Year, whose rhetoric, he claims:

> reproduced many of the stereotypes of the autonomous model: in particular, that 'illiterates' were lacking in cognitive skills, living in 'darkness' and 'backward' and that the acquisition of literacy would (in itself, 'autonomously') lead to major 'impacts' in terms of social and cognitive skills and 'Development'.
>
> (Street 1995: 13)

The strength of Street's objections to the 'autonomous' model is that he recognizes that it is people, rather than literacy, that have the power to cause things to happen in the social world. It does not follow from this, though, that written language has no distinctive properties. Moreover, these properties, since they are emergent, shape the contexts within which people exert the powers they do have. Indeed, this is why it is impossible for us, working as academics in the twenty-first century, to empathize fully with those philosophers who have lived in an exclusively oral society and why Street and the other critics of the 'autonomous' model of literacy have felt obliged to put their ideas into print rather than formulating them exclusively in speech. The 'ideological' model of literacy, we would argue, does not acknowledge sufficiently the emergent properties of written language, thus running the risk of reducing literacy to what people do with it.

The properties of written language

What, then, are the properties of written language? In our terms, written language is a second order cultural emergent property. By this we mean that it is emergent from oral language (which is, of course, temporally prior), human practice and physical resources. It is thus distinct from each, and capable of acting back on any of them.

Various writers have identified the properties of written language which differ from those of speech. Newmeyer (2002), for example, suggests that the features of languages which appear to be linked to their functionality may well change over time, as the practices of their speakers change. In particular, literacy would increase the salience of a constraint on certain formal properties of language, such as parsing pressure, for example, relative to those constraints deriving from face-to-face interaction, such as orderliness and absence of ambiguity. Halliday (1989) discusses how written discourse demonstrates features such as greater lexical density, multiple embedding and grammatical metaphor. This is consistent with Newmeyer's claim (following Givón 1979), that in early language 'discourse pressure was the primary determinant of the ordering of grammatical elements' (2002: 372), and Ong's that '[o]ral structures often look to pragmatics (the convenience of the speaker), whereas chirographic structures look more to syntactics (organization of the discourse itself)' (Ong 1982). Knowledge not mediated by literacy is conceptualized and verbalized with close reference to the human lifeworld, since without writing it is difficult to structure knowledge at a distance from lived experience; and by keeping knowledge embedded within the lifeworld, orality situates knowledge within a context of struggle. Amongst the core features of texts is their suitability for travel, especially once technological developments in typography make possible efficient reproduction. This allows texts, in marked contrast to embodied utterances, to move easily beyond their site of production, thus changing the communicative context dramatically 'both as regards the emitter and as regards the receivers, with consequent implications for the nature of the message' (Goody 1986: 38).

By freeing language from its immediate dependence on human interlocution, writing enables the construction of texts that 'can lead to their contemplation, to the development of thoughts about thoughts, to a metaphysic that may require its own metalanguage' (*ibid.*). So whilst orality can facilitate philosophizing, it cannot produce a library of philosophy texts. In enlarging the possibilities for context-free language, writing makes memory more durable (though not necessarily more reliable): it enables words to have histories, rituals to have rules, texts to have critics.

Writing changes the nature of the World 3 of human intelligibilia by making accessibility to significant parts of it dependent upon literacy. Thus, literate, chirographic societies manifest a different relationship between culture and sociocultural interaction than that expressed in wholly oral societies. The properties of writing are experienced as constraints and enablements by people only *in their practice* in the world. As properties of writing *qua* writing they exist irrespective of the actions of specific readers and writers; they are, in this significant but limited sense, context-independent. They are actualized by specific readers and writers in particular contexts, and are only then experienced as constraints and enablements. That is, it is only when individuals or groups try to modify their circumstances, or resist the efforts of others to change them, that the properties of written language become causally influential. But the causal influence is mediated through agency, through social interaction.

Orality and literacy are emergent properties of human practice; properties say nothing about what human beings do with them, only what is possible (or not possible) when they do. Nor do they produce, in some deterministic fashion, particular types of individuals: literates are not more intelligent, more rational or more accomplished than oralists. It is simply that the contexts that people confront in literate societies and in oral societies present them with different sorts of possibilities for social interaction, whose realization depends on human agency. Indeed, in an important sense writing builds on what was implicit in oral cultures; people have not changed, but the conditions shaping what they can accomplish have.

Constitutions can be written, legal systems can be codified, files can be kept and doctrines can be fought over as a result of writing. When people write things down, the text can be used as evidence for arraignment and banned or burnt. Laws can be passed preventing the publication of certain thoughts and ideas; publishers can be intimidated. One of the important properties of written language is the particular forms of dissent that it makes possible. Not only does writing enable the formation of a continuing tradition grounded in texts, it also permits the development of alternative, dissenting readings of the texts. Furthermore, texts are 'inherently contumacious' because there is no way to directly refute a text (Ong 1982). This emphatically does not mean that the possibilities for dissent in oral-based societies are deficient, merely that individuals and groups pursue other means of resistance.

Moreover, the effects of writing are cumulative. Ideas, plans and traditions become ever more dense as textual commentary builds upon textual commentary and so place greater and greater pressure on those excluded from access to, and participation in, the ever expanding World 3 of textualized human knowledge. Interdiscursivity and intertextuality, both emergent properties of chirographic cultures, permit heightened forms of linguistic reflexivity as well as the commodification of language (Chouliaraki and Fairclough 1999).

A further cultural emergent property of speech and writing in interaction with computer technology is, of course, electronic discourse, and some see a contrast of an equivalent kind between this mode and both of the more established ones (Crystal 2001). We have no space to discuss this issue here, but the approach we would want to take would distinguish, once again, between: the distinctive properties of the cultural, semiotic system which electronic discourse comprises (similarities to, and differences from, the properties of speech and of writing); the constraints and affordances brought about by the structural distribution of material and cultural goods (access to the internet, opportunities to learn and contribute to 'netspeak' conventions); and the properties and powers of the human agents who actualize what is available to them on-line (choice, intentions, propositional knowledge, affective communication).

The next section illustrates the arguments of the chapter with reference to attempts to legislate on the acquisition of literacy and use of a specific language variety (a variety which is tightly linked to written language via the processes of codification and standardization) by young language learners in one country – England.

Language and literacy education policy in England

One phenomenon on which Crystal comments in his discussion of electronic discourse is public concern about a 'decline' in linguistic 'standards', as email and internet users adapt the conventions of written language to these new communicative contexts. The notion of standards in relation to language is always contentious, and applied linguists' work almost inevitably involves responding to it in some way. It has been central to recent events in English education policy, which we present in summary as a case study in which to explore the respective contributions of applied linguistic and social theoretical analysis.

Standard English

The 'standard' variety of a language is notoriously difficult to define, and definitions invariably draw on social criteria, either functions (the variety is identifiable by the purposes for which it is used) or evaluation (the variety is identifiable by the prestige in which it is held). The extent to which linguists are culpable in contributing to the dominant perception of what constitutes standard English is a matter of debate. The orthodoxy is that linguistics, with its aspirations to scientific method, does no more than describe the characteristics of language varieties, with no pretensions to prescription or proscription. This claim is challenged, however, by commentators such as Harris (1980), Crowley (1989, 2003) and Pennycook (1994b). From his position as an applied linguist, Pennycook is particularly keen to point out the difficulties of separating claims about language from sociopolitical goals. It is part of his argument that linguistics and applied linguistics are implicated almost unwittingly in the expansion of English across the globe as a 'neutral' or 'beneficial' resource, as a result of 'the dominance of positivism and structuralism' in these disciplines (p.141). Pennycook's critique is that the maintenance of descriptive neutrality is deceptive, since teaching a standard variety is inherently exclusive. On the other hand, a number of linguists have sought to influence policy-makers in other directions, by appeals to the knowledge base of the discipline, a strategy which has met with very little success, as we shall see. Firstly, however, it is necessary to present the background to the conflict over language and literacy education in English schools at the present time.

Key issues in current English education policy

To summarize very briefly, the last two decades of the twentieth century saw an unprecedented raft of edicts on education policies in England. As Alexander (2000: 257) puts it:

> England's transition from a decentralized to a centralized education system was effected at immense speed. It was sweeping in its range, covering governance, finance, curriculum, assessment, pedagogy, teacher training, local administration and much else besides. It was ruthlessly enforced and policed.

Within this raft of measures, English as a curriculum subject has held a particularly prominent place. Writing in 1989, Stubbs observed that '[i]n the last 15 years, English has been subject to more official enquiries, reports and personal ministerial interest than any other school

168

subject' (Stubbs 1989: 236) – and much more has happened since then. In 1988 the Education Reform Act was passed by the Conservative government of Margaret Thatcher. Among other measures, this established a National Curriculum: publicly-funded schools in all the local authorities of England and Wales became subject to 'Orders' which specified 'attainment targets, programmes of study and assessment arrangements' for each of seven 'foundation subjects', together with the three 'core subjects' (English, Mathematics and Science) to be studied by pupils of statutory school age. In the same year, a committee of enquiry recommended in its report ('The Kingman Report', DES 1988a) a programme of teacher training about the English language. Working groups were established to draft the content which would go into the curriculum Orders, and, also in 1988, the first report of the National Curriculum working group for English (DES 1988b) published its own conclusions, including those about 'knowledge about language' and 'standard English'. A separate teacher training project (as recommended in the Kingman Report) was funded by the government to run alongside the introduction of the new National Curriculum. This project became known as LINC (Language in the National Curriculum), and it produced training materials containing many linguistically focused tasks with accompanying commentaries. However, the government of the day, which had commissioned the materials, reacted against them, deciding not to publish the materials and refusing to allow commercial publication either. The National Curriculum was subsequently reviewed, with a new version introduced in 1995, and yet a third version coming into force in 2000. In 1996, a 'Literacy Task Force' was set up, and this became a National Literacy Strategy (NLS) after the change of government (from Conservative to Labour, under Tony Blair) in 1997. The stated aim of the NLS was 'to raise standards of literacy in all primary schools in England' (DfEE 1998), and a 'framework' document set out 'teaching objectives for Reception [age 4–5] to Year 6 [age 10–11] to enable pupils to become fully literate' (p.2). Commentators such as Street (Bourne *et al.* 1999) have pointed out the ways in which this policy corresponds to an 'autonomous' version of literacy. Although not statutory in the way in which the National Curriculum Orders are, any primary school which chooses not to adopt the Strategy is obliged to demonstrate to inspectors that its own approach to literacy teaching is at least as effective, as measured by test results.

Each of these initiatives has involved politicians, educationalists, linguists and practitioners (from trainers and advisers to classroom teachers) in different configurations, and with different opportunities and resources for influencing policy and practice. Standard English has been a core bone of contention, but by and large the policy which has been made official reflects a version of commonsense nationalism which has changed very little for over a hundred years. Crowley (1989: 221) quotes a nineteenth-century politician advocating the standardization of English:

> It is evident ... that unity of speech is essential to the unity of a people. Community of language is a stronger bond than identity of religion or government, and contemporaneous nations of one speech, however formally separated by differences of creed or political organization, are essentially one in culture, one in tendency, one in influence.
>
> (Marsh 1860)

In 1921, there was a government enquiry into 'The teaching of English in England', resulting in 'The Newbolt Report' (Board of Education 1921). One of the aims it advocated was reducing class distinctions by teaching children 'First systematic training in the sounded speech of standard English, to secure correct pronunciation and clear articulation: second, systematic training in the use of standard English, to secure clearness and correctness both in oral expression and in writing' (Ch.1 para 13). The desire to see English in schools as a means of unifying the population is quite explicit: 'We believe that such an education based upon the English language and literature would have important social, as well as personal, results; it would have a unifying tendency' (Ch.1 para 15). In 1986, Kenneth Baker, who was the Secretary of State for Education in Margaret Thatcher's cabinet, introduced the National Curriculum 'as a way of increasing our social coherence. ... The cohesive role of the national curriculum will provide our society with a greater sense of identity' (Baker, *Guardian*, 16.9.87, quoted in Johnson 1991). Standard English is envisaged in this project as 'a proper model of the language' to be included in a 'national agreement on the aims and objectives of English teaching in schools' (DES Press Notice 16.1.87).

Some linguists and applied linguists have tried to contribute their expertise as these policies have developed. (Widdowson, for example, sat on the Kingman Committee and contributed a 'note of reservation' to its final report; see also Bauer and Trudgill 1998, Bourne and Bloor 1989, Cameron 1995, Carter 1994, Graddol and Swann 1988, Milroy and Milroy 1991.) There have been some minor concessions to this expertise, such as the commissioning of two linguists to correct the worst misconceptions perpetrated in the Glossary accompanying the National Literacy Strategy (although in its on-line version only). One of the changes made in the 'expanded' (not 'revised') version will serve to illustrate the extent of change in descriptions of the standard variety. The definition of 'double negative' is given in the first, printed glossary as follows: 'the use of two negative forms which effectively cancel each other out, as in: *I never took nothing*' (p.78). In the second, on-line version, the definition reads: 'In non-standard English, a double negative may be used. For example: *We didn't see nobody. I never took nothing*. Such double negatives are not acceptable in **standard English**. The equivalent standard forms would be: *We didn't see anybody. I didn't take anything.*'

Despite such modifications, the policies have largely retained the commonsense, prescriptivist conception of English grammar which has influenced education for so long. In 2000, procedures were instituted to ensure compliance of 'trainee' teachers with this official version of language description, in the form of an exit test which all intending teachers must pass if they are to attain qualified teacher status. The specification for these national, computerized, centrally marked 'literacy tests' includes a section on the knowledge of grammar on which 'trainees' are to be tested, which reads as follows:

> **grammar** – required to ensure that trainees can demonstrate that they have sufficient grammatical knowledge to correct their own and others' grammatical errors, e.g.: recognising incorrect/correct usage of grammar generally and editing appropriately ...[1]
>
> http://www.tta.gov.uk/training/skillstests/literacy/
> content/grammar.htm

Different views of language = different discourses?

At another point in the history of events we have been outlining, an attack on what was seen as the abandonment by educators of standard English was published by Honey as *The Language Trap* (1983). Graddol and Swann (1988) provide an account of the debate which followed, examining details of some correspondence between Honey and the linguist Crystal, as well as press coverage of the debate and allegations on both sides that participants' positions had been misrepresented. Graddol and Swann suggest in their article that the populist interpretations of the issues, as represented in the press, are part of one kind of discourse, while linguists' accounts are associated with another. These discourses are then in competition as language education becomes embroiled in a wider political debate. Crowley (1991: 10–11) suggests similarly that it is important to identify and challenge the 'discourse of "proper English"' which holds that there is ... a given, settled and inflexible cultural identity in which language has a crucial determining role'. It is the aim of his collection of writings about 'proper English', he says, 'to demonstrate the ways in which the "fiction" of "true", "real", "proper" English has been constructed'.

As will be clear from what has gone before, we do not think that 'competing discourses' constitute an explanation, and indeed in the discussions to which linguists have themselves contributed there is usually a recognition of the need to distinguish between 'fact' and 'opinion'. For example, Wardhaugh (1999) observes in a discussion of the traditional grammar books which are often consulted as arbiters of 'correct' English: 'In every other serious discipline the practitioners respect their data. Only in language study do many of those who seek to influence others turn their backs on data in favor of opinion' (p.129). Cameron (1995) brings a further dimension to understanding the difference between 'lay' accounts of language and linguists' accounts. With reference to a range of closely analysed case studies, she demonstrates that, although there are discursive differences in what non-linguists and linguists say about language, the issue is not simply about differing discourses. 'The state of the language', she says, is a concern shared by a wide range of people, and

> it produces discourse in which opinions – not to say prejudices – do not merely substitute for facts, but are triumphantly paraded as somehow superior to facts; discourse in which it seems that what linguists *know* about language can simply be dismissed, because linguists do not *care* about language.
>
> (p.xii)

Graddol and Swann identify a similar disjuncture in their analysis of the Honey controversy, where press debate suggests that the 'commonsense' approach is highly valued, while specialist knowledge is represented as irrelevant obfuscation. 'Very many language-users', says Cameron,

> hold passionate convictions about what is right in language, and conversely about what is wrong with it. Unfortunately, the strength of passion with which verbal hygienists express their views and pursue their goals is not often matched by the strength of their arguments.
>
> (Cameron 1995: 236)

From all these accounts, a problem that emerges is the contrast between the linguists' concern with facts, evidence and objectivity and lay actors' concerns about attitudes, values and opinions. Our own approach to understanding this contrast offers a somewhat different perspective from that which sees it as mere variation in the description of language, expressed in different discourses.

A social theoretical explanation

We would wish to stand by the claim that social theory is necessary for an adequate explanation of social action, and that there is good reason to defend linguists' epistemic authority: in other words, linguists know more about the nature of language than those who have not studied language. This does not make the linguist a better human being, or more intelligent, or better placed to make political decisions, but it is a stronger claim about his or her authority to speak about language and its properties – and, in the case of the applied linguist, how it may be taught and learned – than are the claims about alternative discourses. Policy about language in education is declared in language, carried out through language, and intended to operate on language. In no other discipline is the object of study – and of policy – also the medium through which it is discussed, by all parties. This can easily lead to the conflation of practice (being a language user) with different kinds of authority (being a politician, with constitutional authority, or a linguist, with epistemic authority). One of the ways in which a variegated social ontology helps to disambiguate concepts of different kinds, such as these, is by identifying the properties of 'culture' as well as those of 'structure' and of 'agency'. Language may be conceptualized as one element of the cultural stratum of the social world, a resource available to, but pre-existing, its speakers, and some of its systematic properties were discussed in a previous section. Speakers are very adept at deploying its resources in pursuit of their interests, and in any actual interaction both the systematic, structural properties of language and the agential, creative properties of speakers continually combine to produce new meanings, new relationships and emergent linguistic products (in the form of new written texts, and genres of text, for example).

The events discussed here were outcomes of human agency. Specific individuals made decisions and acted upon them, and the kind of actors with whom we have been most concerned are those whose actions have an extensive impact. In 1987, the then Secretary of State for Education, Kenneth Baker, announced that he had been 'struck by a particular gap' in pupils' knowledge about the English language. It is conceivable that many private citizens (employers, teachers, parents, maybe pupils themselves) had already experienced a similar kind of concern, but a key difference between their reaction to any perceived shortcomings in school pupils' knowledge about the

English language and Mr Baker's reaction is that he was enabled by his structural location to cause changes in policy to happen, whereas most people do not have this power.

Baker, of course, had his own individual history: a particular experience of education, certain literary tastes, relationships, ambitions, in short, his 'psychobiography' (see Chapter 6). These individual qualities and characteristics are likely to have influenced his political priorities, but it is his occupation of a role within particular social relations which made it possible for him to instigate a national enquiry into the teaching of English language. The office of Secretary of State existed before Baker assumed it, and continued to exist after he left the government. It is an office which has meaning only in relation to other components of the social structure of which it is itself one component. Members of 'governments' exist *in relation to* the populations they govern. Thus, one property of structures is their relational nature, and although the details of this relationship may change over time, it remains an enduring property of this analytically distinct kind of entity.

Government offices outlast the entire lifetime of any individual, despite the fact that they require living individuals to occupy them and to take actions from within those positions. In this sense, structures have a temporal priority over individuals, and different temporal modalities are relevant to structure and to agency. Within Baker's political career, his role as Secretary of State for Education lasted only a few years, but the projects he pursued as a member of Thatcher's cabinet were heavily influenced by a number of contextual factors operating on government in the UK in the 1980s, and arrangements that were set up during his time in office provide a context for subsequent holders of the office, including the current incumbent.

By 'contextual factors' we mean things like: existing legislation (e.g. the Education Acts of 1902, 1944 and 1962); the fact that many teachers were already organized as members of trade unions, which themselves had existing relationships (and disagreements) with other components of the trade union movement; popular views about 'good' grammar and its relationship to 'good' conduct, and the promulgation of such views in the press and other mass media, and so on. These factors provide a context for attempts to change practice in schools, and while some of them may have helped to pave the way for the kind of change Baker imagined, others provided significant resistance.

Among the properties of social structures, then, is their endurance beyond the actions or intentions of individuals. If we are parents, for example, in a country such as the UK, we are obliged to ensure that our children attend school, facing penalties if we fail to do so. We can seek to exert some degree of choice about *which* school the children will attend, and we can even decide to provide alternative schooling at home, but we cannot without fear of sanction ignore the institutions of our society which contribute to the context of our own actual experience of parenting. Archer (1995) alludes to people's routine recognition of this 'social fact':

> An inescapable part of our inescapably social condition is to be aware of its constraints, sanctions and restrictions on our ambitions – be they for good or evil. Equally, we acknowledge certain social blessings such as medication, transportation and education: without their enablements our lives and hopes would both be vastly more circumscribed.
>
> (p.1)

Whatever Baker's personal vision or individual charisma, he could act only within the social context obtaining at the time. As Archer continues:

> ... we delude one another by the pretence that society is simply what we choose to make it and make of it, now or in any generation, for generically 'society' is that which nobody wants in exactly the form they find it and yet it resists both individual and collective efforts at transformation – not necessarily by remaining unchanged but altering to become something else which still conforms to no one's ideal.
>
> (*ibid.*: 2)

At the point at which Baker made his intervention, there already existed a range of perceptions about: the validity of current practice in the teaching of English; the desirability of different sorts of change to this practice; who was best placed to decide on and bring about such change; and, crucially, the nature of language and how it is learned. Baker did not create these conflicting views, but his actions sparked off a series of sociocultural interactions which themselves contributed to the context for the further reforms which followed. In this account, human agency is crucial, but people's actions are always contextualized by structural relations. The Education Secretary who took up office in the Labour government which then came to power a decade later did so in a context heavily shaped by the events in which Baker had been involved. The minister concerned was David Blunkett, who demonstrated his commitment to the National Literacy Strategy in 1998 by pledging to resign if 'targets' for pupils' test performance were missed. The course set for policy about written English under the Thatcher government changed in some respects but remained remarkably stable in others. (Blunkett subsequently became Home

175

Secretary, and the subject of the English language resurfaced in this later stage of his career, as we shall see.)

The final topic of this chapter is a consideration of the international social context for some debates about language varieties in which there are striking similarities with arguments put forward by protagonists reported here. In particular, we would point to a significant overlap between arguments – some of which were considered above and others which will be considered presently – that treat language policies as an aspect of social governance, and more radical arguments that are concerned with the preservation of languages from extinction or suppression. It is this congruence of views about the nature of languages, what languages themselves can achieve, and their relations to 'national' cultures that is considered in the next section.

Global and threatened languages

Home Office ministers believe that immigrants settled in Britain who apply for British citizenship should be able to demonstrate a 'modest grasp' of English. ... 'If we are going to have social cohesion we have got to develop a sense of identity and a sense of belonging,' said Mr Blunkett yesterday.

(guardianonline.co.uk December 10, 2001)

Surprisingly, perhaps, Blunkett's claims about the unifying potential of the English language find echoes in the discussion of global and threatened languages. For example, consider the following two extracts:

(i) ... languages are expressions of identity: a nation without a language is like a nation without a heart ... languages are repositories of history.

(ii) Every society, every nation is unique. ... It has its own past, its own story, its own memories, its own ways, its own languages or ways of speaking, its own – dare I use the word – culture.

The first quotation is Headland (2002) summarizing Crystal's reasons for caring about language death (Crystal 2002), while the second is the Conservative politician Enoch Powell, quoted in Malik (2000). Both discourses, albeit for quite contrasting political reasons, draw on beliefs about language and identity which are inconsistent with the argument of this book.

Debates about global and threatened languages

A brief summary will have to suffice as a basis for the analysis which follows. Several writers have recently drawn attention to the fact that English teaching can be understood as not simply a pedagogic exchange, but rather as an international commodity with a massive turnover (Pennycook 1994b; Phillipson 1992; Tollefson 1991). The charge has been levelled against those involved in applied linguistics and English Language Teaching that they have, wittingly or not, been exporting their language and culture at the expense of indigenous languages and cultures. This process has been labelled 'linguistic imperialism', and is associated with 'linguicism', defined as 'ideologies and structures where language is the means for effecting or maintaining an unequal allocation of power and resources' (Phillipson 1992: 55). A parallel concern is with the recognition that, while the number of speakers of English is rapidly rising, the numbers of speakers of many other languages are dropping at a similar rate, with the result that approximately two languages a month cease to be spoken by anyone and are thus considered extinct. The processes which 'kill' a language may involve the deaths of its speakers or the prohibition of its use, giving rise to terms such as 'linguistic genocide' and 'linguicide', and, in respect of resistance to these processes, 'linguistic human rights' and 'language rights'. A third strand in the debate is the equivalence claimed between the loss of linguistic diversity and the loss of biodiversity as threats to the well-being of the entire planet.

While participants in these debates hold a range of views, their positions share some assumptions about the nature of language and about the relationship between language and agency. These assumptions are not always made explicit, and a series of metaphors, analogies and rhetorical devices has been deployed in this discourse, some of which obscure ontological claims which we believe are important.

Claims about the properties of languages

The English language, for example, has been characterized as potentially either 'a benevolent bonus or creeping cancer of modernity' (Phillipson 1992: 11, quoting Fishman). The biological metaphor recurs in this debate, sometimes leading to a reification of 'language' and an exaggeration of its properties. Thus, while likening endangered languages to endangered biological species is a seductive rhetorical device, it is deceptive if it leads us to equate the two kinds of things. *Contra* Nettle and Romaine, who claim that 'English, Spanish, French and so on are the monoculture crops of the cultural domain, and they balance just as their biological equivalents, wheat, rice and cattle do', we think it is important to acknowledge that cereals and animals are natural kinds, albeit ones which people have affected by farming them. Languages, on the other hand, are human products, which, as cultural emergent properties, differ in important ways from objects in the material, natural world (cf. Blommaert 2001c: 140). In our view much of the debate concerning language death and linguicide neglects this distinction, making extravagant claims about what language is, what it does and what it signifies.

For example, Phillipson (1992: 279) claims as 'an incontrovertible fact that English has a lot of resources' both 'material' and 'immaterial'. Crystal (2002: 44) claims that 'languages contribute to the sum of human knowledge'. It is not, of course, English *as a language* that has resources, but various groups of speakers of English who do. It is not languages *as languages* that contribute to knowledge, but rather human beings, whose knowledge is linguistically communicated. Rassool (2000) claims that language is the means by which groups of people name the world, and that 'in the process of naming, the world itself is transformed' (p.61). It is not the world which is transformed, however, but people's interpretations of the world, which may be modified by different ways of speaking about them. Global inequalities are not eradicated simply by redescribing them.

The analogy of linguistic diversity with biodiversity is also misleading. The species of animals and plants that are natural kinds, that maintain species boundaries by failing to interbreed, are 'diverse' in a different way from languages, which quite clearly do become intermingled, giving rise to new varieties. If they did not, the linguistic purists who seek to defend the boundaries of particular varieties (be these standard English or a threatened minority language) would be much less exercised than they are, since there would be no possibility of a contact language ('Species A') altering, or being altered by, any feature of another variety ('Species B'). Despite denials from the protagonists (see Skutnabb-Kangas *et al.* 2001), the very notion that varieties are under threat rests on a conceptualization of languages as homogeneous entities with naturally occurring boundaries.

It also entails some commitment to linguistic determinism, if the repositories of knowledge deemed to be realized in particular varieties are lost when the variety is lost. A non-relativistic view, however, recognizes the potential of translatability between languages. Thus while a variety that has separate lexical items to denote a wider range of phenomena – such as colours, or species of plants or animals – affords its speakers direct ways of conveying these meanings, a variety with fewer such distinctions obliges its speakers to take a more circuitous route to the same end, using many words to denote something which is conveyed by a single word in another language. However, so long as we recognize that human beings constitute one species rather than many, the concepts and knowledges expressed through the threatened variety can in principle be available to humanity at large. If such understanding is disregarded, this is likely to be because of the political, not linguistic, priorities of the powerful.

Claims about human groups

In rebutting the belief that linguistic diversity is not worth preserving, because '[i]t is, in short, a total myth that the sharing of a single language brings peace, whichever language it might be', Crystal (2002: 27–8) ironically seems to us to undermine one of his own arguments. From our perspective, no language has the power to 'bring' peace, social cohesion or cultural integration. Neither the strategy of creating a single language, nor of supporting endangered ones, is likely by itself to have a significant effect on social inequalities. It is a property of language that it is available to be mobilized by people who have a varied range of social interests (cf. Holborow 1999). These include people who want to portray the links between language and identity, language and culture, or language and nation in particular ways – but, once again, it is people who describe the world in this way, and not language which determines these links. Nettle and Romaine claim that 'a way of life disappears with the death of a language', but the claim that language is synonymous with way-of-life weakens, or even ruptures, the interplay between culture and agency by conflating the two.

Furthermore, because linguistic conformity indicates very little about social conformity, as we noted in Chapter 6, those who would seek to make a nation culturally homogeneous by seeking to impose linguistic homogeneity are unlikely to be successful. When speakers use any given language variety, they do not automatically and unequivocally proclaim their normative commitment to one particular set of cultural values or propositions. Indeed, speakers can play with and exploit the varieties in their repertoire, as several empirical studies have demonstrated (e.g. Rampton 1995b). Alternatively, linguistic conformity may be a favoured strategy for concealing and even advancing social dissidence. For example, you can choose to learn English in order to stand a greater chance of succeeding in your ambition to carry out acts of 'terrorism' against the English or American state.

A further source of disquiet is the congruence between the discourse of linguistic rights and that deployed by more conventional advocates of nationalism. As Blommaert (2001c: 137) observes, '... a program of ethnolinguistic pluralism is based on exactly the same ideology as the one it claims to combat' (see also Ashcroft 2001). This is manifest in a tendency in the linguistic rights discourse to reify the nation, where 'nation' is linked with ethnicity and notions of shared history – what has been identified as 'ethnonationalism' (Connor 1994). Vuolab (2000: 13), for example, asserts that 'The mother tongue is a chain that binds us to our own history. ... Our personal duty is to transfer the mother tongue to the next generation.' A presupposition here is that there is an identifiable, homogeneous entity called the mother tongue, and that there is a single history to which 'we' are 'bound' by language itself.

Myhill (1999: 34) has drawn attention to one significant problem with tying language to 'identity' in this way. The belief that there is some 'inherent emotional and spiritual connection between a person and his/her native language' may conflict with 'the ideology of *language and territory*'. For example, if English is in the blood of its native speakers, the 'identity' argument would give them the right to take it with them into any supposedly non-English territory; conversely, according to the 'territory' argument, if a threatened minority language is associated with geographical region, its use would necessarily be restricted to this small area. Both such logical extensions of the arguments would presumably be unappealing to champions of language rights. Fraser Gupta (1997), among others, has also raised some objections to such claims:

> Does everyone have a mother tongue that they can identify with? People who are ethnically mixed, people whose ancestors have undergone language shift, and those who are bilingual from infancy often have a very weak sense of identification with a 'mother tongue'.

What this observation points to, in our terms, is a recognition of the salience of the psychobiographical domain, and of the interplay between this and the structured social relations which lead to changing linguistic contexts. Critics also have reservations about the retrospection involved in appealing to culture as unchanging, 'fossilized' [*ibid.*], 'a museum piece' (Chew 1999), 'nineteenth-century Romanticism' (Malik 2000).

Access to linguistic resources – structure

This fossilized view of culture, in emphasizing its supposed homogeneity, overlooks the reality, discussed in Chapter 6, of how access to cultural and linguistic resources is structured, in two senses. Firstly, we need to recognize that there are deep and abiding social divisions among speakers of the same language. As Holborow (1999), for example, has pointed out, it is dangerous to equate interests with countries. Critical of Phillipson for failing to explore 'how national states are themselves enmeshed in global capitalism' (p.76), she recognizes that, while there may be good arguments for the championing of local languages, it is important not to overlook how they can be 'used by local elites for their own purposes' (p.80). Material resources are unequally distributed, and this inequality is linguistically and symbolically mediated. Thus speakers are not equally placed to realize their linguistic assets as 'capital' (Bourdieu 1986), when the 'correct' accent, for example, or native speaker facility in the dominant language is a pre-requisite for social and occupational mobility. This suggests that the notion of a shared 'mother tongue' as the basis for access to a shared history is a far more fractured and contested notion than is acknowledged by the writers we have been discussing (a fact that is similarly obscured by politicians who appeal to 'the national interest' and 'the national way of life'). Secondly, there is the issue of access to World 3. Like the supporters of 'linguistic human rights', we are very much opposed to the barriers which prevent any of the world's citizens from moving around the cultural realm. *Access to* this knowledge is via language – usually written language, and often one of the most widely spoken language varieties, such as English. 'Access to English parallels access to the fruits of society', as Holborow (1999: 58) puts it. But the distribution of this access is a political issue, not an issue of either the nature of language or the nature of knowledge. This is why arguments in favour of 'cosmopolitanism' need a political critique of the current global order and its vast inequities. Such a critique may involve the support of minority language rights, where this is politically progressive.

Human choices and purposes – agency

It is important to emphasize once again that it is human beings – and not languages – which do things in the social world. Human beings, in a socially differentiated world, necessarily pursue complex and conflicting interests. It is these human beings who determine how, and which, linguistic resources remain vital elements of social mediation. Languages will survive only insofar as they have a function in furthering people's social interests (or obstructing those of others), and what is functional for one group of people pursuing particular sets of interests may well not be functional for another group, or for the same group if they choose to pursue different interests. It is important to note here that functionality is not synonymous with instrumentality, and our claims do not rest on a reductive conception of language as merely a channel of communication. There is a wide spectrum of functions which a language may have for speakers which can serve to sustain it. People may use a particular variety predominantly for the interpersonal function of expressing solidarity with a social group; it may have a powerful emotional connotation for them, or be significant in language play or other creative and artistic domains (cf. Cook 2000).

Conclusion

In this chapter, we have analysed four topics in order to set out further our view of the properties and powers of language in relation to social structure and human agency. We have argued that languages are cultural emergent properties and as such are: irreducible to either human agency (that is, languages are able to shape the context of social action) or to the material world (that is, languages are pre-eminently social, which is why we have rejected the biodiversity analogy); partially autonomous of individuals (that is, languages have some properties which are peculiar to them); causally influential in shaping the contexts of human action and linguistic choice.

We have explored how the political struggles between groups with different interests are affected by the second order emergent property which is writing; how these impact on education policy; and how they lead to the spread of some language varieties at the expense of others. We have argued that an analytical distinction between languages, agency and structure facilitates an understanding of, and response to, these issues which brings together key insights from both social theory and applied linguistics.

In the final chapter we explore in detail the methodological implications of this position for research in applied linguistics.

Note

1. The tender document from which this text was taken is, at the time of writing, no longer available on-line. However, the inherent prescriptivism is indicated in the guidance for test takers at http://www.tta.gov.uk/training/skillstests/literacy/content/grammar.htm (accessed 19.09.03).

8 A social realist approach to research in applied linguistics

Introduction

In previous chapters, we have outlined the contribution of a social scientific approach to a range of areas of the applied linguistic enterprise. In this final chapter, we bring together the key ideas we have discussed in an exploration of their potential role in the design of research studies in the discipline.

In Chapter 4 we suggested that research in the most 'well-populated' region of applied linguistics – the teaching and learning of additional languages – has been dominated by an approach which draws on traditional concepts such as falsifiable hypotheses, the identification of dependent, independent and confounding variables, and the measurement and quantification of salient phenomena. We also noted developments in theoretical and methodological debates in applied linguistics which challenge this tradition, and advocate alternatives, including relativist perspectives, qualitative and ethnographic methods and social contructionist assumptions. These two broad alternatives are often presented in open opposition to each other (Block 1996; Gregg *et al.* 1997; Long 1993), but there is a third category of researchers who are not wholly convinced by either. We would locate ourselves amongst them, and will set out in what follows some suggestions for an approach to research which is consistent with the social theory we have been elaborating.

We would like to have illustrated the approach we advocate with references to specific research studies in applied linguistics, but we know of very few as yet which have been developed in accordance with the most contemporary versions of realist social theory (one exception being Belz 2002). Where we are able to do so, we cite studies of direct interest to applied linguistics which seem to us to have elements in common with our own approach, and which have responded in innovative ways to the challenges posed by the two broad traditions described in Chapter 4. At other points, we cite examples of how researchers in a range of different social science disciplines have sought to adopt a realist approach, and here we identify as far as we are able the concepts and themes which may be at least partially transferable to applied linguistics. In other cases, we simply suggest how the kinds of studies often undertaken within applied linguistics and sociolinguistics might be modified if account were to be taken methodologically of the theoretical position we have outlined.

Summary of key claims

The need for *social* theory in applied linguistics

As we have noted, applied linguistics is concerned with language in use. Since using language is a social practice, accounts of language in use must be informed by sociological insights, including social theory and social scientific research methods.

The social world as stratified

The realist model of sociology which we have been advocating entails a recognition of the stratified nature of the social world. That is, the social world comprises structure, agency and culture (including language as a cultural emergent property), and each of these has distinctive properties and powers. We have, following Layder, further distinguished between the two 'domains' associated more with agency (psychobiography and situated activity), and the two associated more readily with structure (social setting and contextual resources). We suggest that for the purposes of analysing and researching social phenomena (including language use), it is possible – and indeed desirable – to distinguish between the different domains, in accordance with their different properties and characteristics.

The limits of the empirical

A further implication of this stratified view of social reality is that its more structural elements are the most abstract and furthest removed from people's direct experience. Thus some aspects of the social world are not directly observable, ruling out approaches to research which rely too heavily on the empirical. To be consistent with our position, research entails *discovering* the world as opposed to *revealing* it. That is to say, the very abstractness of social structural relations makes their theoretical apprehension both more critical and at the same time more fallible. Appeals to empirical evidence in these domains must always be indirect.

The centrality of theory

Many approaches to research rest on an assumption that the social world is already constituted, and can be uncovered, or revealed, by the research process. From this perspective, it is in this process of uncovering that theory has a role, and adjudication between theories is on the basis of how closely they correspond to an already constituted social reality. In contrast to this, we favour an approach which accords some relevance to the role of theory in the *constitution* of the social world. This means that our advocacy of theory is not of the sort whereby the researcher simply looks for empirical data to confirm a prior theory, since how we grasp the world theoretically will in important ways shape what is to count as empirical data. Moreover, as Layder has pointed out, '... if all fieldwork data is interpreted in terms of a prior framework favoured by the researcher then it will lead to a blinkered outlook' (1993: 52).

The relationship between theory and observation in social research is a difficult one. In important ways our theories about the world favour certain observations and rule out others as the basis for confirming or disconfirming evidence; that is, what is to count as evidence is in part defined by the theoretical concepts we are employing. A greater role than is often recognized is therefore played by epistemology in the analysis of the social world (Layder 1990). This might seem to suggest a degree of indeterminacy which is inconsistent with our claim that the world is independent of our cognizing experience. However, we can both acknowledge an independently existing world and yet hold that the representation of it in theoretical terms is provisional and fallible, a matter, as we say, of discovery rather than revelation. There cannot then be a direct appeal to neutral observation as a means of 'proving' or 'disproving' a particular theory. This does not mean, of course, that all theories are equally accurate in their representations of the social world, nor that we cannot make judgements about their veridicality.

A further point to recognize is that the social world itself is partly constituted symbolically. Meanings cannot be observed directly, they have to be inferred from the observation of behaviour, but such inference is always from a position within a theory or a set of theoretical concepts.

A relational view of the world

Since social relations are not observable, and because they are symbolically managed, epistemology has a critical role in social research.

The researcher's task cannot therefore be reduced to the identification of discrete elements – or variables – in the empirically observable world, for two reasons. Firstly, any supposed 'variable' within the social world cannot be taken as empirically given, and cannot be accessed in a theory-neutral way. Thus studies which isolate variables such as ethnicity, say, or distribution of income are likely to be misleading insofar as they neglect to identify the theoretical claims on which they rest: whose definition of 'ethnic group'? based on what criteria? what is to count as 'income'? how is it to be measured? While observable patterns may tell us something, the important part of the researcher's task is to specify what they tell us, rather than to identify the constituents of the patterns. Secondly, patterns are relationally generated, since the world is quintessentially relational. That is, it is the *combination* of the powers and properties of things in the world – and not their individual, isolable operation – that makes the world what it is. 'Social phenomena are what they are', observe Danermark *et al.* (1997: 97), 'by virtue of the internal relations they have to other phenomena.' Thus it does violence to the phenomena in which we are interested (such as the situated language practices of individuals and groups) to attempt to sever parts of the social world (such as the motivation of different language learners, for example) from their relational contexts (such as their relations with each other and their structural location in a particular geo-political moment). As Layder (1993) notes: '... structural features of society are not best thought of simply as measurable variables' (p.29), so that power relations, for example, 'are best thought of as mechanisms which underlie and generate routine activities' (p.30).

Methodological implications

As the focus of this chapter is practical research, it is important to note that the kind of social realism to which we are committed is not tied to a prescriptive methodological programme and is compatible with a range of research methods. A distinctively realist position entails, as a minimum, a recognition of the relational nature of the world, and of its independence from our cognizing experience. An explicitly realist methodological position would seek to employ research methods which are able to investigate a world with the characteristics we have identified in the foregoing.

In the following sections of this chapter, we take each of the claims in this section and enlarge on their significance for the conduct of research in applied linguistics.

Why applied linguistic research questions need social theory

In Chapter 1 we offered a broad interpretation of what constitutes applied linguistics, citing the areas listed by Cook (2003). To complement that list, we reproduce here the list of strands within which the American Association for Applied Linguistics invited papers for its 2003 conference. Again, the discipline, as indicated by such a large international conference, clearly incorporates a wide range of areas, namely: 'Analysis of discourse & interaction; Applied linguistics research methodology; Assessment & evaluation; Bilingual, immersion, heritage, and language minority education; Language acquisition & language attrition; Language & ideology; Language & learner characteristics; Language & technology; Language, cognition & the brain; Language, culture, & socialization; Reading, writing & literacy; Second & foreign language pedagogy; Sociolinguistics; Text analysis; Translation & interpretation' http://www.aaal.org/aaal2003/call.html.

Obviously we cannot present in just one chapter the full implications of the social scientific approach we have been outlining for practical research in all these areas, so instead we have begun by offering some general principles which we believe are of potential relevance for this wide range of interests. To make the discussion less abstract and general, we now present a series of questions which cover the kinds of research problems that the applied linguist might wish to address. These questions are composites, adapted – to indicate broad areas of research – from the kinds of topics which we have encountered in the journals, as supervisors of graduate students, as participants at academic conferences and so on. The questions we cite, of course, do not preclude consideration of the larger issues of interest to applied linguistics as a whole, but are relevant to the small-scale, time-limited research contexts which are familiar to many graduate students and practising academics.

- What works to make English schoolchildren learn foreign languages better?
- Why, on a standardized L2 test, do students in Group A achieve consistently better than students in Group B?
- What kinds of communicative practices characterize public campaigns in health-care promotion, and (how) do these lead to conceptualizations of particular conditions, such as HIV/AIDS?
- How is the relationship between English as a world language and England's history as an imperial power manifest in the language policies in a particular country?

- What constitutes coherence in discourse, and what should learners be taught that will make more coherent their sustained contributions in an interview conducted to assess their competence in English?
- Should advanced learners of English in Chinese universities be encouraged to make use of the more independent style of learning prevalent in English and American universities, and if so, how?
- What are the differences between business letters written in English by business professionals in different countries?
- What are the similarities and differences in the requesting behaviour of the speakers of two different languages (such as Japanese and English, for example)?
- What guidelines should be developed for the protection and development of the cultures and languages of ethnic minorities in a specific country?
- What challenges face bilingual speakers who are called on to interpret between the police and minority language speaker detainees?
- What are the characteristics of synchronous computer-mediated communication among a group of advanced learners of English?

In the sections which follow, we shall make reference to these questions and how studies aimed at answering them might be designed in accordance with the claims about the social world which we adumbrated in the first section. The observation to be made at this point is that all of these questions, as *applied* linguistic questions, depict some form of *social* interaction which by its very nature must be relational, and which will involve people pursuing their interests and projects within social contexts and settings.

The stratified social world and applied linguistic research

The majority of the questions we have cited as examples of applied linguistic research are most obviously focused on the domain of situated activity. This is understandable, since it is situated activity which is the most directly accessible domain of the social world. Such a focus is not in itself problematic for a social realist approach, but it is important to be alert to the limitations of research that concentrates exclusively on this – or indeed any – one domain. We have claimed above that the isolation of specific variables does violence to the relational nature of the social reality under investigation. Similar distortions are likely to result from research approaches which assume an independence of the domains most concerned with agency from the structural domains of social settings and contextual resources. Thus in the absence of the explicit theorizing we propose, it is possible that studies which are most obviously about situated activity – lessons in foreign language classrooms, instances of speakers making requests, exchanges of business letters and so on – confine themselves, in their formulation of hypotheses and collection of data, to only this domain. On our account, the embedded nature of the four domains of the social world requires a research design which takes all of them into account.

One illustration of some research which does implicitly acknowledge the interrelated nature of the different social domains is provided by a comparative study of primary schools in five different locations by Alexander (2000). The 'empirical core' (p.2) of Alexander's study is a comparison of primary education in England, France, India, Russia and the United States, and the analysis is structured at three levels: systems, schools and classrooms. Although its principal focus is on primary school pedagogy, it has direct relevance to applied linguistics because of its recognition of the critical significance of classroom discourse. Language is central to the analysis – as the medium of learning, and thus, in our terms, in the domains of psychobiography and situated activity – but also as a contextual resource:

> By being the principle [*sic*] tool of acculturation language provides a window on culture and in a comparative study to compare how language is used in the classroom is to achieve some insight into the values and worldview of the wider society. ... [I]t seems implausible to suggest that the development of language and the development of social structure are independent and unconnected. ... [I]f we listen to what teachers and children in these five countries say to each other we may understand a little more about what it is to be English, American, Russian, Indian or French. Values will out; identity too, perhaps.
>
> (p. 432)

Alexander conceptualizes the schooling process as involving macro, meso and micro levels, claiming that this is necessary because 'pedagogy connects the apparently self-contained act of teaching with culture, structure and mechanisms of social control' (p.540). He does not elaborate on the properties of the different strata – our account involves a recognition that the differences are not just a matter of scale – nor on the irreducibility of structure, culture and agency; but the empirical work and analysis are entirely consistent with these theoretical claims. Alexander explores both the political and the economic histories of the countries studied, and series of classroom interactions, finding continuities which would seem necessarily to link structure and agency. We shall have more to say about this study in later sections, but its relevance here is in the demonstration it provides of the interaction between domains. Each specific example of classroom interaction ('situated activity', in our terms) is presented within the whole study as explicable partly in terms of aspects of the other domains. Alexander (*ibid.*: 4) identifies a requirement to:

> keep the discussion constantly on the move between micro and macro, school and state, classroom and culture. ... [T]he theory of pedagogy towards which I work depends on an understanding of how nation, school and classroom are intertwined. An account of primary education that neglects this relationship does not take us very far.

So, while, of course, the applied linguistic researcher will be concerned with situated activity (that is, with interviews aimed at assessing language proficiency, or on-line discussions, or encounters between police, detainees and interpreters and so on), we would advocate an awareness also of the relevance of differential distribution of funding for education, the history of relations between national governments – and, indeed, the biographical trajectories of individual participants in these social interactions.

The limits of the empirical in applied linguistic research

Just as we have noted that the majority of the questions we have cited as representing applied linguistic research are likely to be most obviously located in the domain of situated activity, we also suggest that the kind of evidence which is most obviously adduced in answering such questions is empirical evidence. Thus the researcher who wants to know how speakers of a minority language feel about its preservation may interview some of them as a source of data; a comparison of different teaching methods will probably collect test results from students in Group A and those in Group B; the researcher who is interested in coherence in the 'long turns' which candidates are required to produce as part of their test of English language proficiency is likely to collect examples of this speech in the form of recordings and transcripts.

Such data sets are empirical in the sense that what they contain is observable, but of course the real interests of the researchers are frequently in phenomena which are unobservable, for which the data have to serve as traces. So it is important to remember that data which are thought to be 'empirical' are often something other than a collection of instances of the phenomenon under investigation.

Interviews about people's beliefs and attitudes are not only problematic for researchers in being themselves both a research method and a form of social interaction; they also must be deemed to convert something which can never be directly perceived (an attitude) into something which can (a statement or response). This is one of the strengths of ethnography as a means of finding out what people actually do (when and how do they use the variety?) as opposed to what they say they believe (do you think Variety X should be on the school curriculum?). Even so, the behaviour of the speakers under observation still provides evidence only of the empirical, and we refer the reader to Chapter 3, where we discussed the distinction drawn in realist accounts between the empirical, the actual and the real. The implications of this include the fact that accounts which reduce a phenomenon to its empirical manifestations will be seriously misleading. This can be illustrated by reference to the language learners whose test scores are analysed by the researcher comparing two or more teaching methods. By our account, these scores can only be traces of language proficiency: they are not that proficiency in themselves.

Measurement and theory are thus imbricated in a powerful way. For the positivist, measurement provides direct, unmediated information about the world, and its problems lie largely in the area of technical accuracy. From our position, by contrast, measurement must always be understood as a theoretical tool, one by means of which we 'translate' the world into scientifically significant descriptions. It is on the basis of these that we then develop causal accounts. A recognition that '... measurement in social research will always be ... an act of translation' (Pawson 1989: 287) entails a rejection of the notion that measurement is a direct description of the social world – or indeed of the natural world either. One example used by Pawson is the measurement of temperature. The temperature of a physical substance cannot be directly observed, but changes in its temperature are measured indirectly, by observing changes in a measuring instrument, such as a thermometer, which have been devised by previous scientists to 'translate' the presence of heat into something else which is visible, such as the movement of mercury along a marked tube. In response to the recognition that 'measurement is not simply a matter of observation but also of conceptualization' (*ibid.*: 40), there are those who advocate abandoning all forms of empirical measurement as necessarily partial, relativistic and 'socially constructed'. Our position lies somewhere between these two extremes, besieged, as Byrne (2002: 15) provocatively expresses it, by two opposing 'gangs', 'the reductionists' and 'the innumerates':

> The first gang can count but don't know what they are counting, why they are counting, or what to do with what they have counted when they have counted it. The second can't count, won't count, and assert that counting is a vile and perverse activity which ought not to be allowed.

We seek approaches to research which take account of the empirical, but are not limited to it. From this position, we point out a further limitation of empirical data, namely that there are many phenomena of interest to the applied linguist which are inherently refractory to empirical investigation. These include those aspects of the social, cultural, linguistic world which we have described as 'relational' above. To take another example, and one which has a bearing on many branches of social research, how can empirical data shed light on questions about the relationship between social class membership and differential educational attainment?

The initial problem which confronts the researcher who is interested in the significance of social class within some social process, such as benefiting from an education programme, for example, is how 'class' is to be rendered in practical research terms. It is not directly observable – a person's social class membership is not something the researcher can see – so how does he or she utilize class when studying phenomena such as, for instance, making progress towards learning an additional language? Two of the strategies most common across the social sciences draw so heavily on the empirical that they are arguably empiricist, though in different ways.

The better established approach is to theorize class as an attribute, something which people 'have'. Quantitative studies in this tradition may either seek to 'control for' social class, by including only subjects whose measure of this attribute is deemed to be within the same kind of range, or they may investigate how the possession of different degrees of the attribute correlates with different outcomes. This approach can be illustrated by reference to one example of an applied linguistic study in the quantitative tradition. In the research by Fazio and Stevens (1994), cited in Chapter 4, social class was identified as potentially relevant in differential patterns of achievement in French by 'minority children' immigrating to Canada. The schools attended by the children were classified as being of 'low' or 'middle-high' socioeconomic status. This variable 'was determined by the Four

Factor Index of Social Status developed by Hollingshead (1975). The four factors used in the calculation of SES are: occupation ...; education ...; sex ...; and marital status ...' (p.426). Our disagreement with this kind of approach is that it takes variate traces of complex social relations and conflates these with the relations themselves. There is then a loss of ontological depth as the distinction between the world as it is and the world as it appears to us is collapsed. This is not to argue that a study which sets out to measure the correlations between levels of income, say, and indications of educational attainment has no value. It is to claim, though, that the approach taken in such studies does not constitute a measure of social class: it may provide us with traces of the operation of class processes, but the significant challenge in research terms is to connect the traces with the processes, and this means moving beyond the empirical.

The alternative approach we might classify as 'experiential'. 'Class', in this younger tradition, may be theorized not so much as a given attribute as a possession which people use to perform in the world. An example from applied linguistics is provided by Rampton (2002) in his analysis of young people deploying differently valorized accentual varieties of English, in this case stylizations of 'Cockney' versus 'posh', to convey both 'class awareness' and 'class critique'. Again, insofar as this approach reduces social class to what speakers do and are aware of – which, we might add, provides us with a different sort of 'trace' – it has the same kind of effect as the first approach discussed. But now it is experience which is taken as the empirical element – the means by which we know class.

Thus, while the quantitative approach indicates traces of structural distributions in the patterns it identifies, it does not provide evidence of how social class relations are experienced by people themselves. By contrast, the interpretive approach indicates how social actors experience social class processes, but has little to say about the structural features of these. What the approaches share, however, is an emphasis on empirical data, be they aggregated in the form of levels of income or individualized in the form of utterances spoken.

As we have indicated, applied linguistics shares with many other social science disciplines a need to respond to wider debates about how we can know the social world, and, in broad terms, it also participates in the struggle between methodologies which are more inclined towards measurement and those which are more inclined towards interpretation. Debates in the journals suggest that there can be a productive relationship between theory and practice, including both theory about applied linguistics and applied linguistic practices (such as language teaching), and theories about the nature of the social world and the practical challenge of how it may be researched. A recent review of health-care communication as 'a problematic site for applied linguistic research', for example (Candlin and Candlin 2003), reports on how qualitative and quantitative approaches have been combined, and how applied linguists concerned with the study of health-care communication have drawn on studies undertaken by researchers in other academic disciplines as well as those by health-care practitioners in the course of their own work.

Our own position stresses the links between theory and the empirical world, seeking to steer between an approach in which the world tells us, as it were, what theories to have, so that 'the whole thrust and meaning of theory is irresistibly driven by the empirical world as it appears to our senses' (Layder 1993: 61) and an alternative approach which suggests that the connection between the empirical world and theory formation is arbitrary or contingent; that is that theories can be of little help with developing knowledge of the empirical world. Our belief that the world extends beyond our empirical knowledge of it does not imply or entail a reduction of the empirical simply to a portal through which access to 'deeper reality' is enabled. The empirical, in other words, is no less an element of reality for being directly present in ways that other elements of the social world are not. Our central point here is that forms of measurement and classification are critical to research which seeks to explicate the connections between the empirical, the actual and the real dimensions of social relations. The aim, then, is an elaboration of the kind of '... theory which is guided rather than limited by empirical evidence' (*ibid.*: 63).

The centrality of theory in applied linguistic research

Many of the sets of data (interview and questionnaire responses, test scores, recordings of speech in assessment interviews and so on) are not in themselves the phenomena we are trying to investigate, and yet these data sets are useful for research. This is because the empirical data to which we do have access are suffused with theories about categories, measurement and knowledge. All too often, however, these theories are not made explicit, and the emphasis in research design is on the technical adequacy of the questionnaire, sample size or consistency in interview style among researchers, rather than on the theoretical adequacy of the research categories themselves.

Let us explore this a little further with reference to research into differential achievement among language learners. Since learners' motivation is often taken to be a relevant variable in such studies, we will consider briefly the ways in which 'motivation' has been represented in applied linguistic research to illustrate the issue of theoretical concepts. The characteristics of motivation have been discussed, as 'a learner trait' or with reference to 'situated language identity theory' (Noels and Clément 1996 in Dörnyei 2001); researchers debate how accurately different sub-components of motivation have been identified, how to distinguish between goals, motives and orientations, and so on. To exemplify this area, we cite one study into ESL acquisition in Quebec. Belmechri and Hummel (1998) generated a 'Motivational Intensity Score' for each student in their study, and used:

> (a) Factor analyses to determine which orientations clustered together to form general orientations in this particular context, and (b) after delineating general orientations, a multiple regression analysis to find out which combination of these best predicted motivation.
>
> (p.227)

They conclude that 'orientations explained 41 per cent of the variance in motivation' (p.239). The study has many of the characteristics of the traditional approach to SLA research, including the identification of variables, the quantification of their relative weighting, and a quest for some generalizable findings about the nature of motivation in SLA. This goal is evident in much of the relevant literature, so that Crookes and Schmidt, for example, 'suggest ... that a theory of the role of motivation in SL learning ought to be general and not restricted to particular contexts or groups' (1991: 502). On the other hand, the researchers in our example study counsel caution about their findings, 'because our sample was not fully representative ... and was not large enough to be conclusive' (Belmechri and Hummel 1998: 241). Moreover, motivation researchers increasingly recognize the importance of 'context':

> We would certainly not dispute that language learning takes place within a social context, nor that socially grounded attitudes may provide important support (or lack thereof) for motivation. We do not claim that there are no interesting relationships among social contexts, individual attitudes, and motivation.
>
> (Crookes and Schmidt 1991: 501)

However, this position (perhaps revealingly constructed with several double negatives) does not seem to us to resolve the tension inherent within a desire to specify salient variables and draw generalizable conclusions about them, while simultaneously acknowledging the specificity of time, place and social location of the language learners focused on in the research. These authors declare that a desirable goal for 'a theory of the role of motivation in SL learning' is that it be 'general', but the underlying, more implicit, theoretical proposition is that the label 'motivation' names something in the world which can be directly investigated. We suggest that similar problems surround studies which take many superficially unproblematic concepts for granted. These include ethnic categories (discussed in detail in Chapter 5), but also concepts such as ' discourse coherence', 'Japanese/Chinese/English requesting/apology styles', and, in a generic way, the studies involving comparisons between 'learners in Group A' and 'learners in Group B', where membership of the group may mean being taught in a specific country, or by a specific method, or any other supposed 'variable' in the pedagogic experience.

The realist social theorist Byrne (2002: 31) has dramatically declared 'death to the variable – or rather', as he continues:

> let us understand clearly, once and for all, that variables don't exist. They are not real. What exists are complex systems, which systems are nested, intersecting, which involve both the social and the natural, and which are subject to modification on the basis of human action, both individual and social.

In other words, the crucial search is for ways of accessing – both theoretically and empirically – the relational nature of social (including linguistic) phenomena, which is emphatically not the same quest as that for the elusive, definitive list of interacting factors which might, if properly specified and isolated, account for the behaviour, experience and texts in which applied linguistic researchers are interested.

A relational view of applied linguistic issues

We noted in an earlier section of this chapter that '[s]ocial phenomena are what they are by virtue of the internal relations they have to other phenomena' (Danermark *et al.* 1997: 97). Researchers whose practice is consistent with the approach we have been developing should be able to distinguish between those empirical outcomes which are contingent and those which are a necessary product of generative relations. There are echoes here, of course, of the notion of 'confounding variables', but, as we hope we have made clear, a relational approach is not hoping to find which variables make a difference, since the world of social interaction is an emergent, complex, densely symbolic world, where relations themselves, not isolable variables, are constitutive of 'what works'. Applied researchers may feel much better equipped to address the policy-makers' concern with 'what works', if the question can be reformulated as 'what works for whom in what circumstances?'.

Two social researchers who have operationalized this approach provide us with an example which, while it does have some relevance to education, is outside the direct concerns of applied linguistics. In a later section we shall draw out the ways in which we think principles embodied in this study can be built on within applied linguistics.

For Pawson and Tilley (1997: 46), studies based on successionist, variationist models of social research cannot tell us 'what works for whom in what circumstances', precisely because they work:

> with a logic which prioritizes a certain set of observational cate-
> gories and sequences. This framework tends to overlook the real
> engine for change in social programs which is the process of dif-
> ferently resourced subjects making constrained choices amongst
> the range of opportunities provided.

For Pawson and Tilley, research must identify how people are 'dif-ferently resourced'; what choices are open to them – and how these are 'constrained'; and what opportunities are afforded them by virtue of their social location. A recognition of the importance of all these ele-ments (that is, resources, constraints and affordances) is the methodological starting point for designing a research programme, and one that Pawson has incorporated into a long-term study of the impact of the Simon Fraser University Prison Education Program on the rehabilitation of inmates serving in British Columbian penitentiaries.

The first point that Pawson notes about the programme is that it does not 'work' in reducing recidivism in some undifferentiated way. Rather the researcher starts by forming hypotheses about potential generative relations and mechanisms which might underlie educa-tional rehabilitation. Briefly, the point 'is to acknowledge that outcomes of complex programs [such as the Simon Fraser University Prison Education Program] bear the mark of countless contexts and mechanisms' (p.107). Thus in forming theories about what might work for whom in what contexts, the researcher needed to consult both the academic literature and also those who had an 'insider's knowledge' of the programme itself, namely those who had taught on it and those who had been taught in it. This mixture of theorizing and qualitative investigation prepares the way for the main body of the investigation, which is an empirical study of outcomes.

In this particular study this meant building up a quantitative picture of which types of inmates and which types of course experi-ence were associated with lower recidivism. Salient differences between individuals were identified from large numbers of cases, often by means of interviews, and grouped to provide an empirical description of hundreds of sub-groups. Data analysis then involved constructing a 'mosaic of outcome patterns', somewhat as we advocated in our discussion of the sociolinguistic research in Chapter 5. In this research process, there can be no unqualified finding as to 'what works' to make prison education programmes effective in preventing reoffending. Instead, the process of tracing different outcomes back through similar pathways taken by those who were studied leads to a richer and deeper understanding of the particular mechanisms that have operated in specified contexts. This study is innovative, then, in its view of causality and in the methodological means chosen to operationalize it, namely the retroductive tracing of similar outcomes in order to identify which contexts trigger which 'causal mechanisms'.

Another way of approaching the multi-layered phenomena which interest the social researcher is to focus, as Byrne does, on *states* rather than *outcomes*. For Byrne, realist accounts should be concerned less with effects and outcomes, which still smack of linearity and fixity, and more with the state of the system as a whole. Such 'states' are inherently unstable, complex and emergent. The research problem we have drawn from Byrne's work involves health and social class, and it exemplifies an attempt to take account of the stratified character of the social world. To account for the differential incidence of TB amongst urban populations, Byrne (in press) illustrates a methodology which he suggests is more capable than many traditional approaches of grasping the emergent nature of a stratified social reality. In accounting for who gets TB and in what contexts, Byrne argues, we must first acknowledge a biological aetiology (people must be exposed to the bacillus) and a genetic component (some people will have a natural resistance to the bacillus). However, whether particular individuals contract the disease or not will be socially contingent, since it will depend on the interaction between these features and other levels of the social world. Byrne identifies four such levels – the individual, the household, the community and the nation-state – existing in a nested hierarchy.

Interaction between these levels is both outwards and back inwards. Thus for many working people in the 1930s, seeing family members die of TB impelled them towards a radical political critique of inequality. (This critique is an example of what we have called a Cultural Emergent Property.) Such radicalization was a factor in the Labour victory in the General Election of 1945 and in the development of a national health service. This, together with local programmes of housing construction and urban improvement, effectively succeeded in wiping out TB in the UK during the 1950s and 1960s and thereby changed markedly the answer to the question of who gets TB and in what contexts. Byrne's example provides a clear illustration of how the social and the individual intersect, and of how the nature of that intersection is best understood in terms of unstable, nested systems of social relations, where 'feedback' can be in both directions.

A multi-strategy approach in applied linguistic research methods

As we have already observed, the key research issue is not resolved by choosing between qualitative and quantitative methods. In various branches of the social sciences, including applied linguistics, approaches are being developed which cannot be easily categorized under either of these headings. The shortcomings of both measurement and interpretation when either is used exclusively are identified by several applied linguists.

One researcher who provides an account of how and why he has modified his research practice is Spolsky (2000), who has used traditional questionnaires as a means of access to speakers' attitudes to learning additional languages. But he has been frustrated by the limitations of mere correlations and by what is *not* learned by using them. Although not embracing explicitly a stratified ontology or realist philosophy, Spolsky's reflections on his changing attitude to research methodology echo some of the points we – and others we have cited – have been making. As he says:

> To attempt to reduce their [his subjects'] orientation, attitude, and motivation to a single scale is clearly distortion. I do not deny the 'truth' behind simpler models of motivational and attitudinal effects on language learning, but they remain the bare skeleton, . . . unlikely to account for the complexity of language practices and ideology.

> (p.165)

Spolsky has therefore enriched his data collection methods, by not only recognizing the probabilistic qualities of sociolinguistic practices, but also augmenting the traditional correlational study with 'long interviews that give us an opportunity to explore in conversation and through stories and anecdotes the attitudes, identities, and ideologies of our subjects and to gather reports of language use in various domains and with various members of their social networks' (p.162).

Other researchers who feel constrained by the reductionism inherent in translating human behaviour into numbers are also drawn to incorporate more vivid descriptions into their accounts of language practices. Thus Coupland (1997), for example, identifies the short-comings of 'autonomous' applied linguistic research, claiming that the decontextualized patterns of language use revealed by statistical methods cannot illuminate 'how age-salience imbues language in use … [and] is communicatively valorised'. Coupland notes the problems of reconciling the advantages of the qualitative approach he came to develop in his own studies with the loss of 'scientistic, objectivist, expert research practice', and, although his conclusions (in this and subsequent work) are more thoroughly constructionist than we would find convincing, it is worth noting that he feels drawn to a mixture of methods and approaches to analysis, in order to capture the depth of the issues (here, how ageing and language practices are interrelated) with which, as an applied linguist/sociolinguist, he is concerned.

Another factor which leads to the deployment of a range of methodological approaches in applied linguistic studies is the desirability of investigating both the micro and macro dimensions of the social world.

One approach towards achieving this aim is taken by Norton (2000), who explains how the methodological framework she adopted was influenced by researchers seeking to 'investigate the complex relationship between social structure on the one hand, and human agency on the other, without resorting to deterministic or reductionist analyses' (p.21). She provides a powerful description of the experience of immigrant women in Canada, whose progress as learners of English unfolds in the context of 'inequitable relations of power'. She finds the concepts of both 'motivation' – as a fixed personality trait – and 'acculturation' into the target language group – as a process for which the learner is responsible – wholly inadequate to account for the differentiated experiences of her informants, arguing that 'a language learner's affective filter cannot be understood apart from his or her relationship to larger, and frequently inequitable social structures' (p.120). Her ethnographic method enables her to present detailed portraits of these women's psychobiographies – their personal trajectories in the context of their family relationships and expectations, career opportunities in their home countries and the much more limited opportunities for work afforded them as immigrants to Canada. The 'social settings' of these workplaces valorize different languages differently, so we discover why one of the women, of Vietnamese background, came under pressure to learn Italian rather than English, where the former served as a marker of social solidarity among the employees in the factory where she worked. Norton also refers to material resources, glossed as 'capital goods, real estate and money' (p.7), and identifies a key role for history as integral to explanation. However, her analysis gives much less attention to these, the domain of contextual resources, than to those of situated activity and social settings, while, from her 'poststructuralist feminist' perspective, 'discourse' once again assumes a role in social relations which we find unpersuasive, and she appears to underestimate the shaping effects of *material* inequalities on people's choices, opportunities and ambitions.

Another 'critical ethnographer' who disparages the 'ahistorical perspective' of much ethnographic research is Canagarajah (1999), whose four-year study at Jaffna University encompassed the community and classroom settings, and whose data included field notes, formal and informal interviews, recordings of linguistic interaction, textual analysis of written products and questionnaires. Like Norton, Canagarajah describes the different experiences and responses to learning English of various students, but he also provides detailed information about the history of Sri Lanka as a colonized territory. This includes the impact on both official language policy and actual language practice of different interest groups. He explains clearly how local people 'selectively appropriat[ed] the Western culture and values, while benefiting from the economic and social rewards from English education' (p.65), and why the Tamil military had an interest in promoting Tamil and outlawing the use of English. Canagarajah's account also includes evidence of how the 'socially strategic' use of English by the Tamil community acts back on the variety itself, 'modify[ing] the communicative and linguistic rules of English' (p.76), an example of the kind of nonlinear interaction between structure, culture and agency that we have discussed in this text. However, once again we find his theoretical position rather confusing in places, lacking detail about who did what to whom in claims such as 'colonialism and Anglicism had many ways of imposing their reproductive agenda' (p.59), and unhelpful in suggesting that 'language is an active ideological agent that constrains our consciousness' (p.178). In the sense discussed earlier, these claims are conflationary in appearing to endow structural and cultural relations with agency, a power, we have argued, that is possessed only by human beings.

There is a further distinction marking a realist account from those considered above, namely the pursuit of 'a modest form of objectivity', in the sense discussed in previous chapters, as an aim of social research. Therefore we find ourselves in disagreement with both Norton's approving reference to the position that no research can claim to be objective (Norton 2000: 21), and with Canagarajah's claim that '... knowledge is partisan and partial to the communities which construct it' (Canagarajah 1999: 32).

A mix of research methods and of perspectival scale is also evident in a study by Chick (2001). This began as a micro-ethnography of 14-year-old, Zulu-speaking mathematics students in the KwaZulu region of South Africa, where the data at situated activity level was analysed using an interactional sociolinguistic framework. Chick became aware, however, of the 'limitations of explanations of school failure in terms of culturally-specific styles' (p.234), and decided to investigate the macro context too. He points out that in apartheid South Africa '... the discriminatory legislation tended to make visible what is normally hidden in democratic societies, namely the mechanisms in the wider (macro) society through which groups and individuals exercise power and deny it to others' (p.234). His study describes displays in the classroom of 'safe-talk' (chorused responses to teachers' questions, concealing a poor command of English and an absence of learning taking place), which he suggests are visible traces of 'the unpleasant fact that schooling is structured in such a way as to provide access to opportunities for learning for some students and deny it to others' (p.237). Studies such as his, Chick claims, 'show how features of the macro context, namely the institutional ideologies and bureaucratic structures, constrain what takes place at micro level' (p.238).

The stratified nature of the social world, then, as well as its complex and emergent features, make it impossible to apply a single approach to analysing it: '... if the world is complex it is a pointless exercise to try to deal with understanding it on a foundation of abstracted and unreal simplification' (Byrne 2002: 39). There is obviously a risk of seeming to endorse all methodological approaches and none, but the social realist can turn to theoretical principles in the process of discriminating between methods. In making 'judgements about the nature of social life and society', Layder (1993) identifies three main theoretical elements. 'These are, first, the layered nature of social reality; second, the unfolding nature of social activity over time and space, and third, the integrated nature of macro and micro features of social life' (p.108). For Layder, methods that are incapable of grasping the relationship between the macro and micro elements of social life must be ruled out as inadequate.

In sum, then, social realism is not a research method (nor yet a methodology), and studies may well draw eclectically on the extensive expertise developed by social and linguistic researchers during the previous century, including surveys, official statistics, questionnaires, interviews, observation, ethnography and even introspection. The final section of this chapter provides a single worked example of a typical applied linguistic research question, drawn once again from the field of second language teaching and learning, to illustrate the processes a researcher might go through in seeking to investigate it from a social realist perspective.

Social realist research: an applied linguistic example

Research into social processes whose primary focus is the domains of situated activity and social settings is sometimes labelled 'middle range research'. Thus research into the learning of additional languages in educational settings can be thought of in these terms. As it is Pawson who has developed the most explicit model of a realist research programme intended for those interested in carrying out middle range research, we shall draw heavily on his work in what follows. It should not be forgotten, though, that the 'strata', 'domains' or 'nested dimensions' are not conceived of as either hierarchical or impermeable, and will all be implicated in social interactions, whatever the primary focus.

This recognition, again, is implicit in studies which set out to investigate macro differences at the local level. For example, there is a widespread belief that foreign language teaching in the UK is not as successful as it is elsewhere. (See for example the Nuffield Foundation 2000, and a 'green paper' published by the UK government,[1] which states 'We have not in the past taught languages as successfully as many other countries'.) One response of researchers is to look closely at what goes on in foreign language classrooms (e.g. Mitchell 2000). Or teachers of English to foreign learners notice that those in some countries have much less difficulty obtaining high scores on the standardized tests such as IELTS than those in other countries. Research studies aimed at investigating this large-scale phenomenon frequently involve observation and analysis of tiny numbers of nationals from each country, and may use the much more local, accessible data of interactions between learners and teacher, or the texts (such as, in our earlier example, business letters in the target language, English) produced by a 'sample' of learners in each group. Such research designs are operationally 'middle-range', but are rarely explicit about the processes which link the macro concern – the English education system's achievement in teaching and learning foreign languages/the differential average IELTS scores of, say, Greek and Korean learners – with the micro, more observable manifestation of that concern – features of these particular teachers/learners/syllabuses/teaching styles/texts.

To make this section of the chapter manageable, we shall assume a prototypical research problem, derived from these applied linguistic concerns, which we couch in fairly general terms to encompass issues such as those sketched out in the preceding paragraph. So the research question we consider here, from the list with which we opened the chapter, is 'Why, on a standardized L2 test, do students in Group A achieve consistently better than students in Group B?', where belonging to either group may mean being taught in a specific country, or by a specific method, or being male as opposed to female and so on. We shall use this question to illustrate our modified version of Pawson's model, a model which contains a series of stages, and which we have represented diagrammatically in Figure 8.1.

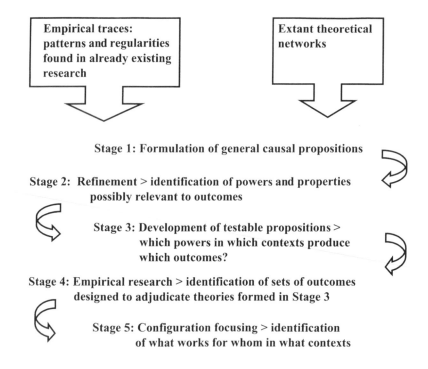

Figure 8.1 A realist research strategy

Firstly, the researcher tries to formulate general causal propositions, on the basis of prior empirical research. What does existing research suggest might be leading Group A students towards consistently better achievements in language learning than Group B students? In Byrne's terms, this investigation consists of the identification and classification of the 'traces' left by real social processes.

The causal propositions generated are necessarily formed within the extant networks of theory. Adopting the modified version of Pawson's approach would start from a recognition, *contra* the empiricist alternative, that it is not the world – directly – that informs the causal propositions formulated at this stage. Therefore, this approach does not seek to identify either 'the typical case' or 'the representative case' as variables-based research seeks to do, thereby subscribing to a theoretical claim (though it is often not explicitly acknowledged as such) that the empirical world is 'given'.

A review of the existing literature might point to a significant role for, among other things, 'motivation' in the differential achievements of the two groups: studies which suggest that many English school students in an increasingly anglophone world are not motivated to study a foreign language, for example, or those which find that student-centred teaching styles motivate learners more, and so on. Traditional approaches might then 'factor in' motivation as a variable, but for Pawson and Tilley, in contrast, motivation is reconceptualized in terms of the complexity of constrained choice in a structured context.

In the second stage of Pawson's research design, when some causal propositions have been identified, the researcher seeks to refine these by simplifying them to an essential core of attributes. The goal at this stage is **the identification of powers and properties, with a view to investigating whether it is the realization of these that produces the outcomes under examination**. Having proposed general causal propositions – for example, that high motivation in L2 learning is associated with the kind of teaching encountered, or with the long-term utility of the L2 for the learner – the next question concerns what powers and properties are involved in the development of motivation generally. The realist explanation would consider the powers and properties of agency, structure and culture, and consideration of agency in relation to motivation would point to intentionality – or purpose – as a core 'power' of human beings (see Chapter 1). It is a distinctive characteristic of human beings that they have reflexivity, the ability, through self-consciousness, to attain a degree of objectivity towards themselves in the world, and therefore not simply to be determined by the world and their instincts. This power leads to the possibility of making decisions among a range of possible choices, and 'motivation' is involved when one course of action is perceived as more desirable than another. The realist's stratified ontology, however, requires consideration of the properties of social structure which act to constrain or enable human intentions. So while learners' assessment of the probability of being able to make use of the L2 may also be involved in motivation, that probability is associated with more macro structural factors such as the global economy, and the likelihood that facility in this particular L2 will lead to secure employment. 'Motivation', then, is conceptualized not as an individual characteristic, nor as a quantifiable variable possessed in different measures by different learners, but as emergent from relations between human intentionality and the social world:

> Without doubt, the interpretive work that individuals do to give direction and substance to social encounters is extremely important, but acknowledging this should not blind us to the part played by the wider social context of positions and locations in which the individual is embedded. Clearly these more encompassing social relations of domination and subordination play a significant role in constraining, as well as enabling, certain forms of behaviour and activity. It is therefore important that field research attempts to incorporate these features.
>
> (Layder 1993: 104)

It is important, too, to note that the impact of structure on agency is not unidirectional: '... systems that "contain" other systems are as potentially liable to be influenced by those contained, as the contained are to be influenced by the container' (Byrne 2002: 33). In this example, if disaffection is demonstrated by a significant proportion of learners, this may well have the effect of altering the context in which some new teaching approach is tried out. Then, learner motivation and teaching style may interact with each other in a sequence which becomes increasingly different from a parallel sequence emerging where the same innovation is also under trial in a neighbouring context. For instance, English school students who opt in sufficiently large numbers *not* to study foreign languages may thereby exert an influence on the distribution of resources to this curriculum area, teaching posts, departments in universities and so on, so that Modern Foreign Languages as a school subject has very different characteristics in England from the equivalent subjects in other European countries.

Because language learning is not simply a matter of motivation, of course, this stage of the research design would also include specification of other important powers and properties, such as 'what needs to be present for people to learn (additional) languages at all?' Answers to this question, again, entail taking account of all the domains of the social world, and include not only the human physiological capacity for language acquisition, but also contextual resources such as access to tuition, the social setting of a productive teaching environment, as well as the situated activity of teaching interactions themselves.

206

The third stage of Pawson's research design is the selection of a conceptual orientation or analytic framework. Returning to the example of motivation, a realist ontology will rule out, for example, those approaches which see it as a fixed trait, because, as we have observed, human reflexivity and purpose are adaptive and motivation is emergent, nonlinear, and subject to feedback mechanisms which can change it. Conversely, it will incline the researcher towards frameworks which are able to accommodate processes of change and emergence.

On the basis of this framework, the researcher then seeks to build up series of testable propositions, framed in terms of outcomes which are emergent from the engagement of powers and properties with contexts. That is, propositions are formulated as suggestions about which things – in combination with each other – in which circumstances, result in the particular outcome under review. We would also be seeking to distinguish the necessary from the contingent. In relation to our example research problem, then, drawing on Bourdieu's claim (1986) that cultural capital shapes the contexts in which social agents act, and the studies which he and others have conducted to investigate these ideas, we might propose at this stage that successful learning of the L2 is an emergent product of cultural capital in combination with a cultured habitus and learners' motivation.

This brings us to the next stage, and the first phase of empirical research. The important feature of empirical work in this realist approach is that it does not set out to refute hypotheses by direct appeal to empirical reality. Rather, data collection and analysis are primarily directed towards testing, refining and adjudicating the middle range theories produced in the previous stage. In this phase we identify as many sources of information as we can in order to develop as rich as possible a set of outcomes. So research investigates distributions of the successful L2 learners (those in 'Group A') in relation to various features of social contexts, exploring whether there are any marked characteristics associated with being in this group, such as age, skin colour, sex, nationality, religion and so on; or, returning to 'motivation', are there consistent patterns among the successful learners' reasons for taking L2 classes? The methods to be used here would be adapted to these questions, probably involving quantifying data such as test results as well as interviewing learners about their aspirations and preferences. The outcomes identified at this stage represent the regularities which form the raw material to be explained: that is, they do *not* constitute the end-point or 'findings' of the research.

The final stage in the first cycle of this realist approach to researching the original problem is that of 'configuration focusing', where we begin to answer the question of 'what works for whom in what circumstances?' Pursuing our illustrative research problem in these terms, let us suppose that investigation of the data demonstrates that a particular style of teaching is associated with successful outcomes (enhanced L2 attainment) at least for some learners – perhaps for most of the females in the group, but only a small proportion of the males. In many studies, the findings would be presented at this point, with an indication of the strength of correlation between these variables. And of course, another study might be published from another researcher which provides counter evidence. What does the realist researcher do? Since we are not seeking to generate covering laws, but rather to develop an explanatory account of social action, we are not confounded by inconsistencies across replicated and near-replicated studies; instead, the next move is a return to the theoretical drawing board. The challenge at this point is to refine the causal hypotheses, to try to explain what contextual features are operating to suppress the realization of those properties and powers identified as causally effective in other contexts or for other learners.

In our hypothetical example, some further interpretive study, such as close observation or interviews, might identify a sub-group of several male and some female learners in the 'student-centred' classroom who find aspects of the social setting in which learning takes place 'demotivating'. Perhaps there is a conflict between winning peer group approval as an adolescent boy and displaying fluency in a foreign language (Barton 2000). Or perhaps the impact of international conflict has led to an increase in racist responses to particular groups of learners, so that some of them in turn begin to develop more negative attitudes towards a target language associated with their detractors. This points to the need to include the most abstract 'domains' of social life (contextual resources) in our causal account of successful L2 learning, and the causal proposition would be further refined. Psychobiographical differences, too, would almost certainly influence different learners in different ways, so that what amounts to a demotivating context for one learner may be an inspiring one for another. The approach avoids reduction to the ideographic, however, because by and large, given the structured contexts of the social world, there will be the patterned regularities identified in the earlier stages of the research process: communities of practice are far-from-equilibric, dynamic systems, constantly perturbed by feedback mechanisms of various kinds. The result of the research cycle is not a 'master theory' of the key causal mechanism, nor a catalogue of inconsistent results, but a typology of broadly based configurations.

Conclusion

In this chapter, we began by summarizing the core claims of a social realism for applied linguistics, and went on to elaborate on each of them. Thus we argued for applied linguistics research problems to be seen as social issues, which require social theoretical insights. To exemplify the range of research problems which arise in the discipline, we provided an illustrative list of the kinds of question with which it is concerned, all of which have components that can be located in each of the 'social domains' discussed in Chapter 6. We reiterated the claim that the social world is stratified, and that what is real about it is not fully accessible to, nor exhausted by, empirical evidence. We advocated the rejection of a variables-based approach to the explanation of social phenomena such as language use, in favour of a relational, emergentist perspective, and explored this contrast with reference to the notion of 'motivation' in second language learning. We explained that social realism is not in itself a methodological approach, and outlined the various social research methods which are best deployed in combination to explain something as complex as human language behaviour. Throughout these sections of the chapter, examples of actual studies were provided, some of which derive from applied linguistics, although we found that we had to turn to other areas of social research, including health and epidemiology, prison education and recidivism, and primary school pedagogy, for examples of studies of an explicitly realist kind. In the final section of the chapter, we returned to a major preoccupation within applied linguistics – the differential progress towards an additional language by different learners – as the ground on which to work through a research problem in a consistently realist manner.

We conclude by summarizing some key points emerging from this discussion which may guide those readers who are convinced by our arguments as they seek to carry out research in applied linguistics.

- Measurement is important in most research programmes, but it does not provide direct access to reality. The implication of this is that, whether you are interested in a learner's current level of proficiency in a 'target' language, or in a speaker's affective identification with a foreign culture, whatever form of measure you use will rest on theoretical claims about social reality. 'Facts' never 'speak for themselves'.
- The social world is complex and emergent. This entails an acceptance of the context-specific operation of causal relations. Byrne (2002: 163) expresses this idea as:

> Localism – the recognition that knowledge is inherently contextual and that a crucial component of the specification of any item or system of things and relations known is the delimitation of the spatial and temporal boundaries within which that knowledge might hold good.

That is to say, some kinds of teaching will work for some learners in some circumstances. The purpose of research becomes to discover which circumstances are associated with progress for which learners. The replicability of studies is much reduced in salience, since the search for covering laws can safely be abandoned. This kind of research entails a case-driven methodology, which is able to connect outcomes with contexts and causes.

- However, 'case-driven' does not equate with 'idiosyncratic', and 'complexity' does not equate with 'randomness'. We would expect studies of many different kinds to illustrate similar kinds of relations between contexts, mechanisms and outcomes. Contexts, such as class relations and global inequalities, are already structured when encountered by new language learners. This is why we are able to predict that people born in less privileged regions of the world are likely to struggle more determinedly to learn a globally dominant language than those born in Western countries to learn a dying one. Empirical data act as a trace of how structures such as international capitalist relations constrain social action consistently in particular directions.

We have provided here a first indication of how a distinctively social realist orientation might have a role in steering applied linguistic research away from the kinds of impasse which seem to threaten many social science disciplines as policy-makers grow increasingly impatient for answers to the question 'what works?' The process has at its heart the explanation of the dynamic relationship between agency and structure; the focus is on people making constrained choices in structured contexts, and what we are proposing is an appropriate research methodology for investigating precisely that.

Note

1. http://www.dfes.gov.uk/14-19greenpaper/download/raisingstandards.doc (accessed 21.10.02)

References

Aitchison, J. (1989) *The Articulate Mammal*. London: Routledge.

Alexander, R. (2000) *Culture and Pedagogy: International Comparisons in Primary Education*. Oxford: Blackwell.

Anderson, P. (1976) *Considerations on Western Marxism*. London: New Left Books.

Archer, M. (1988) *Culture and Agency: The Place of Culture in Social Theory*. Cambridge: Cambridge University Press.

Archer, M. (1995) *Realist Social Theory: The Morphogenetic Approach*. Cambridge: Cambridge University Press.

Archer, M. (1996) Social integration and system integration: developing the distinction. *Sociology* 30 (4), 679–99.

Archer, M. (2000) *Being Human: The Problem of Agency*. Cambridge: Cambridge University Press.

Ashcroft, B. (2003 [2001]) Language and race. In R. Harris and B. Rampton (eds), *The Language, Ethnicity and Race Reader*. London: Routledge, pp.37–53.

Aston, G. and Burnard, L. (1998) *The BNC Handbook: Exploring the British National Corpus with SARA*. Edinburgh: Edinburgh University Press.

Atkinson, P. (1985) *Language, Structure and Reproduction: An Introduction to the Sociology of Basil Bernstein*. London: Methuen.

Auerbach, E. R. (1995) The politics of the ESL classroom: issues of power in pedagogical choices. In J. W. Tollefson (ed.), *Power and Inequality in Language Education*. Cambridge: Cambridge University Press, pp.9–33.

Austin, J. L. (1962) *How to Do Things with Words*. Oxford: Oxford University Press.

Bachman, L. F. (1990) *Fundamental Considerations in Language Testing*. Oxford: Oxford University Press.

Bailey, B. (1997) Communication of respect in interethnic service encounters. *Language in Society* 26 (3), 327–56.

Barratt, M. (1991) *The Politics of Truth: From Marx to Foucault*. Cambridge: Polity Press.

Barthes, R. (1973) *Mythologies*. London: Paladin.

Barton, A. (2000) *Pupils' responses to foreign language learning in the* context of national concern about boys' performance, with specific reference to single-sex classes in co-educational schools. Unpublished PhD thesis, University of Warwick.

Barton, D. (1994) *Literacy: An Introduction to the Ecology of Written Language.* Oxford: Blackwell.

Bates, E. and Goodman, J. C. (1999) On the emergence of language from the lexicon. In B. MacWhinney (ed.), *The Emergence of Language.* Mahwah, NJ: Lawrence Erlbaum Associates, pp.29–79.

Bauer, L. and Trudgill, P. (eds) (1998) *Language Myths.* London: Penguin.

Bauman, Z. (1978) *Hermeneutics and Social Science: Approaches to Understanding.* London: Hutchinson.

Beach, W. A. (1991) Intercultural problems in courtroom interaction. In L. A. Samovar and R. E. Porter (eds), *Intercultural Communication: A Reader.* Belmont, CA: Wadsworth Publishing Co., pp.215–21.

Beaugrande, R. de (1997) *New Foundations for a Science of Text and Discourse: Cognition, Communication, and the Freedom of Access to Knowledge and Society.* Norwood, NJ: Ablex.

Beaugrande, R. de (1999) Linguistics, sociolinguistics, and corpus linguistics: ideal language versus real language. *Journal of Sociolinguistics* 3 (1), 128–39.

Belmechri, F. and Hummel, K. (1998) Orientations and motivation in the acquisition of English as a second language among high school students in Quebec city. *Language Learning* 48 (2), 219–44.

Belz, J. A. (2002) Social dimensions of telecollaborative foreign language study. *Language Learning and Technology* 6 (1), 60–81.

Beretta, A. and Crookes, G. (1993) Cognitive and social determinants of discovery in SLA. *Applied Linguistics* 14 (3), 250–75.

Bernstein, B. (1970) A critique of the concept of 'compensatory education'. In D. Rubinstein and C. Stoneman (eds), *Education for Democracy.* Harmondsworth: Penguin, pp.110–21.

Bernstein, B. (1996) *Pedagogy, Symbolic Control and Identity.* London: Taylor and Francis.

Bhaskar, R. (1978) *A Realist Theory of Science.* Sussex: Harvester Press.

Bhaskar, R. (1979) *The Possibility of Naturalism: A Philosophical Critique of the Contemporary Human Sciences.* Brighton: Harvester Press.

Bhatia, V. K., Candlin, C. N., Engberg, J. and Trosborg, A. (eds) (2003a) *Multilingual and Multicultural Contexts of Legislation: An International Perspective.* Bern: Peter Lang.

Bhatia, V. K., Candlin, C. N. and Gotti, M. (eds) (2003b) *Legal Discourse in Multilingual and Multicultural Contexts: Arbitration Texts in Europe.* Bern: Peter Lang.

Bickerton, D. (1996) *Language and Human Behavior.* London: UCL Press.

Billig, M. (1999a) Whose terms? Whose ordinariness? Rhetoric and ideology in Conversation Analysis. *Discourse and Society* 10 (4), 543–58.

Billig, M. (1999b) Conversation Analysis and the claims of naivety. *Discourse and Society* 10 (4), 572–7.

Block, D. (1996) Not so fast: some thoughts on theory culling, relativism, accepted findings and the heart and soul of SLA. *Applied Linguistics* 17 (1), 63–83.

Blommaert, J. (1998) Different approaches to intercultural communication: a critical survey. Paper presented at *Lernen und Arbeiten in einer international vernetzten und multikulturellen Gesellschaft*, Expertentagung Universität Bremen, Institut für Projektmanagement und Wirtschaftsinformatik.

Blommaert, J. (2001a) Ethnography as counter-hegemony: remarks on epistemology and method. Paper presented at the *International Literacy Conference*, Cape Town.

Blommaert, J. (2001b) *Analyzing African Asylum Seekers' Stories: Scratching the Surface.* Ghent: University of Ghent. http://africana. rug.ac.be/texts/publications/janonlineindex.htm (accessed 05.01.02).

Blommaert, J. (2001c) The Asmara Declaration as a sociolinguistic problem: reflections on scholarship and linguistic rights. *Journal of Sociolinguistics* 5 (1), 131–42.

Bloor, T. and Bloor, M. (1995) *The Functional Analysis of English: A Hallidayan Approach.* London: Arnold.

Board of Education (1921) *The Teaching of English in England ('The Newbolt Report').* London: His Majesty's Stationery Office.

Boas, G. (2001) *Cross-cultural misunderstandings and culture teaching.* Unpublished MA assignment, School of Linguistics and Applied Language Studies, University of Reading.

Botha, R. P. (1992) *Twentieth Century Conceptions of Language: Mastering the Metaphysics Market.* Oxford: Blackwell.

Bourdieu, P. (1986) *Distinction: A Social Critique of the Judgement of Taste.* London: Routledge.

Bourdieu, P. (1991) *Language and Symbolic Power.* Cambridge: Polity Press.

Bourne, J. and Bloor, T. (eds) (1989) *Kingman and the Linguists.* Birmingham: Committee for Linguistics in Education.

Bourne, J., Kress, G., Street, B. and Sealey, A. (1999) The National

Literacy Strategy: a debate. In T. O'Brien (ed.), *Language and Literacies*. Clevedon: BAAL in association with Multilingual Matters, pp.1–13.

Breen, M. (2001 [1985]) The social context for language learning: a neglected situation? In C. N. Candlin and N. Mercer (eds), *English Language Teaching in its Social Context*. London and New York: Routledge in association with The Open University and Macquarie University, pp.122–44.

Breen, M. (2001) Postscript. In M. Breen (ed.), *Learner Contributions to Language Learning*. Harlow: Pearson, pp.172–82.

Bremer, K., Broeder, P., Simonot, M. and Vasseur, M.-T. (1996a) Case studies: the making of understanding in extended interactions. In K. Bremer, C. Roberts, M.-T. Vasseur, M. Simonot and P. Broeder (eds), *Achieving Understanding: Discourse in Intercultural Encounters*. London: Longman, pp.109–58.

Bremer, K., Roberts, C., Vasseur, M.-T., Simonot, M. and Broeder, P. (eds) (1996b) *Achieving Understanding: Discourse in Intercultural Encounters*. London: Longman.

Brislin, R. (1993) *Understanding Culture's Influence on Behaviour*. Fort Worth: Harcourt Brace.

Brown, P. and Levinson, S. (1978) Universals in language usage: politeness phenomena. In E. N. Goody (ed.), *Questions and Politeness: Strategies in Social Interaction*. Cambridge: Cambridge University Press, pp.56–289.

Brumfit, C. (1997) How applied linguistics is the same as any other science. *International Journal of Applied Linguistics* 7 (1), 86–94.

Brumfit, C. (2001) *Individual Freedom in Language Teaching: Helping Learners to Develop a Dialect of their Own*. Oxford: Oxford University Press.

Burnard, L. and McEnery, T. (eds) (2000) *Rethinking Language Pedagogy from a Corpus Perspective*. Frankfurt: Peter Lang.

Byram, M. (1997) *Teaching and Assessing Intercultural Communicative Competence*. Clevedon: Multilingual Matters.

Byram, M. and Fleming, M. (eds) (1998) *Language Learning in Intercultural Perspective*. Cambridge: Cambridge University Press.

Byrne, D. (1998) *Complexity Theory and the Social Sciences*. London: Routledge.

Byrne, D. (2002) *Interpreting Quantitative Data*. London: Sage.

Byrne, D. (in press) Complex and contingent causation – the implications of complex realism for quantitative modelling – the case of housing and health. In B. Carter and C. New (eds), *Making Realism Work: Realist Social Theory and Empirical Research*. London: Routledge.

Callinicos, A. (1989) *Making History*. Cambridge: Polity Press.

Cameron, D. (1995) *Verbal Hygiene*. London: Routledge.

Cameron, R. and Williams, J. (1997) Sentence to ten cents: a case study of relevance and communicative success in non-native/native speaker interactions in a medical setting. *Applied Linguistics* 18 (4), 415–45.

Canagarajah, A. S. (1999) *Resisting Linguistic Imperialism in English Teaching*. Oxford: Oxford University Press.

Canagarajah, A. S. (2001 [1993]) Critical ethnography of a Sri Lankan classroom: ambiguities in student opposition to reproduction through ESOL. In C. N. Candlin and N. Mercer (eds), *English Language Teaching in its Social Context*. London and New York: Routledge in association with The Open University and Macquarie University, pp.208–26.

Candlin, C. N. (ed.) (2002) *Research and Practice in Professional Discourse*. Hong Kong: City University of Hong Kong Press.

Candlin, C. N., Bhatia, V. K. and Jensen, C. H. (2002) Developing legal writing materials for English second language learners: problems and perspectives. *English for Specific Purposes* 21 (4), 299–320.

Candlin, C. N. and Candlin, S. (2003) Health care communication: a problematic site for applied linguistics research. *Annual Review of Applied Linguistics: Language Contact and Change* 23, 134–54.

Carr, P. (1990) *Linguistic Realities: An Autonomist Metatheory for the Generative Enterprise*. Cambridge: Cambridge University Press.

Carter, B. (1996) Rejecting truthful identities: Foucault, 'race' and politics. In M. Lloyd and A. Thacker (eds), *The Impact of Michel Foucault on the Social Sciences and the Humanities*. London: Macmillan, pp.128–46.

Carter, B. (2000) *Realism and Racism: Concepts of Race in Sociological Research*. London: Routledge.

Carter, B. and Sealey, A. (2000) Language, structure and agency: what can realist social theory offer to sociolinguistics? *Journal of Sociolinguistics* 4 (1), 3–20.

Carter, B. and Sealey, A. (in press) Researching 'real' language. In B. Carter and C. New (eds), *Making Realism Work: Realist Social Theory and Empirical Research*. London: Routledge.

Carter, R. (1993) *Introducing Applied Linguistics*. London: Penguin Books.

Carter, R. (1994) Standard Englishes in teaching and learning. In M. Hayhoe and S. Parker (eds), *Who Owns English?* Buckingham: Open University Press, pp.10–23.

Carter, R. (1998) Orders of reality: CANCODE, communication, and culture. *ELT Journal* 52 (1), 43–56.

Carter, R. and McCarthy, M. (1995) Grammar and the spoken language. *Applied Linguistics* 16 (2), 141–58.

Cass, A., Lowell, A., Christie, M., Snelling, P. L., Flack, M., Marrnga-nyin, B. and Brown, I. (2002) Sharing the true stories: improving communication between Aboriginal patients and healthcare workers. *The Medical Journal of Australia* 176 (10), 466–70.

Chambers, J. K. (1995) *Sociolinguistic Theory: Linguistic Variation and its Social Significance.* Oxford: Blackwell.

Charon, J. M. (1998) *Symbolic Interactionism: An Introduction, an Interpretation, an Integration.* New Jersey: Prentice Hall.

Chaudron, C. (1988) *Second Language Classrooms: Research on Teaching and Learning.* Cambridge: Cambridge University Press.

Cheshire, J. (1982) *Variation in an English Dialect.* Cambridge: Cambridge University Press.

Chew, P. G.-L. (1999) Linguistic imperialism, globalism, and the English language. In D. Graddol and U. H. Meinhof (eds), *English in a Changing World.* Oxford: AILA, pp.37–47.

Chick, K. J. (2001 [1996]) Safe-talk: collusion in apartheid education. In C. N. Candlin and N. Mercer (eds), *English Language Teaching in its Social Context.* London and New York: Routledge in association with The Open University and Macquarie University, pp.227–40.

Chomsky, N. (1986) *Knowledge of Language: Its Nature, Origin and Use.* New York: Praeger.

Chomsky, N. (1988) *Language and Problems of Knowledge.* Cambridge, MA: MIT Press.

Chouliaraki, L. and Fairclough, N. (1999) *Discourse in Late Modernity: Rethinking Critical Discourse Analysis.* Edinburgh: Edinburgh University Press.

Cicourel, A. (1973) *Cognitive Sociology: Language and Meaning in Social Interaction.* Harmondsworth: Penguin.

Clear, J. (2000) Do you believe in grammar? In L. Burnard and T. McEnery (eds), *Rethinking Language Pedagogy from a Corpus Perspective.* Frankfurt: Peter Lang, pp.19–30.

Clyne, M. (1996) *Intercultural Communication at Work: Cultural Values in Discourse.* Cambridge: Cambridge University Press.

COBUILD (1990) *Collins COBUILD English Grammar.* London: HarperCollins.

Connor, W. (1994) *Ethnonationalism: The Quest for Understanding.* Chichester: Princeton University Press.

Cook, G. (1989) *Discourse.* Oxford: Oxford University Press.

Cook, G. (1998) The uses of reality: a reply to Ronald Carter. *ELT Journal* 52 (1), 57–63.

Cook, G. (2000) *Language Play, Language Learning.* Oxford: Oxford University Press.

Cook, G. (2001) 'The philosopher pulled the lower jaw of the hen.' Ludicrous invented sentences in language teaching. *Applied Linguistics* 22 (3), 366–87.

Cook, G. (2003) *Applied Linguistics.* Oxford: Oxford University Press.

Cook, V. (1986) The basis for an experimental approach to second language learning. In V. Cook (ed.), *Experimental Approaches to Second Language Learning.* Oxford: Pergamon Press, pp.3–21.

Corson, D. (1997) Critical realism: an emancipatory philosophy for applied linguistics? *Applied Linguistics* 18 (2), 166–88.

Coupland, N. (1997) Language, ageing and ageism: a project for applied linguistics? *International Journal of Applied Linguistics* 7 (1), 26–48.

Coupland, N. (2001a) Introduction: sociolinguistic theory and social theory. In N. Coupland, S. Sarangi and C. N. Candlin (eds), *Sociolinguistics and Social Theory.* Harlow: Pearson Education, pp.1–26.

Coupland, N. (2001b) Age in social and sociolinguistic theory. In N. Coupland, S. Sarangi and C. N. Candlin (eds), *Sociolinguistics and Social Theory.* Harlow: Pearson Education, pp.185–211.

Coupland, N., Sarangi, S. and Candlin, C. N. (eds) (2001) *Sociolinguistics and Social Theory.* Harlow: Pearson Education.

Craib, I. (1998) *Experiencing Identity.* London: Sage.

Crookes, G. and Schmidt, R. W. (1991) Motivation: reopening the research agenda. *Language Learning* 41 (4), 469–512.

Crowley, T. (1989) *The Politics of Discourse: The Standard Language Question in British Cultural Debates.* Basingstoke: Macmillan Education.

Crowley, T. (ed.) (1991) *Proper English? Readings in Language, History and Cultural Identity.* London: Routledge.

Crowley, T. (2003) *Standard English and the Politics of Language.* London: Palgrave.

Crystal, D. (1991) *A Dictionary of Linguistics and Phonetics.* Oxford: Blackwell.

Crystal, D. (2001) *Language and the Internet.* Cambridge: Cambridge University Press.

Crystal, D. (2002) *Language Death.* Cambridge: Cambridge University Press.

Cushner, K. and Brislin, R. W. (1996) *Intercultural Interactions: A Practical Guide.* Thousand Oaks and London: Sage.

Danermark, B., Ekstrom, M., Jakobsen, L. and Karlsson, J. (1997)

Explaining Society: Critical Realism in the Social Sciences. London: Routledge.

Davey, N. (1993) Hermeneutics, language and science: Gadamer's distinction between discursive and propositional language. *Journal of the British Society for Phenomenology* 24 (3), 250–64.

Davies, A. (1991) *The Native Speaker in Applied Linguistics.* Edinburgh: Edinburgh University Press.

Davies, A. (1999) *An Introduction to Applied Linguistics: From Practice to Theory.* Edinburgh: Edinburgh University Press.

Davis, K. A. (1995) Qualitative theory and methods in applied linguistics research. *TESOL Quarterly* 29 (3), 427–53.

Dean, M. (1994) *Critical and Effective Histories: Foucault's Methods and Historical Sociology.* London: Routledge.

de Boer, B. (2000) Emergence of sound systems through self-organisation. In C. Knight, M. Studdert-Kennedy and J. R. Hurford (eds), *The Evolutionary Emergence of Language: Social Function and the Origins of Linguistic Form.* Cambridge: Cambridge University Press, pp.177–98.

DES (Department of Education and Science) (1988a) *Report of the Committee of Inquiry into the Teaching of English Language ('The Kingman Report').* London: Her Majesty's Stationery Office.

DES (Department of Education and Science and the Welsh Office) (1988b) *English for Ages 5 to 11 ('The Cox Report').* London: DES.

Devitt, M. and Sterelny, K. (1987; 1999 second edition) *Language and Reality: An Introduction to the Pphilosophy of Language.* Oxford: Basil Blackwell.

DfEE (Department for Education and Employment) (1998) *The National Literacy Strategy.* London: Department for Education and Employment.

Donato, R. (2000) Sociocultural contributions to understanding the foreign and second language classroom. In J. P. Lantolf (ed.), *Sociocultural Theory and Second Language Learning.* Oxford: Oxford University Press, pp.27–50.

Dörnyei, Z. (2001) New themes and approaches in second language motivation research. *Annual Review of Applied Linguistics* 21, 43–59.

Drew, P. and Heritage, J. (eds) (1993) *Talk at Work: Interaction in Institutional Settings.* Cambridge: Cambridge University Press.

Dreyfus, H. L. and Rabinow, P. (1982) *Michel Foucault: Beyond Structuralism and Hermeneutics.* Brighton: Harvester Press.

Dudley-Evans, T. (1994) Genre analysis: an approach to text analysis for ESP. In M. Coulthard (ed.), *Advances in Written Text Analysis.* London: Routledge, pp.219–28.

Dunn, W. E. and Lantolf, J. P. (1998) Vygotsky's Zone of Proximal Development and Krashen's *i + 1*: incommensurable constructs; incommensurable theories. *Language Learning* 48 (3), 411–42.

Durkheim, E. (1965) *The Elementary Forms of the Religious Life*. New York: Free Press.

Durkheim, E. (1982) *The Rules of Sociological Method*. London: Macmillan.

Eckert, P. (1988) *Jocks and Burnouts: Social Categories and Identity in the High School*. New York and London: Teachers College Press.

Ellis, N. C. (1998) Emergentism, connectionism and language learning. *Language Learning* 48 (4), 631–64.

Ellis, R. (1990) *Instructed Second Language Acquisition*. Oxford: Basil Blackwell.

Ellis, R. (1994) *The Study of Second Language Acquisition*. Oxford: Oxford University Press.

Ellis, R. (1999) Input-based approaches to teaching grammar: a review of classroom-oriented research. *Annual Review of Applied Linguistics* 19, 64–80.

Elman, J. L. (1999) The emergence of language: a conspiracy theory. In B. MacWhinney (ed.), *The Emergence of Language*. Mahwah, NJ: Lawrence Erlbaum Associates, pp.1–27.

Erickson, F. (2001) Co-membership and wiggle room: some implications of the study of talk for the development of social theory. In N. Coupland, S. Sarangi and C. N. Candlin (eds), *Sociolinguistics and Social Theory*. Harlow: Pearson Education, pp.152–81.

Fairclough, N. (1989) *Language and Power*. London: Longman.

Fairclough, N. (1993) *Discourse and Social Change*. Cambridge: Polity Press in association with Blackwells.

Fairclough, N. (1995) *Critical Discourse Analysis: Papers in the Critical Study of Language*. London: Longman.

Fairclough, N. (2001) The discourse of New Labour: critical discourse analysis. In M. Wetherell, S. Taylor and S. J. Yates (eds), *Discourse as Data: A Guide for Analysis*. London and Milton Keynes: Open University and Sage, pp.229–66.

Fazio, L. and Stevens, F. (1994) Using multiple regression to predict minority children's second language performance. *Applied Linguistics* 15 (4), 421–41.

Finch, G. (1998) *How to Study Linguistics*. Basingstoke: Macmillan.

Firth, A. (1996) The discursive accomplishment of normality: on 'lingua franca' English and conversation analysis. *Journal of Pragmatics* 26, 237–59.

Firth, A. and Wagner, J. (1997) On discourse, communication, and (some) fundamental concepts in SLA research. *The Modern Language Journal* 81 (3), 284–300.

Fishman, J. A. (1978) *The Sociology of Language: An Interdisciplinary Social Science Approach to Language in Society.* Rowley, MA: Newbury House.

Foucault, M. (1974) *The Archaeology of Knowledge.* London: Tavistock.

Foucault, M. (1977) *Discipline and Punish: The Birth of the Prison.* Harmondsworth: Penguin.

Foucault, M. (1978) *The History of Sexuality Vol. 1: An Introduction.* Harmondsworth: Penguin.

Fought, C. (1999) A majority sound change in a minority community: /u/-fronting in Chicano English. *Journal of Sociolinguistics* 3 (1), 5–23.

Fought, C. (2002) Ethnicity. In J. Chambers, P. Trudgill and N. Schilling-Estes (eds), *The Handbook of Language Variation and Change.* Oxford: Blackwell, pp.444–72.

Fowler, R., Hodge, B., Kress, G. and Trew, T. (1979) *Language and Control.* London: Routledge & Kegan Paul.

Francis, G. and Sinclair, J. (1994) 'I bet he drinks Carling Black Label': a riposte to Owen on corpus grammar. *Applied Linguistics* 15 (2), 190–200.

Frank, R. A. (2000) Medical communication: non-native English speaking patients and native English speaking professionals. *English for Specific Purposes* 19 (1), 31–62.

Fraser Gupta, A. (1997) Language rights. *English Today* (50), 24–6.

Fromkin, V., Rodman, R. and Hyams, N. (2003) *An Introduction to Language.* Boston, MA: Heinle.

Gadamer, H.-G. (1975) *Truth and Method.* London: Sheed and Ward.

Garfinkel, H. (1967) *Studies in Ethnomethodology.* Englewood Cliffs, NJ: Prentice-Hall.

Gass, S. (2000) Changing views of language learning. In H. Trappes-Lomax (ed.), *Change and Continuity in Applied Linguistics.* Clevedon: British Association for Applied Linguistics/Multilingual Matters, pp.51–67.

Gerth, H. and Mills, C. (eds) (1948) *From Max Weber.* London: Routledge & Kegan Paul.

Giddens, A. (1976) *New Rules of Sociological Method.* London: Hutchinson.

Giddens, A. (1979) *Central Problems in Social Theory: Action, Structure and Contradiction in Social Analysis.* London: Macmillan.

Giddens, A. (1984) *The Constitution of Society: Outline of the Theory of Structuration.* Cambridge: Polity Press.

Gill, M. (2002) Rhetoric in practice: the role of the autonomous/ideo-
    logical dichotomy in literacy studies. Paper presented at the
    British Association for Applied Linguistics, University of Cardiff.
Gilroy, P. (1993) *The Black Atlantic: Modernity and Double Con-
    sciousness*. London: Verso.
Givón, T. (1979) *On Understanding Grammar*. New York: Academic
    Press.
Goffman, E. (1971) *Relations in Public: Microstudies of the Public
    Order*. New York and Cambridge: Harper and Row.
Goffman, E. (1983) The interaction order. *American Sociological
    Review* (48), 1–17.
Goody, J. (1986) *The Logic of Writing and the Organization of Society*.
    Cambridge: Cambridge University Press.
Gordon, C. (ed.) (1980) *Michel Foucault: Power/Knowledge: Selected
    Interviews and Other Writings 1972–1977*. London: Harvester
    Wheatsheaf.
Graddol, D., Cheshire, J. and Swann, J. (1994) (2nd edition) *Describing
    Language*. Buckingham: Open University Press.
Graddol, D. and Swann, J. (1988) Trapping linguists: an analysis of
    linguists' responses to John Honey's pamphlet 'The language
    trap'. *Language and Education* 2 (2), 95–111.
Greenwood, J. D. (1994) *Realism, Identity and Emotion: Reclaiming
    Social Psychology*. London: Sage.
Gregg, K. (1993) Taking explanation seriously; or, let a couple of
    flowers bloom. *Applied Linguistics* 14 (3), 276–94.
Gregg, K. R., Long, M. H., Jordan, G. and Beretta, A. (1997) Rationality
    and its discontents in SLA. *Applied Linguistics* 18 (4), 538–58.
Grice, H. P. (1975) Logic and conversation. In P. Cole and J. L. Morgan
    (eds), *Syntax and Semantics; Volume 3: Speech Acts*. New York:
    Academic Press, pp.41–58.
Grillo, R. D. (1989) *Dominant Languages: Language and Hierarchy in
    Britain and France*. Cambridge: Cambridge University Press.
Gudykunst, W. B. (1995) Anxiety/Uncertainty Management (AUM)
    theory: current status. In R. L. Wiseman (ed.), *Intercultural Com-
    munication Theory*. Thousand Oaks and London: Sage, pp.8–58.
Gumperz, J. J. (ed.) (1982) *Language and Social Identity*. Cambridge:
    Cambridge University Press.
Habermas, J. (1984) *The Theory of Communicative Action Vol. 1*.
    Cambridge: Polity Press.
Habermas, J. (1986) *Knowledge and Human Interests*. Cambridge:
    Polity Press.
Habermas, J. (1987) *The Theory of Communicative Action Vol. 2*.
    Cambridge: Polity Press.

Habermas, J. (1990) *On the Logic of the Social Sciences*. Cambridge: Polity Press.

Habermas, J. (2001a) *The Liberating Power of Symbols*. Cambridge: Polity Press.

Habermas, J. (2001b) *On the Pragmatics of Social Interaction: Preliminary Studies in the Theory of Communicative Action*. Cambridge: Polity Press.

Hacking, I. (1997) *Taking Bad Arguments Seriously*. London Review of Books.

Hakuta, K. and D'Andrea, D. (1992) Some properties of bilingual maintenance and loss in Mexican background high-school students. *Applied Linguistics* 13 (1), 72–99.

Hall, E. T. and Hall, M. R. (1990) *Understanding Cultural Differences: Germans, French and Americans*. Yarmouth, Maine: Intercultural Press.

Hall, K. (1995) Lip service on the fantasy lines. In K. Hall and M. Bucholtz (eds), *Gender Articulated: Language and the Socially Constructed Self*. New York: Routledge, pp.183–216. Cited in Fought 2002.

Halliday, M. A. K. (1978) *Language as Social Semiotic*. London: Edward Arnold.

Halliday, M. A. K. (1989) *Spoken and Written Language*. Oxford: Oxford University Press.

Halliday, M. A. K. (1991) Corpus studies and probabilistic grammar. In K. Aijmer and B. Altenberg (eds), *English Corpus Linguistics*. Harlow: Longman, pp.30–43.

Harris, R. (1980) *The Language Makers*. London: Duckworth.

Harris, R. (2001) Linguistics after Saussure. In P. Cobley (ed.), *Semiotics and Linguistics*. London: Routledge, pp.118–33.

Hatch, E. and Farhady, H. (1982) *Research Design and Statistics for Applied Linguistics*. Cambridge, MA: Newbury House Publishers.

Hatch, E. and Lazaraton, A. (1991) *The Research Manual: Design and Statistics for Applied Linguistics*. Boston, MA: Heinle & Heinle.

Hawkins, J. A. (1994) *A Performance Theory of Order and Constituency*. Cambridge Studies in Linguistics 73, Cambridge University Press.

Headland , T. N. (2002) Endangered hunter-gatherer languages in the Philippines. Paper presented at *The Ninth International Conference on Hunting and Gathering Societies*, Heriot-Watt University, Edinburgh, Scotland.

Hofstede, G. (1991) *Cultures and Organizations: Software of the Mind*. London: HarperCollins.

Holborow, M. (1999) *The Politics of English: A Marxist View of Language*. London: Sage.

Holliday, A. (1999) Small cultures. *Applied Linguistics* 20 (2), 237–64.

Holmes, J. (2001) *An Introduction to Sociolinguistics*. Harlow: Longman/Pearson.

Honey, J. (1983) *The Language Trap*. Middlesex: National Council for Educational Standards.

Hopper, P. J. and Traugott, E. C. (1993) *Grammaticalization*. Cambridge: Cambridge University Press.

House, J. (1989) Politeness in English and German: the functions of please and bitte. In S. Blum-Kulka, J. House and G. Kasper (eds), *Cross-cultural Pragmatics: Requests and Apologies*. Norwood, NJ: Ablex, pp.96–119.

House, J. (1996) Contrastive discourse analysis and misunderstanding: the case of German and English. In M. Hellinger and U. Ammon (eds), *Contrastive Sociolinguistics*. Berlin: Mouton de Gruyter, pp.345–61.

How, A. R. (1995) *The Habermas-Gadamer Debate and the Nature of the Social: Back to Bedrock*. Aldershot: Avebury/Ashgate.

Hoy, D. C. (ed.) (1986) *Foucault: A Critical Reader*. Oxford: Blackwell.

Hudson, R. (1996) *Sociolinguistics*. Cambridge: Cambridge University Press.

Hunston, S. (1995) Grammar in teacher education: the role of a corpus. *Language Awareness* 4 (1), 15–31.

Hunston, S. (2002) *Corpora in Applied Linguistics*. Cambridge: Cambridge University Press.

Hunston, S. and Francis, G. (2000) *Pattern Grammar: A Corpus-driven Approach to the Lexical Grammar of English*. Amsterdam: John Benjamins.

Hymes, D. (1972) On communicative competence. In J. B. Pride and J. Holmes (eds), *Sociolinguistics: Selected Readings*. Baltimore: Penguin, pp.269–93.

Hymes, D. (1974) *Foundations in Sociolinguistics: An Ethnographic Approach*. London: Tavistock Publications.

Itkonen, E. (1978) *Grammatical Theory and Metascience*. Amsterdam: John Benjamins.

Johnson, K. and Johnson, H. (1999) *The Encyclopedic Dictionary of Applied Linguistics: A Handbook for Language Teaching*. Oxford: Blackwell.

Johnson, R. (1991) A new road to serfdom? A critical history of the 1988 Act. In Department of Cultural Studies (ed.), *Education Limited: Schooling, Training and the New Right in England since 1979*. London: Unwin Hyman, pp.31–86.

Johnson, S. (2001) *Emergence*. London: Penguin.

Kasper, G. (1997) 'A' stands for acquisition: a response to Firth and Wagner. *The Modern Language Journal* 81 (iii), 307–12.

Keat, R. and Urry, J. (1982) *Social Theory as Science*. London: Routledge.

Kerswill, P. (1996a) Children, adolescents and language change. *Language Variation and Change* 8 (2), 177–202.

Kerswill, P. (1996b) Milton Keynes and dialect levelling in south-eastern British English. In D. Graddol, D. Leith and J. Swann (eds), *English: History, Diversity and Change*. London: Routledge, pp.292–300.

Kirby, S. (1999) Learning, bottlenecks and the evolution of recursive syntax. In E. Briscoe (ed.), *Linguistic Evolution through Language Acquisition: Formal and Computational Models*. Cambridge: Cambridge University Press, pp.173–203.

Kitching, G. (1988) *Karl Marx and the Philosophy of Praxis*. London: Routledge.

Kluckhohn, F. and Strodtbeck, F. L. (1961) *Variations in Value Orientations*. Westport, CT: Greenwood.

Knight, C., Studdert-Kennedy, M. and Hurford, J. R. (eds) (2000a) *The Evolutionary Emergence of Language: Social Function and the Origins of Linguistic Form*. Cambridge: Cambridge University Press.

Knight, C., Studdert-Kennedy, M. and Hurford, J. R. (2000b) Language: a Darwinian adaptation? In C. Knight, M. Studdert-Kennedy and J. R. Hurford (eds), *The Evolutionary Emergence of Language: Social Function and the Origins of Linguistic Form*. Cambridge: Cambridge University Press, pp.1–15.

Kramsch, C. (1993) *Context and Culture in Language Teaching*. Oxford: Oxford University Press.

Kramsch, C. (2002a) Introduction: 'How can we tell the dancer from the dance?'. In C. Kramsch (ed.), *Language Acquisition and Language Socialization: Ecological Perspectives*. London and New York: Continuum, pp.1–30.

Kramsch, C. (ed.) (2002b) *Language Acquisition and Language Socialization: Ecological Perspectives*. London and New York: Continuum.

Kress, G. (1985) *Linguistic Processes in Sociocultural Practice*. Oxford: Oxford University Press.

Krouglov, A. (1999) Police interpreting: politeness and sociocultural context. *The Translator* 5 (2), 285–302.

Lantolf, J. P. (1996) Review article – SLA theory building: 'Letting all the flowers bloom!' *Language Learning* 46 (4), 713–49.

Lantolf, J. P. (ed.) (2000a) *Sociocultural Theory and Second Language Learning*. Oxford: Oxford University Press.

Lantolf, J. P. (2000b) Introducing sociocultural theory. In J. P. Lantolf (ed.), *Sociocultural Theory and Second Language Learning*. Oxford: Oxford University Press, pp.1–26.

Lantolf, J. P. and Pavlenko, A. (1995) Sociocultural theory and second language acquisition. *Annual Review of Applied Linguistics* 15, 108–24.

LARA (Learning and Residence Abroad). (2003) http://lara.fdtl.ac.uk/lara/ethno.html. (accessed 16.07.03).

Larsen-Freeman, D. (1997) Chaos/complexity science and second language acquisition. *Applied Linguistics* 18 (2), 141–65.

Larsen-Freeman, D. (2002) Language acquisition and language use from a chaos/complexity theory perspective. In C. Kramsch (ed.), *Language Acquisition and Language Socialization: Ecological Perspectives*. London and New York: Continuum, pp.33–46.

Lass, R. (1980) *On Explaining Language Change*. Cambridge: Cambridge University Press.

Layder, D. (1981) *Structure, Interaction and Social Theory*. London: Routledge & Kegan Paul.

Layder, D. (1985) Beyond empiricism: the promise of realism. *Philosophy of the Social Sciences* 15, 255–74.

Layder, D. (1990) *The Realist Image in Social Science*. London: Macmillan.

Layder, D. (1993) *New Strategies in Social Research*. Cambridge: Polity Press.

Layder, D. (1994) *Understanding Social Theory*. London: Sage.

Layder, D. (1997) *Modern Social Theory: Key Debates and New Directions*. London: UCL Press.

Layder, D. (1998) The reality of social domains: implications for theory and method. In T. May and M. Williams (eds), *Knowing the Social World*. Buckingham: Open University Press, pp.86–102.

Lazaraton, A. (1995) Qualitative research in applied linguistics: a progress report. *TESOL Quarterly* 29 (2), 455–72.

Le Page, R. B. and Tabouret-Keller, A. (1985) *Acts of Identity: Creole-based Approaches to Language and Ethnicity*. Cambridge: Cambridge University Press.

Lévi-Strauss, C. (1958) *Structural Anthropology*. London: Allen Lane.

Lévi-Strauss, C. (1966) *The Savage Mind*. Chicago: University of Chicago Press.

Lewis, M. and Wray, D. (1997) *Writing Frames: Scaffolding Children's Non-fiction Writing in a Range of Genres*. University of Reading: Reading and Language Information Centre.

Lieb, H.-H. (2002) *Basic Characteristics of Integrational Linguistics: A Brief Summary.* http://camelot.germanistik.fu-berlin.de/il/+en/basic-en.html (accessed 28.12.02).

Lightbown, P. M. (2000) Classroom SLA research and second language teaching. *Applied Linguistics* 21 (4), 431–62.

Lightbown, P. M. and Spada, N. (2001 [1999]) Factors affecting second language learning. In C. N. Candlin and N. Mercer (eds), *English Language Teaching in its Social Context.* London and New York: Routledge in association with The Open University and Macquarie University, pp.28–43.

Lightfoot, D. (1991) *How to Set Parameters: Arguments from Language Change.* Cambridge, MA: MIT Press.

Linell, P. (2001) Dynamics of discourse or stability of structure: sociolinguistics and the legacy from linguistics. In N. Coupland, S. Sarangi and C. N. Candlin (eds), *Sociolinguistics and Social Theory.* Harlow: Pearson Education, pp.107–26.

LNC (Language in the New Capitalism) (2003) http://www.cddc.vt.edu/host/lnc/LNC.htm (accessed 16.07.03).

Lockwood, D. (1964) Social integration and system integration. In G. K. Zollschan and W. Hirsch (eds), *Explorations in Social Change.* London: Routledge and Kegan Paul, pp.244–57.

Long, M. H. (1993) Assessment strategies for second language acquisition theories. *Applied Linguistics* 14 (3), 225–49.

Long, M. H. (1997) Construct validity in SLA research: a response to Firth and Wagner. *The Modern Language Journal* 81 (iii), 318–23.

Lopez, J. and Scott, J. (2000) *Social Structure.* Buckingham: Open University Press.

MacWhinney, B. (1998) Models of the emergence of language. *Annual Review of Psychology* 49, 199–227. http://psyling.psy.cmu.edu/papers/annual.pdf (accessed 04.12.02).

MacWhinney, B. (ed.) (1999) *The Emergence of Language.* Mahwah, NJ: Lawrence Erlbaum Associates.

Malik, K. (2000) Let them die. *Prospect.* http://www.kenanmalik.com/essays/die.html (accessed 25.03.02).

Martin, J. R. (1989) *Factual Writing: Exploring and Challenging Social Reality.* Oxford: Oxford University Press.

Marx, K. (1959) *Economic and Philosophical Manuscripts.* London: Lawrence and Wishart.

McCarthy, M. (1991) *Discourse Analysis for Language Teachers.* Cambridge: Cambridge University Press.

McCarthy, M. and Carter, R. (1994) *Language as Discourse: Perspectives for Language Teaching.* Harlow: Longman.

McDonough, J. and McDonough, S. (1997) *Research Methods for English Language Teachers*. London: Arnold.

McEnery, T. and Wilson, A. (1996) *Corpus Linguistics*. Edinburgh: Edinburgh University Press.

McGroarty, M. (1998) Constructive and constructivist challenges for applied linguistics. *Language Learning* 48 (4), 591–622.

Mead, R. (1994) *International Management: Cross-cultural Dimensions*. Oxford: Basil Blackwell.

Meier, A. (1997) Teaching the universals of politeness. *ELT Journal* 51 (1), 21–8.

Miller, J. (1993) *The Passion of Michel Foucault*. London: Harper-Collins.

Milroy, J. and Milroy, L. (1991) *Authority in Language: Investigating Language Prescription and Standardisation*. London: Routledge.

Milroy, J. and Milroy, L. (eds) (1993) *Real English: The Grammar of English Dialects in the British Isles*. Harlow: Longman.

Milroy, L. (2001) The social categories of race and class: language ideology and sociolinguistics. In N. Coupland, S. Sarangi and C. N. Candlin (eds), *Sociolinguistics and Social Theory*. Harlow: Pearson Education, pp.235–60.

Milroy, L. and Milroy, J. (1992) Social network and social class: toward an integrated sociolinguistic model. *Language in Society* 21, 1–26.

Mitchell, R. (2000) Applied linguistics and evidence-based classroom practice: the case of foreign language grammar pedagogy. *Applied Linguistics* 21 (3), 281–303.

Mitchell, R. and Myles, F. (2001 [1999]) Second language learning: key concepts and issues. In C. N. Candlin and N. Mercer (eds), *English Language Teaching in its Social Context*. London and New York: Routledge in association with The Open University and Macquarie University, pp.11–27.

Mouzelis, N. (1991) *Back to Sociological Theory: The Construction of Social Orders*. London: Macmillan.

Mouzelis, N. (1995) *Sociological Theory: What Went Wrong? Diagnosis and Remedies*. London: Routledge.

Mouzelis, N. (1997) Social and system integration: Lockwood, Habermas, Giddens. *Sociology* 31 (1), 111–19.

Myhill, J. (1999) Identity, territoriality and minority language survival. *Journal of Multilingual and Multicultural Development* 20 (1), 34–50.

Nagel, T. (1986) *The View From Nowhere*. Oxford: Oxford University Press.

Nattinger, J. R. and DeCarrico, J. S. (1992) *Lexical Phrases and Language Teaching*. Oxford: Oxford University Press.

Nettle, D. (1999) *Linguistic Diversity*. Oxford: Oxford University Press.

Newmeyer, F. J. (2002) Uniformitarian assumptions and language evolution research. In A. Wray (ed.), *The Transition to Language*. Oxford: Oxford University Press, pp.359–75.

Niedzielski, N. and Preston, D. (2000) *Folk Linguistics*. Berlin and New York: De Gruyter.

Nisbet, R. A. (1966) *The Sociological Tradition*. London: Heinemann.

Norton, B. (2000) *Identity and Language Learning: Gender, Ethnicity and Educational Change*. Harlow: Longman.

Norton, B. (2001) Non-participation, imagined communities and the language classroom. In M. Breen (ed.), *Learner Contributions to Language Learning*. Harlow: Pearson Education, pp.159–71.

Nuffield Foundation (2000) *Languages: The Next Generation*. London: The Nuffield Foundation.

Ong, W. J. (1982) *Orality and Literacy: The Technologizing of the Word*. London: Methuen.

Outhwaite, W. (1994) *Habermas: A Critical Introduction*. Cambridge: Polity Press.

Owen, C. (1993) Corpus-based grammar and the Heineken effect: lexico-grammatical description for language learners. *Applied Linguistics* 14 (2), 167–87.

Owen, D. (1994) *Maturity and Modernity: Nietzsche, Weber, Foucault and the Ambivalence of Reason*. London: Routledge.

Parsons, T. (1937) *The Structure of Social Action*. New York: McGraw-Hill.

Parsons, T. (1951) *The Social System*. New York: The Free Press.

Pateman, T. (1987) *Language in Mind and Language in Society*. Oxford: Oxford University Press.

Pawson, R. (1989) *A Measure for Measures: A Manifesto for Empirical Sociology*. London: Routledge.

Pawson, R. and Tilley, N. (1997) *Realistic Evaluation*. London: Sage.

Pennycook, A. (1994a) Incommensurable Discourses? *Applied Linguistics* 15 (2), 115–38.

Pennycook, A. (1994b) *The Cultural Politics of English as an International Language*. London: Longman.

Pennycook, A. (2001) *Critical Applied Linguistics: A Critical Introduction*. Mahwah, NJ: Lawrence Erlbaum Associates.

Phillipson, R. (1992) *Linguistic Imperialism*. Oxford: Oxford University Press.

Phillipson, R. and Skutnabb-Kangas, T. (1999) Englishisation: one dimension of globalisation. In D. Graddol and U. Meinhof (eds),

English in a Changing World. London: The English Company, pp.19–36.

Pinker, S. (1999) *Words and Rules: The Ingredients of Language*. London: Phoenix.

Pleasants, N. (1999) *Wittgenstein and the Idea of a Critical Social Theory: Giddens, Habermas and Bhaskar*. London: Routledge.

Popper, K. R. (1972) *Objective Knowledge: An Evolutionary Approach*. London: Oxford University Press.

Popper, K. R. and Eccles, J. C. (1977) *The Self and its Brain*. Berlin: Springer.

Potter, J. (2000) Realism and sociolinguistics: response to Carter and Sealey. *Journal of Sociolinguistics* 4 (1), 21–3.

Poulisse, N. (1997) Some words in defense of the psycholinguistic approach: a response to Firth and Wagner. *The Modern Language Journal* 81 (iii), 324–8.

Preston, D. R. (ed.) (1999) *Handbook of Perceptual Dialectology*. Amsterdam: John Benjamins.

Rabinow, P. (ed.) (1984) *The Foucault Reader*. Harmondsworth: Penguin.

Rampton, B. (1990) Displacing the 'native speaker': expertise, affiliation, and inheritance. *ELT Journal* 44 (2), 97–101.

Rampton, B. (1995a) Politics and change in research in applied linguistics. *Applied Linguistics* 16 (2), 233–56.

Rampton, B. (1995b) *Crossing: Language and Ethnicity among Adolescents*. Harlow: Longman.

Rampton, B. (1997) Retuning in applied linguistics. *International Journal of Applied Linguistics* 7 (1), 3–25.

Rampton, B. (2000) Continuity and change in views of society in Applied Linguistics. In H. Trappes-Lomax (ed.), *Change and Continuity in Applied Linguistics*. Clevedon: British Association for Applied Linguistics/Multilingual Matters, pp.97–114.

Rampton, B. (2002) Stylisation and the meaning of social class. Paper presented at *Sociolinguistics Symposium 14*, Ghent, Belgium.

Rassool, N. (2000) Language maintenance as an arena of cultural and political struggles in a changing world. In R. Phillipson (ed.), *Rights to Language: Equity, Power and Education*. Mahwah, NJ: Lawrence Erlbaum Associates, pp.57–61.

Rickford, J. R. (1999a) The Ebonics controversy in my backyard: a sociolinguist's experiences and reflections. *Journal of Sociolinguistics* 3 (2), 267–75.

Rickford, J. (1999b) *African American Vernacular English: Features, Evolution, Educational Implications*. Oxford: Blackwell.

Roberts, C. (2001 [1998]) Language acquisition or language socialization in and through discourse? Towards a redefinition of the domain of SLA. In C. N. Candlin and N. Mercer (eds), *English Language Teaching in its Social Context*. London and New York: Routledge in association with The Open University and Macquarie University, pp.108–21.

Roberts, C., Davies, E. and Jupp, T. (1992) *Language and Discrimination: A Study of Communication in Multi-ethnic Workplaces*. London: Longman.

Roberts, C. J. and Sarangi, S. (eds) (1999) *Talk, Work and Institutional Order: Discourse in Medical, Mediation and Management Settings*. Berlin: Mouton de Gruyter.

Roberts, C., Sarangi, S., Southgate, L., Wakeford, R. and Wass, V. (2000) Oral examinations, equal opportunities and ethnicity: fairness issues in the MRCGP. *British Medical Journal* 320 (7231), 370–5.

Romaine, S. (1984) *The Language of Children and Adolescents: The Acquisition of Communicative Competence*. Oxford: Blackwell.

Rosenau, P. (1992) *Postmodernism and the Social Sciences*. New Jersey: Princeton University Press.

Rothery, J. (1989) Learning about Language. In R. Hasan and J. R. Martin (eds), *Language Development: Learning Language, Learning Culture. Meaning and Choice in Language: Studies for Michael Halliday*. Norwood, NJ: Ablex Publishing Corporation, pp.199–256.

Salkie, R. (2001) The Chomskyan revolutions. In P. Cobley (ed.), *Semiotics and Linguistics*. London: Routledge, pp.105–17.

Sarangi, S. (2000 (1995, 1996, 1997 & 1999 Instalments)) Culture. In J. Verschueren, J.-O. Östman, J. Blommaert and C. Bulcaen (eds), *Handbook of Pragmatics*. Amsterdam: John Benjamins.

Sarangi, S. (2001) A comparative perspective on social theoretical accounts of the language-action interrelationship. In N. Coupland, S. Sarangi and C. N. Candlin (eds), *Sociolinguistics and Social Theory*. Harlow: Pearson Education, pp.29–61.

Sarangi, S. and Candlin, C. N. (2001) 'Motivational relevancies': some methodological reflections on social theoretical and sociolinguistic practice. In N. Coupland, S. Sarangi and C. N. Candlin (eds), *Sociolinguistics and Social Theory*. Harlow: Pearson Education, pp.350–85.

Sayer, A. (1992) *Method in Social Science: A Realist Approach*. London: Routledge.

Sayer, A. (2001) Reply to Holmwood. *Sociology* 35 (4), 967–84.

Schegloff, E. A. (1991) Reflections on talk and social structure. In D. Boden and D. H. Zimmerman (eds), *Talk and Social Structure:*

Studies in Ethnomethodology and Conversation Analysis. Cambridge/Oxford: Polity Press/Blackwell, pp.44–70.

Schegloff, E. A. (1999) 'Schegloff's texts' as 'Billig's data': a critical reply. *Discourse and Society* 10 (4), 558–72.

Schmitt, N. (ed.) (2002) *An Introduction to Applied Linguistics.* London: Arnold.

Schmitt, N. and Celce-Murcia, M. (2002) An overview of applied linguistics. In N. Schmitt (ed.), *An Introduction to Applied Linguistics.* London: Arnold, pp.1–16.

Schumann, J. H. (1993) Some problems with falsification: an illustration from SLA research. *Applied Linguistics* 14 (3), 295–306.

Schutz, A. (1943) The problem of rationality in the social world. *Economica* X, 130–49.

Schutz, A. (1953) Common-sense and scientific interpretation of human action. *Philosophy and Phenomenological Research* XIV (1), 1–38.

Schutz, A. (1967) *The Phenomenology of the Social World.* Evanston, IL: North Western University Press.

Scollon, R. (2002) Cross-cultural learning and other catastrophes. In C. Kramsch (ed.), *Language Acquisition and Language Socialization: Ecological Perspectives.* London and New York: Continuum, pp.121–39.

Scollon, R. and Scollon, S. W. (2001) *Intercultural Communication.* Oxford: Blackwell.

Sealey, A. and Carter, B. (2001) Social categories and sociolinguistics: applying a realist approach. *International Journal of the Sociology of Language* 152, 1–19.

Sealey, A. and Carter, B. (forthcoming) Research in Applied Linguistics: a realistic way forward? Submitted to *Applied Linguistics.*

Searle, J. R. (1995) *The Construction of Social Reality.* London: Allen Lane.

Seedhouse, P. (forthcoming) *The Interactional Architecture of the Language Classroom: A Conversation Analysis Perspective.* Oxford: Blackwell.

Seidenberg, M. S. (1997) Language acquisition and use: learning and applying probabilistic constraints. *Science* 275 (1602). http://www.sciencemag.org (accessed 18.12.02).

Shotter, J. (1993) Becoming someone: identity and belonging. In N. Coupland and J. Nussbaum (eds), *Discourse and Lifespan Identity.* London: Sage, pp.5–27.

Simons, J. (1995) *Foucault and the Political.* London: Routledge.

Sinclair, J. (1991) *Corpus, Concordance, Collocation.* Oxford: Oxford University Press.

Skutnabb-Kangas, T., Phillipson, R. and Kontra, M. (2001) Reflections on scholarship and linguistic rights: a rejoinder to Jan Blommaert. *Journal of Sociolinguistics* 5 (1), 143–55.

Smagorinsky, P. (2001) Rethinking protocol analysis from a cultural perspective. *Annual Review of Applied Linguistics* 21, 233–45.

Snow, C. E. (1999) Social perspectives on the emergence of language. In B. MacWhinney (ed.), *The Emergence of Language*. Mahwah, NJ: Lawrence Erlbaum Associates, pp.257–76.

Spolsky, B. (2000) Language motivation revisited. *Applied Linguistics* 21 (2), 157–69.

Steels, L. (2000) Language as a complex adaptive system. In M. Schoenauer, K. Deb, G. Rudolph, E. L. X. Yao, J. J. Merelo and H.-P. Schwefel (eds), *Parallel Problem Solving from Nature – PPSN VI*. Berlin: Springer-Verlag, pp.17–26.

Stewart, P. (2001) Complexity theory, social theory, and the question of social complexity. *Philosophy of the Social Sciences* 31 (3), 323–60.

Street, B. V. (1984) *Literacy in Theory and Practice*. Cambridge: Cambridge University Press.

Street, B. V. (1995) *Social Literacies: Critical Approaches to Literacy in Development, Ethnography and Education*. Harlow: Longman.

Stubbs, M. (1989) The state of English in the English state. *Language and Education* 3 (4), 235–50.

Stubbs, M. (1996) *Text and Corpus Analysis*. Oxford: Blackwell.

Stubbs, M. (1997) Whorf's children: critical comments on critical discourse analysis (CDA). In A. Ryan and A. Wray (eds), *Evolving Models of Language*. Clevedon: British Association of Applied Linguistics/Multilingual Matters, pp.100–16.

Stubbs, M. (2001a) *Words and Phrases: Corpus Studies of Lexical Semantics*. Oxford: Blackwell.

Stubbs, M. (2001b) Texts, corpora and problems of interpretation. *Applied Linguistics* 22 (2), 149–72.

Swales, J. M. (1990) *Genre Analysis: English in Academic and Research Settings*. Cambridge: Cambridge University Press.

Taylor, C. (1985) *Human Agency and Language: Philosophical Papers 1*. Cambridge: Cambridge University Press.

Teschendorff, J. (1994) Intercultural communication: Philippine nurses and the Australian nursing subculture. *Australian Journal of Communication* 21 (2), 31–40.

Teubert, W. (1999) Corpus linguistics – a partisan view. *International Journal of Corpus Linguistics* 5 (1). http://tractor.bham.ac.uk/ijcl/teubert_cl.html (accessed 28.12.02).

Thomas, G. (1991) *Linguistic Purism*. Harlow: Longman.

Thompson, E. P. (1978) *The Poverty of Theory and Other Essays.* London: Merlin.

Tollefson, J. W. (1991) *Planning Language, Planning Inequality.* Harlow: Longman.

Trompenaars, F. (1993) *Riding the Waves of Culture.* London: The Economist Books.

van Dam, J. (2002) Ritual, face, and play in a first English lesson: bootstrapping a classroom culture. In C. Kramsch (ed.), *Language Acquisition and Language Socialization: Ecological Perspectives.* London and New York: Continuum, pp.237–65.

van Lier, L. (1988) *The Classroom and the Language Learner: Ethnography and Second-language Classroom Research.* London: Longman.

van Lier, L. (1990) Ethnography: bandaid, bandwagon, or contraband? In C. Brumfit and R. Mitchell (eds), *Research in the Language Classroom.* Basingstoke: Macmillan, pp.33–53.

van Lier, L. (2001) Constraints and resources in classroom talk: issues of equality and symmetry. In C. N. Candlin and N. Mercer (eds), *English Language Teaching in its Social Context.* London and New York: Routledge in association with The Open University and Macquarie University, pp.90–107.

Volosinov, V. N. (1973) *Marxism and the Philosophy of Language.* New York: Seminar Press.

Vuolab, K. (2000) Such a treasure of knowledge for human survival. In R. Phillipson (ed.), *Rights to Language: Equity, Power and Education.* Mahwah, NJ: Lawrence Erlbaum Associates, pp.13–16.

Wardhaugh, R. (1992) *An Introduction to Sociolinguistics.* Oxford: Blackwell.

Wardhaugh, R. (1998) Déjà vu? A response to Schachter. *Language Learning* 48 (4), 585–9.

Wardhaugh, R. (1999) *Proper English: Myths and Misunderstandings about Language.* Oxford: Blackwell.

Weber, M. (1964) *The Theory of Social and Economic Organization.* New York: Free Press.

Weber, M. (1974) *The Protestant Ethic and the Spirit of Capitalism.* London: Unwin.

Weber, M. (1978) *Economy and Society.* Berkeley: University of California Press.

Wen, Q. and Johnson, R. K. (1997) L2 learner variables and English achievement: a study of tertiary-level English majors in China. *Applied Linguistics* 18 (1), 27–48.

Wetherell, M. and Potter, J. (1992) *Mapping the Language of Racism:*

Discourse and the Legitimation of Exploitation. Hemel Hempstead: Harvester Wheatsheaf.

White, R. (1999) *Inter-cultural Communication: Course Materials*. Reading: Centre for Applied Language Studies, the University of Reading.

Wichmann, A., Fligelstone, S., McEnery, T. and Knowles, G. (eds) (1997) *Teaching and Language Corpora*. Harlow: Addison Wesley Longman.

Widdowson, H. G. (1996) *Linguistics*. Oxford: Oxford University Press.

Widdowson, H. G. (2000) On the limitations of linguistics applied. *Applied Linguistics* 21 (1), 3–25.

Wierzbicka, A. (1985) Different cultures, different languages, different speech acts. *Journal of Pragmatics* (9), 145–78.

Wierzbicka, A. (1991) *Cross-cultural Pragmatics: The Semantics of Human Interaction*. Berlin: Mouton de Gruyter.

Williams, G. (1992) *Sociolinguistics: A Sociological Critique*. London: Routledge.

Williams, M. (2000) *Science and Social Science*. London: Routledge.

Williams, R. (1976) *Keywords: A Vocabulary of Culture and Society*. London: Fontana.

Wong, J. (2002) Applying conversation analysis in applied linguistics: evaluating English as a Second Language textbook dialogue. *International Review of Applied Linguistics* 40 (1), 37–60.

Wooffitt, R. (2001) Researching psychic practitioners: conversation analysis. In M. Wetherell, S. Taylor and S. J. Yates (eds), *Discourse as Data: A Guide for Analysis*. London and Milton Keynes: Open University and Sage, pp.49–92.

Wray, A. (ed.) (2002) *The Transition to Language*. Oxford: Oxford University Press.

Index

agency 4, 5–12, 113–14, 118, 123, 181–2
Aitchison, J. 20
Alexander, R. 147, 168, 189–90
American Association for Applied Linguistics 187
analytical dualism 4, 49, 149
Archer, M. 6, 9, 12, 14, 41, 54, 70, 80, 82, 111, 123, 130, 132–4, 136, 137–9, 145, 148–9, 151, 152, 175
Atkinson, P. 56
Austin, J.L. 53
autonomous linguistics 19
autonomy of language 157–63

Bailey, B. 128
Baker, K. 170, 173–5
Bank of English 61, 64
Barthes, R. 7, 44
Barton, D. 164
Bates, E. 83, 159
Bauman, Z. 43–4
Beaugrande, R. de 69, 74, 97, 120, 160
Belmechri, F. 195
Bernstein, B. 55–7
Bhaskar, R. 16, 67, 79–80
Bickerton, D. 78, 80, 157, 163
Billig, M. 28, 58
Black English 120–2, see also Ebonics
Blommaert, J. 29, 130, 132, 141, 147, 150, 152, 180
Bloor, M. 23
Bloor, T. 23
Blunkett, D. 175–6
Board of Education 170
Boas, G. 141–3
Bourdieu, P. 52–5, 181, 207
Breen, M. 98

Bremer, K. 152–3
Brislin, R.W. 129–30, 131, 135–6, 137–8
Broeder, P. 152–3
Brumfit, C. 17, 32, 61, 63, 105, 128
Byram, M. 139, 143
Byrne, D. 92, 104, 126, 192, 196, 198, 202, 206, 209–10

Callinicos, A. 36
Cameron, D. 172
Canagarajah, A.S. 153, 201
CANCODE 64
Candlin, C.N. 10, 15, 17, 194
Candlin, S. 194
Carr, P. 68–70, 80–1
Carroll, L. 159
Carter, B. 112
Carter, R. 17, 23, 65, 66
causality 3, 197–8, 205, 208
  generative models of 88–9, 105
  successionist models of 87
Celce-Murcia, M. 85
Chambers, J.K. 29, 107, 113, 124
Charon, J.M. 27
Chaudron, C. 93, 103
Cheshire, J. 21
Chew, P.G-L. 180
Chick, K.J. 202
Chomsky, N. 19, 52, 60–1, 65, 66, 71
Chouliaraki, L. 23, 27, 55, 167
Cicourel, A. 40–2
COBUILD 61, 64
complexity 72, 77–84, 89, 97, 196, 198, 202, 209–10
Connor, W. 180
contextual resources 140–1, 147–50
conversation analysis 26, 42–4, 58

Cook, G. 17, 25, 61, 64, 65, 187
Cook, V. 89, 91
corpus linguistics 23–5, 28, 73–6, 160
Corson, D.D. 100
cosmopolitanism 154, 181
Coupland, N. 42, 44, 94, 113, 200
critical discourse analysis 27, 58
critical realism 100
Crookes, G. 195
Crowley, T. 170, 171–2
Crystal, D. 19, 167, 176, 178, 179
cultural emergent property *see*
    emergent properties
cultural resources 119
Cultural System 134–5, 150
culture 130–9, 141, 153–5, 180
Cushner, K. 129–30, 135–6, 137–8

D'Andrea, D. 91, 95
Danermark, B. 186, 196
Davies, A. 17, 31
Davis, K.A. 98
de Boer, B. 158
DES (Department of Education and
    Science) 170
Devitt, M. 68–70, 83
DfEE (Department for Education &
    Employment) 169
discourse 45–9, 58
discourse analysis 25–6
domains *see* social domains
Donato, R. 99
Dörnyei, Z. 195
Drew, P. 28
Dunn, W.E. 26
Durkheim, E. 35

E-language 61
Ebonics 30, 120, 127n.1, *see also*
    Black English
Eccles, J.C. 81
Eckert, P. 114
ecological theory 26, 98, 99
Education Reform Act 169
Ekstrom, M. 186, 196
Elman, J.L. 78, 79

Ellis, R. 86, 87, 89–90, 93, 97, 102
emergence 3, 12–14, 76–84, 120, 126,
    198, 202, 207, 209
emergent properties 3, 12, 16, Chapter
    3, 156, 158, 165, 182, 198
English Language Teaching 177, *see
    also* language teaching; SLA;
    instructed language learning
epistemic authority 21, 173
ethnicity *see* social category
ethnography 28–9, 103–5, 191, 200–2
ethnomethodology 25, 38–42

face 143–4
Fairclough, N. 23, 25, 27, 46, 47, 55,
    167
Farhady, H. 90–1, 95
Fazio, L. 91, 192–3
Finch, G. 20, 161
Firth, A. 96
Fishman, J.A. 57, 177
forensic linguistics 31
Foucault, M. 45–7
Fought, C. 115–17, 121
Foundation for Endangered
    Languages 154
Francis, G. 24
Fraser Gupta, A. 180
Fromkin, V. 158
functional linguistics 22

Gadamer, H.-G. 50–1
Garfinkel, H. 39–40
Gass, S. 86
generative mechanisms 60
Giddens, A. 8–10
Gill, M. 163
Goffman, E. 40, 133
Goodman, J.C. 83, 159
Goody, J. 165
governing laws 92–6
Graddol, D. 21, 171
Greenwood, J.D. 110–12
Gregg, K.R. 19, 102
Grice, H.P. 129
Grillo, R.D. 56

Gudykunst, W.B. 135
Gumperz, J.J. 29

Habermas, J. 49–51, 136
habitus 53–4, 154
Hacking, I. 94
Hakuta, K. 91, 95
Hall, K. 121
Halliday, M.A.K. 22, 73–4, 75, 165
Harris, R. 22, 66, 163
Hatch, E. 90–1, 95
Headland, T.N. 176
Heritage, J. 28
hermeneutics 50
Hofstede, G. 148, 149
Holborow, M. 181
Holliday, A. 133, 139
Holmes, J. 118
Honey, J. 171
House, J. 143–4
Hummel, K. 195
Hunston, S. 24, 25, 160
Hurford, J.R. 161–2
Hyams, N. 158
Hymes, D. 28, 128

I-language 61, 161
instructed language learning 86,
    194–196, *see also* language
    teaching
integrationism 22
interactionism 8
Itkonen, E. 82

Jakobsen, L. 186, 196
Johnson, H. 85
Johnson, K. 85
Johnson, R.K. 91
Johnson, S. 77, 89

Karlsson, J. 186, 196
Kerswill, P. 113, 115
Kingman Report *see* LINC
Kirby, S. 157
Knight, C. 161–2
Kramsch, C. 26, 98, 99

Labov, W. 117
language death 176–9
Language in the New Capitalism 27
language learning, *see* instructed
    language learning
language teaching 17, 25, Chapter 4,
    130
Lantolf, J.P. 26, 97, 99
Larsen-Freeman, D. 79, 89
Layder, D. 9, 37, 40, 43, 53, 90,
    139–41, 142–5, 151, 152, 185,
    186, 194, 202, 206
Lazaraton, A. 96
Le Page R.B. 122–3, 126
Lévi-Strauss, C. 7, 44
Lighbown, P.M. 87, 89, 92–3
Lightfoot, D. 71
LINC (Language in the National
    Curriculum) 169
linguistic imperialism 177
literacy 163–76
Lockwood, D. 137
Long, M.H. 94, 101
Lopez, J. 6

McCarthy, M. 65, 66
McDonough, J. 94, 102
McDonough, S. 94, 102
McGroarty, M. 97, 98, 100
MacWhinney, B. 78
Malik, K. 176, 180
Marx, K. 16, 36
Mead, G.H. 36–7
Mead, R. 128
measurement 95–6, 125, 191, 209
Meier, A. 143
Milroy, J. 124
Milroy, L. 107, 115, 124
Mitchell, R. 86, 93, 100
motivation (in SLA) 195–6, 200,
    205–8
Myhill, J. 180
Myles, F. 86

Nagel, T. 15, 16, 126
National Curriculum 169

National Literacy Strategy 169, 170–1, 175
Nettle, D. 72–3, 157, 159, 161, 177–8, 179
Newbolt Report, *see* Board of Education
Newmeyer, F.J. 165
Norton, B. 98, 104, 200–1
Nuffield Foundation 203

objective knowledge 14, 15
objectivity 14–16, 108, 201, 205
Ong, W.J. 165, 166

Parsons, T. 7, 39, 110
Pateman, T. 62–3, 81–2
Pavlenko, A. 97, 99
Pawson, R. 95–6, 102, 104, 125, 191, 197, 203–10
Pennycook, A. 168
Phillipson, R. 177–8
Pinker, S. 19
Popper, K.R. 14, 15, 37, 81, 119
postmodernism 8, 44, 47, 108
post-structuralism 44ff, 99
Potter, J. 48–9
psychobiography 139–41, 151–3

Rampton, B. 27, 94, 119, 193
Rassool, N. 178
'real' language 3, 61–7ff
realism 10–12, 60, 125–7
reflexivity 11, 205
Rickford, J.R. 30, 127n.1
Roberts, C. 94, 100, 152–3
Rodman, R. 153
Romaine, S. 177–8, 179
Rosenau, P. 47

Salkie, R. 19
Sarangi, S. 10, 15, 130
Saussure, F. de 52–3
Sayer, A. 12, 15, 88
Schegloff, E.A. 42–3
Schmidt, R.W. 195
Schmitt, N. 85

Schutz, A. 38–9
Scollon, R. 131, 132, 139
Scollon, S.W. 131, 132, 139
Scott, J. 6
Searle, J.R. 12, 82, 109
second language acquisition 19, 86, 92–4, 96, 98, 195–6
Shotter, J. 103–4
Simonot, M. 152–3
Sinclair, J. 23, 75, 160
situated activity 140–1, 142–4, 188
social aggregates 110–19, 122
social category 3, 4, Chapter 5
  age as 109–10, 112–15
  class as 117–19, 124, 192–3
  ethnicity as 109, 115–17, 120–4
  race as 115–16
social collectives 111–19, 122
social constructionism 108
social domains 4, 139–55, 184, 190, 208
social networks 124
social realism 1, 60, 130, 153, 186, 202–10
social roles 137–8
social settings 140–1, 144–7
social structure(s), *see* structure
sociocultural theory 26, 98–9
sociolinguistics 29–30, Chapter 5
Spada, N. 89, 92–3
Spolsky, B. 199
standard English 168–9, 170
Sterelny, K. 68–70, 83
Stevens, F. 91, 192–3
Stewart, P. 77
Street, B.V. 163, 164, 169
Studdert-Kennedy, M. 161–2
structural functionalism 39, 40, 110
structuralism 7, 44–5
structuration 8–10
structure 4, 5–12, 137–8, 174–5, 180–1
Stubbs, M. 28, 58, 75–6, 161, 168–9
Swann, J. 21, 171
symbolic interactionism 36–8

Tabouret-Keller, A. 122–3, 126
Taylor, C. 47, 80
Teubert, W. 27
Thomas, G. 158
Tilley, N. 197
Trompenaars, F. 146

van Dam, J. 99
van Lier, L. 97, 102, 103
variables 3, 89, 90–2, 95–6, 97, 102–3,
    107–8, 118, 125, 126, 186, 196,
    208
Vasseur, M-T. 152–3
Volosinov, V.N. 81
Vuolab, K. 180
Vygotsky, L.S. 98

Wagner, J. 96
Wardhaugh, R. 92, 97, 120–1, 172
Weber, M. 35, 38
Wen, Q. 91
Wetherell, M. 48–9
White, R. 146
Widdowson, H.G. 19, 20, 28, 74–5,
    170
Williams, G. 117
Williams, M. 126
Wooffitt, R. 43
'World 3' 37, 49, 50, 54, 81, 119–20,
    123, 125, 154–5, 166, 181
writing 163–7